M000314270

A SAGA OF THE NEW SOUTH

A SAGA OF THE NEW SOUTH

Race, Law, and Public Debt in Virginia

BRENT TARTER

University of Virginia Press

CHARLOTTESVILLE AND LONDON

University of Virginia Press
© 2016 by the Rector and Visitors of the University of Virginia
All rights reserved
Printed in the United States of America on acid-free paper

First published 2016

9 8 7 6 5 4 3 2 1

Library of Congress Cataloging-in-Publication Data

Names: Tarter, Brent, 1948- author.
Title: A saga of the New South : race, law, and public debt in Virginia / Brent Tarter.
Description: Charlottesville : University of Virginia Press, 2016. | Includes
        bibliographical references and index.
Identifiers: LCCN 2015048304| ISBN 9780813938776 (cloth : alk. paper) |
        ISBN 9780813938769 (e-book)
Subjects: LCSH: Debts, Public—Virginia—History—19th century. | Debts,
        Public—Law and legislation—Virginia—History—19th century. |
        Virginia—Politics and government—1865–1950.
Classification: LCC HJ8483 .T37 2016 | DDC 336.3/40975509034—dc23
LC record available at http://lccn.loc.gov/2015048304

CONTENTS

Acknowledgments   vii

Introduction   1

1. Origins of the Debt Controversy   11

2. The Funding Act of 1871   22

3. Funders and Readjusters   35

4. The Readjuster Party   53

5. Readjustment, Reform, and Reaction   69

6. The Coupon Killers   82

7. The Coupon Cases   102

8. The Coupon Crusher   117

9. The Olcott Act of 1892   130

10. Unfinished Business   143

11. *Virginia v. West Virginia*   153

12. Legacies of the Debt Controversy   174

Notes   185

Index   211

ACKNOWLEDGMENTS

For valuable advice and assistance I happily thank Gail Warren and E. Terry Long, of the library of the Supreme Court of Virginia; Catherine O'Brien, archivist of the Supreme Court of Virginia; my colleagues and friends Emily J. Salmon, Matthew Gottlieb, Marianne E. Julienne, and John G. Deal, of the Library of Virginia; Wythe Holt, University of Alabama Law School, retired; Warren M. Billings, University of New Orleans, retired, and William and Mary School of Law; John O. Peters, retired Richmond attorney and legal scholar; and Peter Wallenstein, of Virginia Tech, and George Harrison Gilliam, of the University of Virginia, who read the manuscript for the press and offered excellent comments and suggestions.

A SAGA OF THE NEW SOUTH

INTRODUCTION

Among the many challenges that confronted Virginians of both genders and of all ages, classes, races, political backgrounds, and places of residence when the Civil War ended in April 1865, few people could have predicted at the time that the state's prewar public debt would play the important role that it did in shaping Virginia's postwar future. The Virginia debt controversy, as it has often been referred to in the literature of Virginia's history, began in the 1860s and dominated the state's politics during the 1870s and 1880s. It also included two separate legal contests, one that lasted from 1872 until 1898 and the other until 1919. The conflicts about the Virginia debt had a longer and more dramatic political history than did the nineteenth-century public debt crisis in any other state, and its legal history was even longer. It was an unusually important episode in Virginia's history and a peculiarly interesting one in Southern history.

Government debts have always been important and have often been controversial. During the long term of a public debt, a government will often pay more in interest than the amount of the original principal, much as does a person who borrows money to buy a house. Those obligations impose long-term burdens on taxpayers and reduce revenue available for other purposes as well as transfer money from taxpayers to creditors. In spite of the large long-run cost, nation-states have necessarily borrowed money to pay for wars, and most American states and localities have borrowed money to construct schools, water and sewer systems, roads, subways, airports, and cultural amenities such as sports arenas and convention centers. In almost every instance, the decisions to borrow money have created controversy because they involved establishing priorities among competing public policy objectives as well as determining who pays and how much.

Political problems with public debts have a long history. The difficulties that English kings faced with their debts in the seventeenth century led to the creation of the Bank of England, which paid the debt in exchange for a cut of the national revenue. That created a permanent national debt, and the intimate and intricate links between the government and the financiers enabled each to influence the other. That fueled what many subjects in that kingdom, including men in the American colonies, regarded as a corrupt system that favored a few wealthy and influential insiders at the expense of everybody else who paid the taxes. In the 1790s, Alexander Hamilton's plans to pay the national and state debts incurred in the fight for independence produced American echoes of the English controversies and played an important role in creating the new nation's first political parties. Suspicions of similar corruption threw a shadow over payment of the debt in post–Civil War Virginia too.

During the decades between the American Revolution and the American Civil War, many of the states created public debts to subsidize construction of expensive road systems, canals, and railroads. Several state governments defaulted on, or repudiated, part or all of their public debt before the Civil War. All the states of the former Confederacy defaulted on some or all of their debts afterward in part because their tax bases were severely reduced as a consequence of the abolition of slavery. In deciding how to pay or whether to repudiate any or all of the state debts, political and business leaders throughout the region had to choose between honoring old legal and financial obligations and assigning higher priorities to other needs in order to pursue new postwar objectives. In every instance, proposals to repudiate debt encountered strong opposition. Bankers and financiers, attorneys and business leaders, and every person engaged in commerce, including shopkeepers and both large and small farmers, relied on payment of debts and enforcement of contracts as absolutely essential to the effective functioning of the capitalist economy.

In all the states that had been part of the Confederacy, African Americans entered politics and supported public policies that appeared to benefit them and their families and opposed proposals that did not. Many of them probably believed and some in Virginia stated that they had no moral or legal responsibility to pay the prewar debt created for the construction of railroads and canals from which they derived no obvious benefits. That created new political dynamics that complicated the attempts of white Southern political leaders, planters, businessmen, industrialists, and financiers to rebuild their old economies or to refashion them on new models.

Thousands of white men and women in Virginia shared the views of African Americans that paying the old debt did not benefit them and their families either, especially after attempts to pay the accruing interest severely reduced the amount of money available for supporting the popular new public school system. Hence, the especially disruptive consequences of the biracial Readjuster Party, which formed in 1879 to refinance the debt—*readjust* was the word they used—to reduce both the rate of interest and the amount of the principal to be paid. Readjusters appealed to farmers and working people of both races and in 1881 formed a coalition with African American Republicans.

The problem in Virginia was more complicated than in any other state because when West Virginia became a state in 1863 it agreed to pay a portion of the Virginia debt that then existed, but after the war the two states could not agree on whether or how West Virginia would pay. No other state faced a similar complication with its debt, which was the reason why even after 1894, when the Virginia government made the final substantive modifications to its settlement with its creditors, the legal controversies continued for another quarter century.

The Virginia debt controversy had two main story lines. One began with the inability of the governments of Virginia and West Virginia to agree on how much of the debt was West Virginia's share. After some ineffective first steps at a negotiated political settlement, it lay dormant for more than twenty years, and neither government did anything effective toward its resolution for more than thirty years. It was finally resolved late in the second decade of the twentieth century through a protracted lawsuit that Virginia filed against West Virginia in the Supreme Court of the United States requiring the justices to review two bulky reports of a special master and issue eight formal opinions and one decree. The case very nearly brought on a serious constitutional confrontation after Virginia's attorney general requested a writ of mandamus from the Supreme Court to compel the West Virginia Legislature to pay the debt, a writ that the court had the authority to issue but no legal or practical means to enforce.

That important litigation has been the subject of very little scholarship. James G. Randall in the *Political Science Quarterly* in 1915 and Rosewell Page in the *Virginia Law Register* in 1919 published summary histories of the case after the Supreme Court issued its last two important rulings.[1] William C. Coleman wrote about the case in the *Harvard Law Review* in 1917, and in the *Michigan Law Review* in 1918 the legal scholar Thomas

Reed Powell specifically addressed the constitutional questions then being argued about whether Virginia could compel West Virginia to pay or whether the Supreme Court could order the West Virginia Legislature to appropriate money and then force the legislature to act.[2] Elizabeth J. Goodall wrote a series of five articles published in *West Virginia History* between October 1962 and January 1964 on West Virginia's response to the suit,[3] and in 1984 John V. Orth published an essay that focused on the role of the Eleventh Amendment in that part of the debt controversy,[4] but nobody has written in detail about how and why that litigation was important to Virginia and why and how the state's public officials filed and prosecuted the suit to protect the state's interests.

The other story line involved a long sequence of changes that the General Assembly of Virginia made to the method of paying what it acknowledged was its portion of the debt and the interest on it. Chief among the proposed changes were the Readjusters' proposals to reduce both the rate of interest and the amount of the principal to be paid. That outraged bondholders and the political leaders who placed full payment of the principal and interest above all other priorities. In addition, the tax-receivable character of the interest-bearing coupons on the bonds the state issued when refinancing the debt in 1871 and 1879 created a chronic budget deficit and starved the public schools of revenue. For fifteen years legislators passed and governors signed bills to prevent payment of taxes with coupons in spite of early rulings by the Virginia Supreme Court of Appeals and repeated later rulings by the Supreme Court of the United States that the Constitution guaranteed men and women the right to pay taxes with the coupons. Those laws generated a cascade of litigation. At least eighty-five cases concerning their constitutionality or enforcement reached the Virginia Supreme Court of Appeals, and twenty-nine reached the Supreme Court of the United States. The attorney general of the state even spent time in jail as a direct consequence of one of those laws.

That part of the history of the Virginia debt controversy has never been fully recounted and is so important that it deserves a prominent place in the longer narrative of Virginia's sometimes troubled relationship with the federal government and its courts. Legislators and governors of both political parties repeatedly defied the federal courts and evaded their rulings. In drafting and defending their laws, the politicians and attorneys employed a great deal of ingenuity and displayed a strong determination in what might have been a good cause insofar as the majority of the population was then concerned, preventing budget deficits and providing adequate money for the public schools. Their prolonged efforts were at least as ingenious and determined as the better-known attempts of the state's politicians in the third quarter of the twentieth century in the worse cause to defy the Supreme Court and avoid obeying its rulings prohibiting racial segregation. So large a part does the legislation and litigation about the coupons occupy in the overall narrative of the debt controversy that it requires three full chapters here and parts of three others to lay it out fully.

The proposals to refinance the debt and the attempts to prevent payment of taxes with coupons repeatedly disrupted the state's politics, and political alliances shifted as the particular issues and the intensity of the debates changed. The dramatic political contests of the 1870s and early 1880s fundamentally reshaped the political landscape of Virginia twice. They created a biracial political party with an emerging egalitarian ideology that gained control of the state government; and then they created an elitist, undemocratic political party based on white supremacy. The Democratic Party apparatus that formed for the overthrow of the Readjuster Party early in the 1880s was as much committed to traditional antebellum elite values and support of the business and commercial leaders of the state as it was to white supremacy, and it dominated the state's politics and government until the 1960s.[5]

There is no scholarly historical narrative that treats the entire history of the debt controversy in anything like its full complexity, not even the political history but especially not the legal history. It is unpleasant to have to say so, but very few of the historians who have published scholarly books or articles on any aspects of the controversy have carefully read or fully understood even the most important statutes or any of the scores of appellate court decisions. Thus they have ignored, slighted, or misrepresented most of the post-1883 events of consequence—and there were many, and they were consequential. Almost the only exception is a portion of a chapter in John O. Peters's history of the federal court in eastern Virginia, *From Marshall to Moussaoui: Federal Justice in the Eastern District of Virginia* (2013), which treated some of the coupon cases that the United States Circuit Court for the Eastern District of Virginia handled during the 1880s.[6] In fact, the legal documents are the one most important source for learning about and understanding what happened, even though the surviving manuscripts of most of the political leaders and attorneys of the time contain many private comments on the evolving issues, partisan recitations of the politics of the debt controversy filled decades of newspaper columns, and participants published numerous pamphlets and self-serving chapters in their memoirs about the debt and its related issues.

At the beginning of 1892, when it appeared that the state had finally resolved most of the major difficulties with the portion of the debt Virginia was willing to pay, the Virginia Debt Commission issued an extremely lean chronology of the laws and court cases.[7] At almost exactly the same time, William A. Scott wrote a chapter-length summary of the political and legal aspects of the Virginia debt controversy for his 1893 book, *The Repudiation of State Debts*. His chapter on Virginia is the longest on any state's nineteenth-century public debt, but it is incomplete and somewhat superficial.[8] Very soon thereafter, in *History of the Virginia Debt Controversy: The Negro's Vicious Influence in Politics* (1897), the bond attorney William L. Royall wrote reliably but very selectively (deceptively so) about a few of the critical coupon cases in which he had taken part. Royall's characterizations of people and events were bitterly personal and partisan and to that extent unreliable. He also included some undocumented and almost certainly exaggerated references to Readjuster incompetence and corruption that made the Readjusters and their leaders appear worse than they were and by inference made their opponents look better.[9]

Royall's book provided much of the contextual political background that appears in the early-twentieth-century histories of the period and therefore influenced later scholarship on the debt controversy and interpretations of the Readjusters. The earliest of them is Charles Chilton Pearson's *Readjuster Movement in Virginia* (1917), the first scholarly historical account of the party, which includes much good detail on the politics and laws of the 1870s and very early 1880s as the state's politicians struggled with how to pay the debt. For good reasons, Pearson devoted much less space to the West Virginia issue, which played itself out long after the Readjusters had disappeared and was not finally settled until after he published his book.[10] Pearson's study remains valuable, but it relies heavily on Royall's characterizations of the Readjusters, and like the works on the period after the Civil War by many other former graduate students of William A. Dunning and their contemporaries, it is lightly laced throughout with the distasteful racism that appeared in much of the historical scholarship on the American South early in the twentieth century, which to that extent undermines its interpretive value.

Through reliance on Royall's and Pearson's books, two of the leading twentieth-century studies of nineteenth-century state debts, Reginald Charles McGrane's *Foreign Bondholders and American State Debts* (1935) and Benjamin Ulysses Ratchford's *American State Debts* (1941), incorporated parts of Royall's and Pearson's characterizations of the Readjusters into their respected standard scholarship on nineteenth-century state debts. McGrane's and Ratchford's otherwise excellent books include longer treatments of the Virginia debt than of any other nineteenth-century state's debt, clearly reflecting its unusual importance and the complexity of the financial, political, and legal complications that arose from it.[11]

Like Pearson, most historians have concentrated on how the debt controversy wrecked the Conservative Party of Virginia, which formed during Congressional Reconstruction in the 1860s, or on the programs and personalities of the Readjuster Party, which arose largely within the Conservative Party during the 1870s. Two fine books published in 1968, Allen W. Moger's *Virginia: Bourbonism to Byrd, 1870–1925*, and Raymond H. Pulley's *Old Virginia Restored: An Interpretation of the Progressive Impulse, 1870–1930*, traced a long narrative arc, as the titles of their books suggest, between the reestablishment of the state's traditional political elite—Redeemers, as people at the time called them and many historians still refer to them—at the end of Congressional Reconstruction in 1870 and the restoration of that elite to almost unchallengeable dominance late in the nineteenth century and early in the twentieth.[12] So do the corresponding sections in my *Grandees of Government: The Origins and Persistence of Undemocratic Politics in Virginia* (2013).[13]

Historians of the debt controversy have not always interpreted that part of the history in the same way, and their differences of opinion have influenced how other historians writing about the South after the Civil War have understood the Redeemers and reformers elsewhere and consequently how they interpreted the whole region and period.[14] Jack P. Maddex Jr. in *The Virginia Conservatives, 1867–1879: A Study in Reconstruction Politics* (1970) characterized the Conservatives, who dominated the state's politics during most of the 1870s, as devoted to commercial and business interests and resistant to African American suffrage as well as to the democratic ethos that in mid-nineteenth-century Virginia had undermined the old political elites. He characterized the base of support for the Readjusters as agrarian unease with the new commercial and business order.[15] On the other hand, James Tice Moore in *Two Paths to the New South: The Virginia Debt Controversy, 1870–1883* (1974) also recognized the Conservatives

as heirs of the prewar commercial and professional leadership class, but
he noted the Readjusters' appeals to urban working men of both races as
well as to farmers. That appeal blurred class and racial lines, drew in men
from a wide variety of backgrounds, and also attracted supporters of the
Grangers and the Greenback Party, agrarian movements that had sought to
reform or regulate the changing national marketplace, not reject it. Moore
characterized the supporters of the Readjusters as producers and working people who believed themselves to be victims of financiers and their
political agents.[16]

The politics of race rather than the debt itself or its legal history has
been the central theme of most of the scholarship on the debt controversy.
Charles E. Wynes in *Race Relations in Virginia, 1870–1902* (1961) and
Jane Dailey in *Before Jim Crow: The Politics of Race in Postemancipation
Virginia* (2000) most clearly illuminated the central importance of race in
the politics of the 1870s and 1880s. Wynes was one of the first scholars to
attend closely to the Readjusters' appeals to and reliance on white farmers
and working men, and Dailey noted how in the beginning the Readjusters
shrewdly and successfully subordinated race to other issues, specifically
the issue of public education, which appealed to both black and white men
and women.[17] Carl N. Degler in a brilliant essay on the Readjusters in *The
Other South: Southern Dissenters in the Nineteenth Century* (1974) and
Steven Hahn in two substantial sections on them in *A Nation under Our
Feet: Black Political Struggles in the Rural South, From Slavery to the
Great Migration* (2003) accurately portrayed the Readjusters as attempting to carry out a unique but ultimately doomed experiment that could
have provided a model for a radical reformation of traditional Southern
politics and life.[18] So did the authors of the two most sweeping and influential accounts of the late-nineteenth-century South, C. Vann Woodward
in *Origins of the New South, 1877–1913*, published in 1951, and Edward L.
Ayers in *The Promise of the New South: Life after Reconstruction*, published in 1992.[19]

The Virginia debt controversy did not spring so much, as Woodward's
work suggests, from an attempt of the old plantation elite to restore its
dominance in opposition to a new order of commercial and finance capitalism. Neither did opposition to that new order come so much, as Maddex suggested, from residents of the countryside who were suspicious of
economic innovation. The economy and political culture of Virginia had
made the transition away from planter domination by the middle of the

nineteenth century, and by then the old planter elite had virtually disappeared as a major force in Virginia politics.[20] Virginia's political leadership was closely allied with the state's large-scale commercial farmers, bankers, railroad executives, and attorneys both before and after the Civil War. The state's politicians for the most part represented Southern capitalists, not locally minded or backward-looking agrarians. After the Civil War, white political leaders in Virginia strove to preserve, revive, and build on their old commercial and financial institutions, of which the state's antebellum support for railroad and canal construction was an essential component and for which the government had created the troublesome debt.

African American suffrage and the new dynamics of a changed regime of race relations after the abolition of slavery complicated their attempts. The leaders of the Conservative Party insisted on the cultural and therefore political superiority of the state's traditional white elites, even though they relied on the votes of non-elite white farmers to win elections. Their vision initially excluded the state's African Americans from any but subordinate, menial participation in economic change or politics,[21] but forces outside their control made that impossible and contributed to the formation of the biracial Readjuster Party. The speedy rise and speedier fall of the Readjusters and the long legal contests about the debt illuminated the choices Virginians and other Southerners faced in the post–Civil War South and revealed the formidable obstacles in the way of some of the possible alternatives.

That part of the political phase of the Virginia debt controversy is reasonably well treated in the historical literature, although in most instances without exhibiting clearly enough how and why the leaders of the Readjuster Party became as radical as they did, within the long traditions not only of Virginia's politics but also of the South's and the nation's. The other phase, the legal clashes about the tax-receivable coupons, which lasted for nearly two decades, is almost entirely missing from Virginia's historical literature and public memory. The passing references to those laws and lawsuits leave the Readjusters primarily and unjustly blamable for both and therefore for the long-drawn-out, expensive, and vexatious litigation for which Democratic Party legislators and attorneys for non-resident bondholders were actually responsible. That has produced some serious misunderstandings about the Readjusters and also about the late-nineteenth-century Democrats. Those important lawsuits led directly to the last of the funding acts, that of 1892, which is either completely missing from most political narratives or poorly characterized because historians have not clearly understood its origins. Consequently, the history of the Virginia debt controversy has remained incomplete and its importance and its consequences therefore misunderstood or misrepresented. Attending properly to its legal history and placing the events in a longer historical perspective presents a different interpretive narrative of that long and important saga and the implications for understanding the dynamics of late-nineteenth-century Southern politics and race relations.

The elusive phrase *New South* in the title deserves a word of explanation. Historians have not agreed on when a New South came into being or how long it lasted, much less what its defining characteristics were or even how to write about it.[22] Whatever the New South was or was imagined to be and whenever it existed, it was a different thing in each state because of the particular economic, political, and legal conditions in each of them. What was inescapably new in all of them beginning in the 1860s was the absence of slavery and the participation of African Americans in politics. That changed or influenced everything. The Virginia debt controversy shaped both the political and the economic reconstruction of the state after the Civil War as well as the future of the large, important, and influential Southern state of Virginia, which was then definitely new in several fundamentally important ways.

1 ORIGINS OF THE DEBT CONTROVERSY

B y 1 January 1861, which is the date on which calculations of the Virginia public debt became important, the state had sold bonds worth almost $34 million to enable the Board of Public Works to purchase stock in publicly chartered companies that constructed canals, toll roads and bridges, and railroads.[1] The state began the purchases in 1822 but had created about two-thirds of the debt in the 1850s to support construction of railroads. The debt was in the form of bonds that matured in thirty-four years, the maximum term allowed under the Virginia Constitution of 1851, and paid 6 percent annual interest, about typical for state debts incurred at that time.[2] The money derived from the issue of the bonds paid for investments that were the central component of the state's program to stimulate economic growth and development by improving travel networks in Virginia and promoting agricultural, industrial, and commercial prosperity.

Most other states did something similar, but Virginia's public-private partnership was unusual, and in its extent it may have been unique. By purchasing as much as 40 percent of the stock in the railroad and canal companies, the state government assisted materially in rapid capital accumulation and construction, but that made the state vulnerable to the same extent if the companies failed, which some of the railroads chartered in the 1830s and 1840s did. The state government also acquired substantial stock in the banks and in some of the other corporations that it chartered.[3]

The Virginia debt was by far the largest in any Southern state or any Ohio valley state when the Civil War began—at that time Virginia was an Ohio valley state as well as a Mid-Atlantic state and a Southern state. By small margins the Virginia debt was the third largest in the whole United States, after only Pennsylvania's and New York's.[4] Per capita, the Virginia debt was actually two or three times the Pennsylvania or New York debt, and per taxpayer the

Virginia debt was much larger still because about 30 percent of the population was enslaved people, who paid no taxes. In 1861 the debt did not appear to present a potential future problem for Virginia. Its creation reflected the overall confidence of the state's business and political leaders that Virginia would prosper as a full participant in the increasingly sophisticated and integrated national economy. Railroads were the key to that national and state prosperity, and the taxes and dividends they paid to the state could contribute toward paying off the debt.

The Civil War ruined that optimistic vision for Virginia. The state fractured into two states beginning in 1861 as a direct consequence of the fracture of the nation. In May and June 1861, shortly after a state convention in Richmond submitted an ordinance of secession to the voters for ratification, the first of a series of conventions of men who remained loyal to the United States met in the northwestern city of Wheeling, appointed a new governor and other state officers, and reorganized the state government to restore Virginia to the Union. On 4 July 1861, President Abraham Lincoln recognized the government in Wheeling as the legitimate government of all the loyal people of Virginia,[5] and the United States Congress seated senators and representatives from the Restored Government of Virginia, as it was commonly called, during the first years of the Civil War.

In August 1861, the last of the series of conventions in Wheeling authorized the creation of a separate, new state and summoned a convention that met in November to draft a constitution for what became West Virginia. The authorizing resolution pledged that the "new State shall take upon itself a just proportion of the public debt of the Commonwealth of Virginia, prior to the 1st day of January, 1861, to be ascertained by charging to it all State expenditures within the limits thereof, and just proportion of the ordinary expenses of the State government, since any part of said debt was contracted, and deducting therefrom the monies paid into the treasury of the Commonwealth from the counties included within the new State within the same period."[6]

The language about the debt that the constitutional convention included in the new constitution that became effective on 20 June 1863 was broader and less specific, leaving the new state more leeway to decide what to do and how to do it. Article VIII, Section 8, of the Constitution of West Virginia declared, "An equitable proportion of the public debt of the Commonwealth of Virginia, prior to the first day of January in the year one thousand eight hundred and sixty-one, shall be assumed by this State, and the Legislature shall ascertain the same as soon as may be practicable, and provide for the liquidation thereof, by a sinking fund to pay the accruing interest, and redeem the principal within thirty-four years."[7] Throughout the process of creating the new state, western Virginians clearly understood that promising to pay a portion of Virginia's antebellum debt was essential to gain support of Northern financiers and political leaders for admission of West Virginia into the Union.[8]

In May 1862 the General Assembly of the Restored Government of Virginia gave its consent, as required by the Constitution of the United States, for the formation of the new state out of the old.[9] It also appropriated one hundred thousand dollars for deposit in the West Virginia treasury at the time of statehood, and it ordered that all dividends and "all money from any source whatsoever due the State" and all taxes collected prior to statehood from the counties and cities that were to become West Virginia be paid to the new state. As if with the resolution adopted in Wheeling in August 1861 for a negotiated agreement of the respective portions of the debt in mind, the law concluded, "All of the appropriations made by this Act, shall be charged to the State of West Virginia, in the settlement between the States of Virginia and West Virginia."[10]

In the next session of the Restored Government's assembly early in 1863, the legislators passed An Act Transferring to the Proposed State of West Virginia, When the Same Shall Become One of the United States, All This State's Interest in Property, Unpaid and Uncollected Taxes, Fines, Forfeitures, Penalties and Judgments, in Counties Embraced Within the Boundaries of the Proposed State Aforesaid.[11] The assembly also replaced the 1862 law making the $100,000 appropriation with an appropriation of $150,000 and an allocation of all the money collected or owed to Virginia within the new state as of the date of statehood, but it omitted the reference to a future settlement between the two states.[12]

Early in 1864, the General Assembly of the Restored Government, which moved in the summer of 1863 from Wheeling to Alexandria, summoned a constitutional convention, principally for the purpose of abolishing slavery in the loyal state of Virginia. Article IV, Section 27, of the new constitution that took effect on 7 April 1864 prohibited the government from creating a debt for any purpose other than self-defense in time of war or insurrection. It also stated that the "general assembly shall provide by law for adjusting with the state of West Virginia the proportion of the public debt of Virginia, proper to be born [sic] by the states of Virginia and of West Virginia respectively; and may authorize, in conjunction with the state of West Virginia, the sale of all lands and property of every description, including all stocks and other interests owned and held by the state of Virginia in banks, works of internal improvement, and other companies at the time of the formation of the state of West Virginia, and no ordinance passed by the convention which assembled at Wheeling . . . adjusting the public debt between Virginia and West Virginia, shall be binding upon this state."[13] That left the government of the loyal state of Virginia just as unrestrained as the government of the new state of West Virginia with respect to how to pay the debt.

During the war, the government of the Confederate state of Virginia in Richmond refused to recognize the legal existence or legitimacy of the Restored Government of Virginia, which remained one of the United States, or the government of the new state of West Virginia.[14] The collapse of the Confederacy in the spring of 1865 and the simultaneous collapse and disappearance of the government of the Confederate state of Virginia left the Restored Government of Virginia as the only government of what remained of the old commonwealth.[15] Afterwards, acting under the Constitution of 1864, the sole remaining government of Virginia attempted to negotiate with West Virginia about how to calculate the two states' respective portions of the whole debt and how to pay the principal and accruing interest. At the same time, though, the General Assembly of Virginia took several steps that alienated authorities in West Virginia and made them less willing to negotiate with any authorities in Virginia. Early in 1866 the assembly repealed the laws giving consent for the formation of West Virginia and authorizing referenda in Berkeley and Jefferson Counties, among others, to allow the residents to decide whether their counties would be part of Virginia or part of West Virginia.[16] The attorney general of Virginia filed suit against West Virginia in the Supreme Court of the United States to negate West Virginia's acquisition of Jefferson and Berkeley Counties and to prohibit the government of that state from collecting taxes in those counties pending the outcome of the suit.[17] By filing the lawsuit, Virginia implicitly recognized the constitutional existence of West Virginia in spite of the repeal of the authorization law, and the Supreme Court's decision in favor of West Virginia in 1870 validated the constitutionality of the creation of West Virginia and its acquisition of the two counties.[18]

Neither of the Virginia state governments paid any significant amount of interest on the debt during the Civil War. Even though the United States

Army helped rebuild some of Virginia's railroads soon after the end of the war and the railroads began making profits within two years, they paid no dividends to the state.[19] Nor did the state receive dividends from banks it had chartered before the war. Some of them no longer existed. The economic condition of Virginia at the end of the war seriously reduced the options for political leaders who hoped to resume payment of the interest. The poor condition of the state government and the poorer condition of the state's economy made payment on the principal and rapidly accumulating outstanding interest on the debt both more urgent and more difficult. If the state could not recover rapidly, tax revenue would likely remain too low to permit payments on the debt, but without establishing a new, good reputation for financial probity by paying the debt, neither the state nor the state's bankers and businessmen could hope to attract adequate private capital from outside the state with which to revive the economy.

One of the complicating factors was the abolition of slavery, which destroyed a very valuable source of prewar tax revenue. Nearly half a million Virginians lived in slavery when the Civil War began, and those people were taxable property, the most valuable property in the whole state, only the land itself excepted. Since the seventeenth century the government had relied on money collected from taxes on that property for a large portion of its revenue. Local governments had too. Had the rapid increase in the value of slave property as a consequence of the brisk demand for laborers in the lower Mississippi valley continued the trend established during the 1850s, the value of the state's slave property might even have eclipsed the value of its land. The importance of slavery to the Southern economies was widely recognized, but the equally important influence of slavery on Southern taxation may not have been so conspicuous at the time.[20] The postwar consequences of the reductions in revenue were immediately obvious in Virginia and elsewhere.[21] Without the unpaid labor of slaves, both the productive value and the taxable value of the land also dropped.

Throughout much of the controversy about the Virginia debt, people alluded to the damaging effects of the abolition of slavery on public revenue and consequently on the ability of the state to raise sufficient money to pay the interest and principal. Many, perhaps a majority, of white Virginians believed that the federal government and the Northern states were responsible for the Civil War, the abolition of slavery, and the loss of the western counties to West Virginia. Those people concluded that Northerners should not receive payment on the part of the state's debt that they owned or should have their payments reduced by an amount proportional to the reduced value of the taxable property in the postwar state of Virginia. Some of those people advanced arguments similar to those that Thomas Jefferson and Patrick Henry, among others, had made following the American Revolution and that were derived from principles of contract law. Because it had been the deliberate policy of the British government then to carry away slaves and destroy property in Virginia, which had eliminated some of the resources with which Virginia's planters could have paid their prewar debts to British merchants, the planters could not or should not be required to pay those old debts.[22] Many influential post–Civil War Virginians saw an irresistible parallel between the actions of the British and those of the United States.

The economic consequences of the defeat of the Confederacy and the abolition of slavery were profound throughout the South. Many white Southerners as well as some banks and other businesses had invested their capital in Confederate securities, but the end of the war made those investments and all the slave capital equally worthless. The old planter families and owners of mid-sized farms who attempted to operate with hired rather than with enslaved laborers encountered new problems with their private finances. They had to learn how to operate in a free labor economy and could no longer lease enslaved laborers or borrow money using their slaves as collateral. Neither could railroads or canals, timber companies, mine operators, or other businesses that had owned or leased enslaved laborers before the Civil War.

Many old credit relations changed with the abolition of slavery, and freed people and white farmers also operated in a changed credit environment. They all needed to borrow money from time to time or ran up bills for purchase of seeds or supplies. Sharecroppers, an increasingly large proportion of the rural population, fell into debt to landowners or to local shopkeepers. Both men and women had accounts at shops in cities and towns or at country stores, and thousands of men and women owned and operated small businesses or shops. War widows or women with disabled husbands could quickly get mired in debt and incur other obligations just trying to keep their families housed, clothed, and fed. Forced sales of the houses and farms of broken or bankrupted families were commonplace events in all Virginia communities, providing constant reminders of the perils of debt or the loss of resources. Men and women of both races could easily see the immediate effects of personal debt on their families,[23] and even though some of the debate about the public debt and the later laws and court cases were filled with complicated legal and technical financial language, most people easily came to understand the consequences of that problem for their personal lives too. There is no doubt that the state's women followed the political news closely and let their voting male relatives know what they thought.[24]

The debt was high on the agenda of Governor Francis H. Pierpont[25] immediately after the war. In December 1865, in his first annual message to the General Assembly after the Restored Government moved from Alexandria to Richmond, he reported that as of 1 July the public debt of Virginia, including unpaid interest, which had continued to accrue, had stood at more than $41 million. "The holders of Virginia state bonds," he informed the legislators, "are pressing for the payment of the interest due."[26] The assembly passed a law allowing owners of bonds on which interest had not been paid to receive new bonds, to be issued in multiples of one hundred dollars in value to the amount of the unpaid interest. The new bonds paid the same 6 percent interest for thirty-four years from the date of issue.[27] The assembly also authorized the appointment of three commissioners to open negotiations with West Virginia to ascertain the two states' respective portions of the debt,[28] but the West Virginia Legislature appointed no commissioners to negotiate with the Virginians.

When the General Assembly reconvened at the beginning of December 1866, Pierpont cautioned the legislators against undertaking any new spending. None of the many proposals that he anticipated being introduced had "any merit," he argued, "to compare with the demand on the state for the payment of the interest on the public debt." Pierpont also cautioned against temptations to reduce the portion of the debt to be paid. "There has been some vague talk about repudiating or scaling the public debt," he warned. "This I am satisfied proceeds from want of consideration. To say nothing of the morality of the act, no step would be so prejudicial to all our future interests as a serious discussion of the subject. To commit the deed, would be to cut off all private credit from without the state, and erect a bar to future influx of capital. If so fatal a step should be taken, no gentleman would hereafter be particularly anxious, when abroad, to be recognized as a Virginian."[29] The legislators passed a joint resolution strongly condemning repudiation[30] and debated but did not adopt a proposal to promise payment of two-thirds of the debt and assign West Virginia responsibility for the other third.[31] In the spring, with three separate bills they authorized a one-time 2 percent payment on the outstanding interest.[32]

The General Assembly of Virginia did not meet between the adjournment of that session in April 1867 and October 1869, while the state was under military rule during Congressional Reconstruction. Congress, frustrated at the unwillingness of white Southern political leaders to protect the rights of the freed people, required most of the states of the former Confederacy to hold conventions and write new state constitutions—even Virginia, which had a state government that had been loyal to the United States during the Civil War and that was even then operating under the Constitution of 1864, which the loyal government had promulgated. Congress directed that African American men be permitted to vote and run for seats in the convention,[33] and two dozen black men won election to and served in the Virginia Convention of 1867–68.[34] Together with men of Northern birth who moved to Virginia during or soon after the war (called by the insulting name *carpetbaggers*) and a contingent of white Virginians who had remained loyal to the United States during the war (called by the other insulting name from the period, *scalawags*), that gave the convention a membership of radically different composition than any previous Virginia constitutional convention.[35]

The presence of African Americans and the prominence of some of the immigrants provided focal points for people who condemned the constitution the convention wrote. Sharp criticism of the convention and the constitution it produced flourished unabated until long after the constitutional convention that met in 1901 and 1902 revoked many of the democratic reforms embodied in the Constitution of 1869. In the public discourse of the time and in much of the later scholarly literature it was called the Underwood Constitution, for federal judge John C. Underwood, the radical Republican president of the convention.[36]

The new constitution of Virginia made no changes with respect to the public debt and prohibited the state from creating a new debt,[37] meaning that the prewar policy of state purchase of part of the equity of private companies was definitely at an end. The 1864 and 1869 constitutions may have reflected a new concern about the mounting size of the debt during the war years and immediately thereafter. Pierpont's warnings and the constitutional prohibition meant that unlike some other Southern states, Virginia created no new public debt after the Civil War.

The new constitution made other important changes. One of the most important was the requirement that the General Assembly create a new free public school system for all children. The constitution also reformed the structure of local government on the more democratic model of the New England township. For the first time since the American Revolution, the constitution granted the governor authority to veto bills that the General Assembly passed, subject to a two-thirds vote in both houses, which could override a veto. As it happened, some of the first and most controversial vetoes that Virginia governors issued involved the public debt.

The changes of most immediate importance to Virginia's politics were provisions that granted the vote to adult African American men and denied the vote to many men who had taken part in the Confederate army and government. Some influential prewar Virginia political leaders, members of Congress, and President Ulysses S. Grant eventually negotiated an agreement to allow the section disfranchising former Confederates to be voted on separately from the remainder of the constitution at the time of the ratification referendum. That permitted voters, again including African American men, to ratify the constitution with black suffrage intact but without the restrictions on former Confederates.[38]

Soon after the constitutional convention began its work, white Virginia political leaders organized the Conservative Party to unite men who disapproved of what the convention was beginning to do, what Congress had begun doing, and what they feared Congress might do later. Most of the state's prewar Democrats and many of its leading former Whigs supported the Conservative Party. The party's first state leaders had long records of experience in prewar politics as Whigs, and many of them were attorneys closely connected with the state's banks, railroads, and industrial and commercial interests. In addition to opposing Congressional Reconstruction, they hoped to preserve elite white leadership in the state and to revive the state's prewar economy.[39]

In the beginning, though, the Conservatives focused their attention on the constitutional convention. In organizing the state party, Raleigh Travers Daniel,[40] a prominent prewar Whig who identified himself as chief director of the state committee, issued instructions in a series of printed "Circulars." The fourth, dated 12 February 1868, urged local party organizers to stress the dangers the convention posed. It included an explicit link between political issues involving race and personal debt. "Attempts are being made," he wrote, "to engraft in the constitution measures looking to the relief of people from debt, being a *bribe* by which it is hoped white votes can be bought for negro suffrage, negro office-holding, and negro equality generally. Let us hope that these base influences will be lost upon a people determined, for themselves and their posterity, that this is, and ever shall be, *'a white man's government.'* But leave no door open by which danger can enter. Men who are already enrolled with a pledge to vote against a negro constitution, will be less apt to fall away from duty than those who stand uncommitted."[41]

Many of the state's Republicans shared the same economic objectives as the Conservatives, and some also favored allowing former Confederates to return to political office as a measure of reconciliation, but the Republican Party was seriously divided on that and other important issues. The more radical Republicans were sympathetic to the radical Republican reformers in Congress and opposed allowing former Confederates to return to public office soon or at all. In preparation for the election of statewide officers and members of the General Assembly in the summer of 1869, the Republican Party state convention nominated a slate of radical candidates, including an African American for lieutenant governor.

Moderate Republicans were disgusted and convinced that the party would therefore lose the election. They separately nominated Gilbert C. Walker, a former New York attorney and banker then residing in Norfolk, for governor and white Virginia Unionists for lieutenant governor and attorney general. The Conservative Party endorsed the moderate Republican ticket to present a united opposition to the radicals. Walker's ticket won the statewide election, and Conservatives won large majorities in both houses of the General Assembly, abruptly bringing the brief reform period of Congressional Reconstruction in Virginia to an end and restoring governmental control to native white Virginia men who had grown to political maturity before and during the Civil War.[42]

Thus, with reluctance and under duress, a majority of the white political leaders in Virginia accepted universal manhood suffrage, including African Americans, as an unavoidable necessity in the new postwar, postslavery era. Most of the white Conservatives and Republicans in the General Assembly joined about thirty African American members in voting to ratify the Fourteenth and Fifteenth Amendments to the Constitution, which Congress required before it seated senators and representatives from the state. That fully restored Virginia to the Union early in January 1870.[43]

The first political acts of the Virginia debt controversy began the following year in an unprecedented political environment. Most of the state's veteran political leaders, both Whigs and Democrats, were united in the new Conservative Party, and the state's newly enfranchised African Americans joined with outsiders and native white Unionists in an energized but outnumbered Republican Party.

2 THE FUNDING ACT OF 1871

A clause in the Fourteenth Amendment to the Constitution of the United States, which was ratified in 1868, prohibited states from paying debts incurred during the Civil War in support of the rebellion, but it did not apply to the prewar or postwar debt of any state. The government of the Confederate state of Virginia had somehow managed to run a surplus and from March 1864 to February 1865 actually suspended collection of property and license taxes.[1] That state government ceased to exist in April 1865, and what had to that time been called the Restored Government succeeded it and acknowledged that it had inherited the prewar debt.

By 1 January 1870 the Virginia public debt, with its swelling unpaid interest, had risen to more than $45.6 million.[2] It was the largest state debt in the country then and remained the largest until the 1890s. It was therefore the most important of all the states' debts. The inability of Virginia to pay the interest and the uncertainty about what the government would do about the principal depressed the value of the bonds in the immediate aftermath of the Civil War to 50–60 percent of face value.[3] Speculative investors were therefore able to purchase Virginia bonds for a fraction of their face value and then combine their influence to advocate legislation to pay the bonds and interest in full. If they succeeded, that would almost certainly drive up the market value of the bonds.

Early in 1870 the legislators in Richmond resumed discussions about what to do and appointed new commissioners to negotiate with West Virginia to determine the two states' respective responsibilities for the debt. They appointed more commissioners early in 1871 with powers to suggest that the amount be settled by independent arbitration,[4] but after preliminary conversations nothing of importance happened for decades.[5]

Governor Walker[6] sent a long special message to the Virginia General

Assembly in March 1870 enumerating reasons why the state should pay the interest and find a means to pay the principal of the debt. He included several specific suggestions for reducing the cost of operating the state's government and increasing its tax revenue.[7] In his annual message to the next session of the assembly on 7 December 1870, Walker repeated his recommendations and made a strong argument for resuming payment on the interest of the debt and raising some taxes to provide the money. He rejected suggestions that because the state's bonds were trading at a substantial discount the state should consider paying the debt at the reduced market value rather than at its larger face value. "The bond held for the benefit of the poor orphan," the banker-governor lectured the legislators, "and the bond owned by the rich speculator, are of equal dignity, and equally binding upon the State. Each is her solemn obligation to pay. . . . But it matters not where or by whom our bonds are held, or at what rates they were obtained, so far as your duty is concerned. That duty is to reinstate our dishonored credit. The people of this Commonwealth will never permit the blighting stain of repudiation to tarnish her escutcheon. A neglect, however, to provide the means for meeting the obligations of the State is as much repudiation as would be an absolute refusal of payment, and far less manly."[8]

Walker's invocation of the state's honor echoed what Pierpont had told the assembly four years earlier. Virginia's two postwar Unionist-Republican governors urgently advocated paying the full principal and accrued interest on the debt and invoked the honor of the state as a primary motivation. The importance of personal honor in Virginia and the preservation of the state's honor and public credit already were, and for many more years remained, key arguments for paying the full principal and interest on the debt. If the state's honor had not already been emphasized enough, Walker's December 1870 message gave the state's legislators and creditors the language with which to argue that no matter how high the immediate cost to the state, the long-term prosperity of Virginia and Virginians required payment of both the outstanding interest and the full principal. Perhaps as a consequence, hopeful speculators and large-scale investors began buying Virginia bonds, which drove up the average market price in 1870 and 1871 from 50–60 percent to 65–70 percent of par.[9]

Walker's suggestions contained echoes of the arguments of Secretary of the Treasury Alexander Hamilton during President George Washington's first administration when he proposed paying the Revolutionary War debt at face value rather than at the significantly lower market price at which the debt certificates then traded. At that time, influential Virginia political leaders, including Thomas Jefferson and James Madison, had objected that investors and speculators who had purchased the debt certificates from the original owners at much lower prices than the first purchasers had paid should not receive as an unearned bonus from the public treasury the difference between the lower market price and the higher face value. Hamilton argued that if the new U.S. government paid the full debt, foreign investors would perceive the country and its citizens as good future business partners. Hamilton won his case in Congress, and Walker won his in the General Assembly.

In March 1871 the assembly passed An Act to Provide for the Funding and Payment of the Public Debt, which was then known and has thereafter been known as the Funding Act of 1871. It passed in the Senate of Virginia by a vote of 25 to 10 and in the House of Delegates by a vote of 78 to 42,[10] and the governor signed it on 30 March 1871. The law prohibited payment of any interest or principal on any of the then existing public securities and encouraged—as a practical matter, required—owners of the old bonds to exchange them for new bonds dated 1 July 1871. The new bonds paid the same 6 percent annual interest as the old, half payable every six months. The Funding Act also provided for the exchange of a much smaller issue of old 5 percent bonds for new 5 percent bonds. All the bonds were to mature in thirty-four years, with the state reserving an option to redeem them at any time after ten years. The law levied a tax of 2 percent on the value of all property beginning in 1880, to be paid into a sinking fund for retiring the principal when the bonds matured. It also required that the proceeds of all sales of public property be paid into the sinking fund. Virginia was even then selling most of its depreciated stock in the state's railroads at what some critics charged were scandalously low prices.[11]

The new bonds funded—that is, provided for paying—two-thirds of the face value of the old bonds. Without any participation by or approval from any West Virginia officials, the Virginia General Assembly set Virginia's portion of the principal at two-thirds of the whole and West Virginia's at one-third. The Funding Act required that at the time of the exchange of old bonds for new the state issue certificates (each equal to one-half the value of the bond issued at the same time) to the investors, stating that West Virginia's third of the principal would be funded after the two states agreed on how West Virginia would pay its portion. In effect, the Funding

Act made a bond owner's acceptance of the new bonds and certificates, which later came to be called Virginia Deferred Certificates, signify agreement to all the terms, including the temporary abatement of a creditor's claims against Virginia and West Virginia for the third of the principal that Virginia declared was West Virginia's portion.

At the time of exchange of old bonds for new, the bondholders could select bonds with coupons or bonds without coupons and could later exchange bonds of either kind for bonds of the other. Owners of bonds without coupons, called registered bonds because the auditors kept registers of who purchased them and who later owned them, received the full face value and all accrued interest when the bonds matured thirty-four years after the date of issue. Owners of bonds with coupons could receive their interest payments semiannually by clipping the coupons from their bonds and presenting them at the treasury in Richmond for payment of the interest then due. The sixty-eight coupons on a thirty-four-year bond bore dates of maturity at six-month intervals, allowing the owners to receive 3 percent interest twice each year. The coupon bonds were in effect bearer bonds that men and women could buy and sell without recording the transactions with the state's auditors, and whoever owned them at maturity could cash them in for payment of the full principal. The assembly authorized coupon bonds to make them attractive to investors who wished to receive their earnings at regular intervals. Coupon bonds were a popular method that governments and businesses in the nineteenth century used to borrow money, and the phrases *coupon clippers* and *clipping coupons* commonly referred to people who did not labor but lived off income from investments. What quickly became the most troublesome and controversial provision of the law declared that the coupons be "receivable at and after maturity for all taxes, debts, dues, and demands due the state, which shall be so expressed on their face."[12]

Consolidating the entire debt, which had been made up of numerous small bond issues, into a new debt with one set of bonds pleased the banker-governor, and it also pleased people who owned the old prewar bonds and had received few or no interest payments for more than a decade. During the months following passage of the law, owners of about two-thirds of the old bonds exchanged them for the new. Some people had no doubt lost their bonds or forgotten about them, which to a small extent effectively reduced the whole portion of the two-thirds of the principal that Virginia funded with the 1871 bonds. And after the initial exchange of old bonds from numerous prewar issues for the new bonds was completed, the Funding Act also promised to simplify the work of the auditors in keeping track of the state's fiscal obligations.

For the reasons Walker had adduced, the Funding Act of 1871 appeared to make good, solid business sense and therefore appealed to the leading Conservative politicians and also to most Republicans. Almost all the African Americans who were serving in the assembly joined a majority of white legislators in voting for it. The bill did not pass without opposition, though. Some legislators and some influential observers objected that the state's struggling economy had not recovered sufficiently to allow the government to pay 6 percent interest on such a large principal and that the attempt to do so would deplete the treasury to such an extent that the state could not allocate enough money to the new public school system and also pay for other necessary state expenses. Then, and increasingly thereafter, people who opposed the measure believed or charged that the state's creditors had procured its passage by making improper behind-the-scenes offers to members of the assembly. Nobody every conducted a proper investigation to establish the facts, and the allegations clung to the Funding Act throughout its life and afterward. The charge provided arguments for white Virginians who wanted to deprive black Virginians of the vote on the ground that passage of the Funding Act proved that they were easily corrupted and therefore a corrupting influence in politics.[13]

It is not at all clear that anybody could have conducted an unbiased investigation or that a generally acceptable definition of corruption could have been agreed to, so close were the relationships between corporate interests, party leaders, and legislators in that part of the nineteenth century virtually everywhere in the United States. Indeed, they were often the same people, as critics of the role of the Bank of England in British politics had charged in the eighteenth century and critics of Alexander Hamilton's plans for creating a national bank and paying the Revolutionary War debt had charged later. Although Virginia had quickly passed through its period of Congressional Reconstruction without any of the serious financial corruption that occurred in several other Southern states, the period between the American Civil War and the end of the nineteenth century exhibited many intimate relationships between corporate and government officials that contemporaries characterized as improper or corrupt.

Virginia's government was not immune. Favoritism and nepotism were commonplace, and political leaders of all stripes engaged in shady practices.

Railroads in particular, the largest and most influential business-industrial complex in the state—in the nation—vied with one another for favorable legislation and favors from the assembly and probably provided money, alcohol, or women to influence legislators. The sale of the state's railroad stock at the beginning of the 1870s almost certainly involved bribes to legislators.[14] Whether representatives of the bondholders acted similarly in 1871 to encourage members of the assembly to vote for the Funding Act is not certain, but it is entirely possible.[15] Any investigation would probably have resulted in pots calling kettles black, and opponents of the Funding Act as well as its advocates may have backed away from offering the other side an opportunity to retaliate in kind.

The 6 percent interest rate and the tax-receivable character of the coupons may have received inadequate consideration during the legislative deliberations. Walker's estimates of revenue turned out to be unrealistically high,[16] but even then a few simple calculations would have shown just how injurious to the state's budget the interest rate was. The principal of the debt was then about nine times the state's annual revenue and still rising because the state had not been paying the interest on it, and old unpaid interest became new debt. As of 30 September 1872, the end of the first full fiscal year during which the Funding Act was in force, total state revenue was about $3.2 million, and the whole of the debt, less the one-third assigned to West Virginia, stood at nearly $30.5 million.[17] If all the old bonds had been exchanged for new 6 percent bonds, the state would have had to pay more than $1.8 million in interest, more than half the annual revenue. Moreover, every dollar paid into the treasury in the form of a coupon was a dollar the treasury could not use to pay public salaries, to operate the government, or to buy buildings and books or pay teachers and administrators for the new public schools system—or even to pay interest on the debt.

One of the most experienced and outspoken of Virginia's old political leaders objected to the funding bill strenuously. Former governor Henry A. Wise believed that the state could not afford to pay 6 percent interest and also pay for the new public school system and that Walker and the bondholders had conspired to force the bill through a corrupted legislature. Wise suggested an alternative method of freeing the state from the whole debt by renouncing it in a way he considered honorable. "The State that owed it is dead," he argued. "The State that owed it went to war with the United States. The United States, by force of arms and military occupancy, wrested two-fifths of the territory of the State of Virginia from her and erected it into a new State called West Virginia. . . . At a later stage, the United States conquered the remnant of Virginia and displaced the Government of her choice first by a Government of military usurpation, then by a Civil Government of its own dictation, altogether different from that which contracted this debt." The only things the prewar state and government of Virginia shared with the postwar state and government, Wise concluded, were a name and a specific geographic area. Therefore, the postwar state government, not having borrowed the money, was neither legally nor morally responsible for paying it back. If the bondholders had any remedy or hope for payment at all, they should appeal to the U.S. government, which had destroyed the old state government that had borrowed the money.[18] Wise was not unusual among white Virginians in blaming the Northern states or the United States for the decisions of some Southern states to secede in 1861 and therefore for all the consequences of the resulting Civil War.

The ability of people to pay their taxes with the interest coupons that matured every six months very quickly became a huge financial problem for the state and greatly magnified the difficulties the law's critics had foretold. During its first year in operation, taxpayers paid about one-sixth of their taxes with coupons, but during the second year almost half.[19] That revenue was essentially worth nothing. In the autumn 1871 legislative elections, opponents of the law won additional seats in the General Assembly.

When the legislators convened a few weeks later, Walker proposed that the assembly make additional cuts in spending to prevent the state from reducing the amount of money available for the schools or missing interest payments on the debt.[20] A few days later, though, the assembly members adopted a joint resolution to suspend operation of the Funding Act "until proper steps have been taken to ascertain the entire amount that will be required to pay the current expenses of the State Government and the interest upon the State debt, as provided for by the funding act, and increased rate of taxation it may necessitate, should the whole debt be funded." The resolution directed that "the Second Auditor should be, and he is hereby instructed to discontinue any further issue of the new bonds until such time as these facts can be ascertained, and such legislation be perfected in the premises, should any be necessary, as the public good may require."[21]

Walker vetoed the joint resolution, calling it difficult to understand, unwise in that it unsettled the minds of the public and the state's creditors, and unjust in that owners of more than two-thirds of the bonds had already exchanged their old bonds for the new, leaving the other bondholders no equitable remedy.[22] The legislators failed to override the veto,[23] but they then attacked the part of the law that created the worst immediate problem, the flood of coupons into the treasury in payment of taxes, and passed a law that Walker also vetoed.

An Act Declaring What Shall be Received in Payment of Taxes or Other Demands Due the State, which the assembly passed over the governor's second debt-related veto of the session, prohibited collectors "of taxes or other demands of the state, due now or that shall hereafter become due, to receive in payment thereof any thing else than gold or silver coin, United States treasury notes or notes of the national banks of the United States."[24] Walker objected to almost every clause of the bill and pronounced the clause making treasury notes and bank notes equal to gold and silver for payment of taxes a violation of Article I, Section 10, Paragraph 1, of the Constitution of the United States, which prohibited states from making anything but gold and silver "a Tender in Payment of Debts."[25] The bill repealed all other acts or parts of acts inconsistent with it, which definitely meant the language in the Funding Act of 1871 that allowed for payment of taxes with coupons.

A few days later the assembly passed a law that as of 1 January 1873 reduced the annual interest to be paid on the bonds from 6 percent to 4 percent by ordering the treasurer to pay 2 percent for each of the semi-annual 3 percent interest coupons presented for payment that year. The law also correspondingly reduce the amount of interest accruing on the non-coupon bonds.[26] The former Confederate general Bradley T. Johnson, then a prominent Richmond attorney and advocate for full implementation of the Funding Act, published a pamphlet while the interest reduction bill was before the Senate of Virginia. He reported that "certain friends of the Funding Bill in the Senate" had agreed to vote to override the governor's veto of the resolution to suspend operations of the Funding Act in exchange for the lower rate of interest.[27] He was probably correct. During the following years, some people who placed full payment of the debt at the top of their political agendas showed a willingness to reduce interest payments moderately and temporarily in order to prevent a default.

The Act Declaring What Shall be Received in Payment of Taxes or Other Demands Due the State led to the first important court case in the saga of the debt controversy. The Richmond resident Andrew Antoni presented a matured three-dollar interest coupon to the city sheriff, John W. Wright, in partial payment of his real estate tax, but the sheriff, citing the 1872 law, refused to receive it. Antoni and Austin Smith, who also tried to pay his city tax with a coupon at about the same time, appealed to the Virginia Supreme Court of Appeals to issue writs of mandamus to direct the sheriff to receive the coupons. Bradley T. Johnson and an ambitious and persistent young attorney, William L. Royall, a Confederate veteran who later wrote a history of the debt controversy from the creditors' perspective, represented Antoni. Attorney General James Craig Taylor represented the sheriff.

On 13 December 1872, Judge Wood Bouldin[28] delivered the opinion of the court in *Antoni v. Wright.* In his preliminary recitation of the history of the public debt, he did not let pass an opportunity to shift some of the blame for Virginia's problems with its public debt onto the United States, as Wise had done. Bouldin gave a brief account of the creation of the debt during the decades "prior to the late war between the United States and the Confederates States," before the "violent dismemberment" of Virginia, which the state "was powerless to resist," by which "about one-third of the territory and population of the State was cut off, and formed into a new State called West Virginia." Bouldin relied on several recent relevant decisions of the Supreme Court of the United States to conclude that, as in several like instances elsewhere, including Tennessee and some other states of the former Confederacy, when Virginia issued and the creditors accepted the new bonds under the Funding Act of 1871, the two entered into a legal contract that included the wording of the statute and the text printed on each coupon, which allowed owners of coupons to pay state taxes with them. He declared that the act of 1872 was therefore an impairment of the obligations of contract and consequently a violation of Article I, Section 10, Paragraph 1, of the Constitution of the United States. He could have declared, but did not, that it was also a violation of the identical language in Article V, Section 14, of the Virginia Constitution of 1869.[29]

Judge Waller Redd Staples issued a long, almost angry dissenting opinion that gave a preview of some of the political, legal, and public policy issues that later gained acceptance among opponents of the Funding Act. A former member of the Confederate House of Representatives, he too could have blamed the state's financial problems on the federal government, but he did not. Instead, he denied that creditors' acceptance of the 1871 bonds created a legally binding contract between the creditors and the state, because in the exchange of old bonds for new the state received nothing of value. The transaction was missing an essential characteristic of a legal contract, the exchange of goods or services of value. The 1872 law therefore did not unconstitutionally impair any contract. Staples sharply criticized the other members of the court for believing themselves bound "to follow, with blind submission, the decisions of the Supreme court of the United States, however erroneous and unjust we may consider them," in declaring the coupons constitutionally protected contracts.

Staples also declared that because the 1871 funding law permitted fines to be paid into the state's old Literary Fund with coupons rather than with money, the law violated Article V, Section 8, of the state constitution, which required that fines paid into the Literary Fund be expended solely for the benefit of the public schools, which was not the case with fines received in the form of coupons. He also stated, without giving any details, that the Funding Act of 1871 violated Article X, Sections 7, 8, and 9, of the state constitution, which specified in general terms how the state was to pay the debt.

Staples's other constitutional objection to the Funding Act of 1871 was that if the coupons did indeed constitute a binding contract, the law thereby unconstitutionally impaired the sovereign rights of future assemblies. "According to the theory and practice of our government," he wrote, "the whole subject of taxation, the raising and collecting public revenue, and its appropriation, are under the exclusive control of the representatives of the people. These are sovereign powers, which no Legislature is competent to surrender; nor can it, by any contract or enactment, deprive any future Legislature of the right to adopt any laws, to impose any burdens, and apply the public revenue in any manner the public interest may require, not prohibited by the constitution."[30] William L. Royall later wrote that no Virginia judge had ever asserted that one legislature could not adopt a law that entirely prohibited a later legislature from acting on a subject.[31] Royall might even have made that suggestion during the argument of the case.

When Bouldin delivered the opinion for the court, and Staples his dissent, Judge Francis T. Anderson[32] made some oral comments from the bench that the attorney general believed expressed reservations about Bouldin's opinion. The attorney general therefore asked for a rehearing of the case. In a written opinion that the court reporter appended to the official printed report of the case, Anderson stated that he fully concurred in the decision of the court. The court therefore denied the attorney general's request for a rehearing.[33] The Supreme Court of Appeals issued the writ of mandamus to the sheriff, directing him to accept the coupon in payment of three dollars' worth of Antoni's taxes as the Funding Act of 1871 required.[34]

The following year, a second case arose that required the Supreme Court of Appeals to take another look at the effect of the 1872 law. *Antoni v. Wright* had made it legal again for men and women to pay their taxes with coupons clipped from the 1871 bonds they then owned, but people continued to exchange old bonds for new bonds after passage of the 1872 act. On 17 December 1873, in *Wise Bros. &c. v. Rogers,* the court gave opponents of tax-receivable coupons their first judicial victory. The judges unanimously ruled that the act of 1872 was a constitutionally permissible change to the act of 1871 with respect to people who acquired 1871 bonds from the state after passage of the 1872 law. At the time of that later exchange the state and the bondholders entered into a different contract that was based on the laws that then existed, in spite of what the act of 1871 had stated and what was printed on the face of the coupons. In a brief opinion with no dissents, the judges stated "that the act of March 7th, 1872, is valid and binding upon all those who did not avail themselves of the provisions of the funding bill, before the passage of that act." Men and women who "delayed the presentation of their bonds until *after* the passage of the act March 7th, 1872, must be held bound by the provisions of that act" and could not pay taxes with the coupons.[35]

The 1872 law and the 1873 court decision created two classes of owners of 1871 bonds: a large group who could use their coupons for payment of taxes and a smaller group who could not. In public and private discussions and beginning very soon in official documents (and even in some court decisions), the registered bonds and the coupon bonds issued before the act of 1872 came to be called *consols,* short for *consolidated bonds,* a common nineteenth-century term for securities issued to consolidate or refinance debts.[36] The bonds issued after March 1872 came to be called *peelers,* occasionally spelled *pealers.*[37] In 1874 an Alexandria newspaper published a definition: "A 'peeler' bond is a coupon bond issued after the Legislature had repealed the act making the coupons of State bonds receivable for taxes. Consequently the coupons of 'peelers' are not receivable for taxes and other public dues, and in this respect they differ from the other coupons. 'Peeler' is a corruption of repealed, and the term is used by State officials and brokers to economize words."[38]

The Funding Act of 1871 initially appeared to simplify and settle the state's complex public indebtedness, but within two years the controversies that it generated complicated and muddled the state's public finances, its laws, and its politics. And then in mid-1872 West Virginians ratified a new state constitution that omitted any reference to the old debt and did not acknowledge that the state had any moral or legal responsibility for it at all. Article X, Sections 4 and 5, of the new state constitution (which resembled the corresponding articles of the West Virginia Constitution of 1863 and the Virginia Constitutions of 1864 and 1869) prohibited West Virginia from creating a public debt for any purpose other than paying for defense in time of war or domestic insurrection and authorized the legislature to pay the debt; but with the omission of the earlier language acknowledging responsibility to pay part of Virginia's prewar debt, that appeared to eliminate the legislature's constitutional responsibility to pay any of the debt of old Virginia.[39]

In 1872 the West Virginia Constitutional Convention converted the payment of the debt from a constitutional obligation to a discretionary political act. The unilateral decision of the Virginia General Assembly in declaring that West Virginia was liable for payment of one-third of the whole original principal definitely alienated the West Virginians and reduced the chances that they would voluntarily pay any or all of that amount.

Late in 1873 the Committee on Finance of the Senate of West Virginia reported on the fiscal history of the debt. The committee's chair was Jonathan McCally Bennett, a lifelong resident of western Virginia, who had been treasurer of the government of the Confederate state of Virginia, which had run a surplus during the latter part of the Civil War. He knew better than anybody else where to find the facts and figures. His committee reported that the amount of money the residents of what became West Virginia had paid to Virginia in taxes in 1860 was $525,000 greater than the amount of money the government of the old state had spent in the western portion of the state that year. The committee confidently predicted that deeper analysis of the archival records in Richmond would disclose that western Virginians had regularly paid much more than they had received between 1822 and 1861, when the state incurred the debt. The senatorial committee therefore concluded that the state of West Virginia "is not indebted" to the state of Virginia. That effectively ended any realistic possibility that in the near term the Virginia General Assembly and the West Virginia Legislature would be able to agree about whether or how West Virginia should pay part of the antebellum Virginia debt.[40]

A host of questions then arose and remained unanswered until the twentieth century. Was West Virginia liable for any part of the debt at all? Who should decide whether or how much West Virginia should pay if the two legislatures could not agree? Was the two-thirds, one-third allocation fair or enforceable? If not, should the proportions be calculated based on the two states' respective land areas, on the populations of those land areas as of 1 January 1861 or as of statehood on 20 June 1863, on the value of the taxable property in each on one or the other date, or on a combination of those factors? Should the value of public property in what became West Virginia be deducted from the whole before calculating its portion? Should West Virginia receive credit for a proportional amount of the value of the stocks and bonds and other securities that Virginia had then owned? Should West Virginia's government assume responsibility for paying its portion to the creditors or pay it to Virginia, which would then pay it to the creditors?

Should the long-term difference between the amount of taxes westerners had paid and the size of the expenditures that the assembly had authorized in the western portion of the state, which Bennett's committee had identified, be taken into account? What about the disproportion between the value and the extent of the canals and railroads actually constructed in the regions that became separate states? Before the Civil War, western Virginians had often complained that even though the stated purpose of the subsidies was to improve transportation networks throughout Virginia, most of the projects had begun at navigation points in eastern Virginia and had not reached the western cities and counties by 1861. That meant that prior to the creation of West Virginia, western Virginians had paid a proportionately larger amount of tax money than eastern Virginians and had become responsible for a proportionally larger share of the debt to subsidize construction of projects from which the westerners received a disproportionately smaller benefit. In fact, all the railroads and almost all the canals constructed with money raised from the sale of public bonds had been built in the eastern region of Virginia.[41]

And what options did the owners of the Virginia Deferred Certificates have? Did they have any at all? They had no success in trying to persuade the West Virginia Legislature to accept responsibility for paying any of the old Virginia debt, and when some owners tried to sell their certificates in order to realize something then rather than wait and perhaps receive nothing later, the best they could obtain in some markets was five or ten cents on the dollar.[42]

3 FUNDERS AND READJUSTERS

In December 1872, a few days before the Supreme Court of Appeals issued its ruling in *Antoni v. Wright,* Governor Gilbert C. Walker complained to the General Assembly that its failure to adopt his proposals to raise taxes and reduce spending, together with changes made to the Funding Act in 1872, had created a public financing mess and an increase in confusion. He also responded to a new criticism from opponents of that law who charged that its language and the Virginia Deferred Certificates issued with the new bonds could be interpreted to saddle Virginia with liability for the third of the original whole that the law had unilaterally declared was West Virginia's part. If that were so, the public debt of Virginia was actually half again as large as officially calculated. The governor made a special point of stating for the record that "our public debt has not been increased one dollar since 1861, except from the accretions of interest, which we have not been able to pay."[1]

Walker sent another message to the Senate of Virginia later in the session in which he repeated at length that his recommendations for reducing public spending could make new taxes to pay the debt unnecessary.[2] Late in January, though, the auditor of public accounts forecast that by the beginning of the following October the state could be in danger of running a deficit.[3]

In March the assembly passed and the governor signed An Act to Provide for the Payment of Interest on the Public Debt. Much as the act of the previous session of the assembly had done, it authorized the treasurer to pay 2 percent rather than 3 percent on the semiannual interest coupons for the ensuing year.[4] A few days later the governor signed a law that required the treasurer to deduct the amount of a tax of one-half of 1 percent on the market value of the bonds when creditors submitted coupons to be redeemed. It also authorized the auditor of public accounts and the second auditor to begin in April an annual estimation of the current market value of all coupon bonds to ascertain the amount of tax due.[5]

The General Assembly also invited "the holders of the bonds of the state of Virginia, either in person or by proxy" to meet in conference with the assembly in February 1873 "to consider the existing liabilities of the state of Virginia, with a view to a fair, just, equitable, honorable, and certain settlement of the same."[6] The state government published announcements in the Virginia press, but influential creditors in England learned of the offer to negotiate too late to accept it. That and the reduction in interest payments led the frustrated investors to conclude that the assembly's and consequently the state's conduct during 1873 had been deplorable.[7]

Meantime, Walker had concocted a new scheme. After corresponding with governors of the other states about their public debts, he sent a long special message to the General Assembly recommending that the U.S. government assume and pay off all the public debts in the country—somewhat but not exactly as the federal government had done when it assumed the states' Revolutionary War debts—and simultaneously submit to the states a constitutional amendment prohibiting any state from creating a debt. Walker's reasoning did not resemble that of Henry A. Wise two years earlier. Instead, Walker argued that the federal government could afford to pay the debts of the states but that many of the states could not. If all the states' debts were paid, the economic condition of the entire country would be significantly improved, and all the governments in the country would be strengthened.[8] Both houses of the assembly endorsed Walker's proposal,[9] but nothing ever came of it, nor is it evident that very many people actually expected the federal government to pay the debts of the states.

Walker's proposal effectively concluded his official involvement with the public debt. Virginia's constitution prohibited governors from running for reelection, limiting every governor to one four-year term. Walker's term extended until 1 January 1874, but after the General Assembly adjourned in the spring of 1873, he had little to do with and made no new proposals about paying the interest on the debt, increasing revenue, or reducing spending. Too small a remnant of his official papers survives in the state's archives to reveal much about his personal opinions or any other actions that he may have wanted to take on those persistent problems.[10]

One related complication that arose during Walker's last months in office in 1873, though, could have given him cause to needle members of the legislature for neglecting his recommendations for reducing the costs of operating the government and improving the collection of revenue. Among them, he had suggested that city and county tax collectors be required to deposit the money in the state treasury immediately after they collected it.[11] Since the seventeenth century, tax collectors had retained the money in their own hands until they were required to pay it in, and some had delayed to do so for a very long time. That allowed them to use the money for personal purposes and deprived the treasury of the revenue during the interim.[12] The assembly did nothing at that time, and as late as January 1901 the then governor of Virginia again requested the assembly to correct "a system under which officials can get far in arrears with the public funds, as have occurred in many counties of the State."[13]

Evidently, well before the end of 1872 some tax collectors had begun using tax money they collected to buy coupons and later submitted the coupons to the treasury. They made a profit that way because soon after passage of the Funding Act of 1871 brokers began buying coupons in quantity from bondholders in New York, London, and other cities where banks and other owners of large numbers of bonds resided. People at a distance from Richmond had to travel to the city to redeem their coupons or sell them at a discount to brokers, who would redeem them or sell them at a profit to people who then paid their taxes with them. Tax collectors therefore had opportunities to purchase coupons for much less than their full value but could later submit them to the treasury at face value and pocket the difference as a personal profit. A bill that Walker signed on 24 December 1873 specifically prevented all tax collectors from doing precisely that,[14] suggesting that more than a few already had.

Another, extremely embarrassing problem came to light early in March 1874, a little more than two months after Walker retired from the governorship. During the months following the passage of the Funding Act of 1871, the state treasurer and the second auditor (who oversaw the sinking fund and audited the accounts of the state debt) hired several inexperienced men to assist with the increase in office business that the exchange of bonds required. The staff of the treasury and the second auditor received and manually canceled thousands of old bonds and issued thousands of new bonds. They also, as the law allowed, exchanged coupon bonds for registered bonds, and vice versa, and the sinking fund acquired bonds to enlarge its resources. Nobody oversaw the work of the treasurer, and the

Commissioners of the Sinking Fund never even met as a body, nor did they oversee their employees.[15]

Some men found an opportunity to profit from the chaos in the two offices. Joseph Mayo, the state treasurer, and William D. Coleman, the secretary of the Commissioners of the Sinking Fund, began exchanging bonds of one kind for another and made a profit in the process. On one of the exchanges, Coleman retained $1,350, and Mayo $1,851. Coleman also began exchanging or taking bonds that he did not own and using them to finance his drinking and gambling in the faro houses of Richmond, which was what brought the scandal to light. As a consequence, the state may have funded as much as $30,500 in bonds twice. Following the discovery of Coleman's actions, he was tried, convicted, and sentenced to jail, and Mayo made a fool of himself by testifying drunk at Coleman's trial and then spent several years in a state insane asylum.[16] The following year the legislature strengthened oversight in the offices.[17]

The Coleman malfeasance came to light early in the administration of Governor James Lawson Kemper,[18] who was elected in the autumn of 1873, took office on 1 January 1874, and had more to worry about than the criminal behavior of Coleman. The national economic depression that begin with the Panic of 1873 hit the Virginia economy hard, and it had not fully recovered from the damage done during the Civil War. Throughout Kemper's four-year term the national and state economies performed sluggishly, exacerbating the state's already serious problem of how to pay interest on the debt, keep appropriations for the public schools at an adequate level, and also pay for all the other responsibilities of the government. The proportion of the state's taxes collected in expendable money dropped even further. In April 1874 the assembly again authorized payment of 2 percent instead of 3 percent semiannual interest on the 1871 bonds if the governor, treasurer, and the auditors certified that the treasury contained enough money.[19]

While the assembly was in session during Kemper's first months as governor, representatives of some of the principal foreign bondholders met in London and denounced the government of Virginia for the financial injuries they had sustained since engaging in the exchange of bonds that the Funding Act of 1871 authorized and in effect required. The governing council of the recently established Corporation of Foreign Bondholders, representing the leading British investment houses that had large holdings in government debts throughout the world, were especially worried that the political climate in Virginia jeopardized their speculative investments. By the middle of the decade the reductions in interest payments had caused the market value of Virginia bonds to drop dramatically.[20] "The bondholders," their tart statement declared in part, "now find themselves sufferers by the confidence and reliance they have shown in Virginia." They asked that the General Assembly "without delay, restore the funding bill to its full efficiency, or substitute such other measures as may tend to the restoration abroad of the credit and honor of the ancient Commonwealth of Virginia."[21]

The governor forwarded the bondholders' request to the assembly, noting that all the state's securities were selling well below par in domestic and foreign markets, that the creditors had impugned the state's honor based on what he characterized as misrepresentations of the condition of its finances, and that it was impossible to raise enough tax money to pay all the interest on the debt. "The problem you are called upon to solve," Kemper quite unnecessarily informed the assembly members, "is, how to restore the credit of the State without imposing upon our own people burthens impossible to be borne." He therefore called for a full conference to be attended by representatives of both the state and the bondholders. Kemper never suggested raising taxes, and he and most members of the General Assembly of whatever political persuasion took it for granted or as a matter of political faith that the taxpayers of the state could not pay more than they already paid or would not tolerate an increase in tax rates or reelect legislators who increased them.[22]

Not so all the citizens of Virginia. The Women's Association for the Liquidation of the State Debt endorsed full payment of the interest and principal. Its officers published a circular letter "To the Daughters of Virginia" indicating their willingness to pay an increased tax of 10¢ on every $100 valuation of property in the state, a 20 percent increase, to provide enough revenue to pay the full interest. "Now, while the women of the State might endeavor directly to raise a large amount of this balance by self-denial," they proclaimed, "yet it seems better and more honorable for the men to do it. They who incurred these obligations should be the ones to discharge them, and we, the women of Virginia, can greatly aid and encourage them in this attempt by our economy, self-denial and sacrifice."[23] The officers of the association were members of prominent white Virginia families and were no doubt more capable of economizing in their households or of paying higher taxes than the women of ordinary white and black households.

Men and women in several of the state's cities formed similar associations to advocate full payment of the state's debt.

In April 1874, one month after Kemper recommended negotiating with the bondholders, he suggested that the assembly name a commission to suggest amendments to the state constitution to simplify the structures of state and local government in order to save money.[24] Among the proposals that the assembly recommended to the voters and that they ratified were several to roll back some of the democratic reforms of the Constitution of 1869, including reducing the number of elected local officials, reducing the number of members of the assembly, and making the assembly's meetings biennial instead of annual. Kemper also revived a suggestion that Cameron had made in 1871, to amend the constitution and make payment of the poll tax a prerequisite for voting. For more than 250 years the government had imposed a tax on heads of households and all laboring people at a rate of so much per person, or head, called a *poll tax*. Ratified in 1876, the amendment denied the vote to men who had not paid the poll tax. Another amendment adopted at the same time deprived men who had been convicted of petty crimes of the right to vote.[25]

Supporters of the two amendments designed them to make it more difficult for black men to vote. Both racism and political expediency suggested the amendments. They were rooted in an understanding that many poor black families could not afford to pay the tax and in a racist belief that black men were inherently less honest than white men. Payment of the poll tax became difficult, and many poor men undoubtedly relinquished the right to vote in order to support their families. Supporters of the crime amendment believed that African American men were more likely than white men to commit petty criminal acts, such as stealing chickens, on the supposition that African Americans were stealing from white people in the same way that before the end of slavery they had often simply taken food from their owners.[26]

The government did not publish statistics of voter registration or of voting by race, but it is very likely that the two amendments functioned as intended. Even though the population of Virginia increased between 1870 and 1880,[27] the number of voters declined by about 10 percent immediately after ratification of the amendments, from 236,989 in the presidential election of 1876 to 212,281 in the election of 1880.[28] The amendments no doubt contributed significantly to the reduction in the number of African Americans who won election to the General Assembly. In the 1869 general election, the last before the end of Congressional Reconstruction, thirty black men won election to the assembly, and eighteen to twenty won in the elections in 1871, 1873, and 1875. Following ratification of the poll tax and crime amendments, the number fell sharply to eight in 1877. It is possible that a corresponding reduction in the number of African Americans who won election to local offices also occurred during that time, but no systematic and thorough research has sufficiently documented black local officeholding. The reduction in the electorate probably strengthened the political hands of friends of the Funding Act of 1871 and weakened the political hands of its opponents.

Meanwhile, Kemper and the new state treasurer, Robert Mercer Taliaferro Hunter (who had served in both the United States Senate and the Confederate States Senate), met in the Capitol in Richmond on 10 November 1874 with Hugh McCulloch, a former secretary of the United States Treasury, and other representatives of the principal foreign bondholders. The printed record of the day's negotiations indicates that they had what later diplomats would call a frank exchange of views, clearly setting out their different interests and perspectives, pulling no punches, and not cordially accepting one another's statements of fact. The governor made a very long speech justifying Virginia's behavior and explaining the state's inability to pay the whole 6 percent interest promised in the Funding Act of 1871. He described the rate as "a stupendous and disastrous mistake." Kemper also straightforwardly criticized English bondholders for questioning the good faith of Virginia and Virginians and incorrectly presuming that Virginia had enough taxable property to pay the full rate of interest. McCulloch on behalf of the bondholders reluctantly accepted the reality as Kemper stated it.

Together the negotiators adopted a recommendation that the state pay the 4 percent interest in semiannual installments and make it permanent and consider refinancing the whole debt with bonds that paid 4 percent for ten years and then 5 percent for twenty years, the new bonds to be payable in gold in London, New York, Baltimore, and at the state treasury in Richmond; and that the state establish a new sinking fund for paying the principal. They predicted that refinancing the debt in that manner would remove perhaps three-fourths or four-fifths of the coupon bonds from circulation.[29] During the subsequent three days Kemper also exchanged letters with John J. MacKinnon, acting for the American Bond-Funding and Banking Association, Ltd., of London. They agreed to refinance the whole debt with new bonds payable in London in gold in thirty years at 4 percent interest for the first ten years and 5 percent for the next twenty years, rather than at 5 percent for the full term as MacKinnon had originally suggested.[30]

When the General Assembly convened in December 1874, the governor informed the members of his satisfaction with the agreements he had negotiated, which for the most part conformed to his initial suggestions. Repeating his recommendations for strict economy in public spending, Kemper stated that in part because of the sluggish economy after the Panic of 1873 the state and its creditors had but one final opportunity to solve the many problems arising from the state debt. "In an important sense," he concluded, "the state has now reached the crisis of its fortunes. We cannot longer postpone the inevitable task of grappling decisively with the financial problem. It must be mastered by a solution which will settle it at once and forever. . . . The tax-receivable coupons, while wholly unsatisfactory to creditors who really hold them as an investment, are fast becoming mere pabulum for vicious speculation and stock-jobbing among our own people. They are being bought up and thrust upon the treasury, in large amounts, at the most inopportune periods of each fiscal year, and thus they periodically threaten to suspend the operations of the government; and their further effect is to create, in our midst, combinations interested in resisting any readjustment of the debt."[31]

As it had done in the previous years, the assembly authorized the governor, the auditor, the second auditor, and the treasurer to certify that if there was sufficient money in the treasury, the treasurer could pay 2 percent interest semiannually for the next year.[32] That fourth admission in four years that Virginia could not meet its full legal obligations cannot have been reassuring to the owners of the state's bonds, even though it was generally consistent with the agreements they and Kemper had concluded. That the legislators did not then refinance the debt indicated that a broadly acceptable solution to the debt problems was not evident, that the political divisions had grown deeper, and that the problem was going to last longer.

Throughout his term, Kemper used the words *readjust* and *readjustment* when discussing proposals to refinance the debt and reduce the payment of the interest in a manner fair and agreeable to the bondholders and without having to raise taxes on Virginia's farmers and businesses. He was willing, almost eager, to reduce the rate of interest for a limited time while the state's economy recovered, but he insisted on repudiating none of the principal. The words *readjust* and *readjustment* gradually gained common usage to identify proposals for a more radical set of changes than Kemper preferred. During the mid-1870s, the state's politicians split into two factions: Funders, who insisted on paying the full rate of interest and providing for the whole principal, and Readjusters, who preferred to reduce the cost of paying the debt more drastically by permanently reducing the rate of interest and also the amount of the principal to be funded.

Public and private discussions of the issues became as heated and bitter as the differences of opinion between radical Republicans and the founders of the Conservative Party had been during Congressional Reconstruction in the 1860s. Funders denounced Readjusters for proposing to repudiate some or all of the debt, which would destroy the public credit and alienate Northern and foreign investors, whose money the businesses and industries of the state needed in order to flourish. Readjusters denounced Funders for neglecting the interests of Virginia's taxpayers, impoverishing the new public schools, and in effect being tools and agents of Northern and foreign bond speculators and putting their interests ahead of the interests of the men, women, and children of Virginia.

In spite of the obvious divisions between Funders and Readjusters within the dominant Conservative Party, the political allegiances of Virginians were more complicated than a simple Conservative-Republican or Funder-Readjuster dichotomy. The Republican Party continued to exist and competed for legislative seats and statewide offices. It sent delegations to the party's national conventions and often won more than 40 percent of the vote in presidential elections. Some Conservatives ran for and won election to Congress as Democrats, attended the party's national conventions, and opposed Republicans at every opportunity, even though some of those Conservatives were committed Funders and some supported Readjustment. Nearly everyone who was politically active was formally or informally affiliated with one of the two national parties, but within the state, especially at the time of legislative elections, one might or might not be a Conservative, a Republican, or a Democrat and might also be either a Funder or a Readjuster. In 1880, for instance, Republicans, with support from some Readjusters, nominated a slate of candidates for presidential elector pledged to James Garfield and Chester A. Arthur; Democrats and Conservatives nominated a slate pledged to Winfield Scott Hancock and William English; and other Conservatives, with support from Readjusters, nominated a different slate of candidates pledged to Hancock and English.[33]

For nearly a decade, political alignments in Virginia were complex and fluid. The longer the controversies dragged on about how to pay the interest and whether to repudiate any of the principal, the more alignments changed, and individual men shifted from one faction to another or into and out of temporary coalitions of political convenience. Personal animosities between political leaders also developed or intensified, and some prominent politicians shifted their political allegiances for personal as well as policy reasons.

One of the emerging spokesmen for the Readjusters was John E. Massey, of Albemarle County, a retired Baptist minister and increasingly vocal advocate of making major changes to the state's public finances. In September 1875 he revised a series of newspaper articles he had recently written on aspects of the debt controversy and published a sixteen-page pamphlet entitled *Debts and Taxes, or Obligations and Resources of Virginia.* Parson Massey, as he was usually called, distilled the essence of the Readjusters' arguments into that one pamphlet. He attacked Funders for saying that they were protecting the honor of the state, when they were actually doing the work of and looking after the interests of bondholders, most of whom lived outside the state. He accepted and repeated the essence of Henry A. Wise's theory of the death of old Virginia during the 1860s. As far as Massey was concerned, the new state of Virginia therefore owed none of the old debt of the old state, and its creditors should appeal for payment to the federal government, which was responsible for the dismemberment and death of the old state and with those acts acquired responsibility for paying its debt.

Massey knew that the federal government would never accept that responsibility. He proposed instead that because the federal government and the Northern states had been responsible for what happened to Virginia during the 1860s, Virginia and Virginians had no moral or legal responsibilities to bondholders in Northern states and at most should pay a reduced principal and interest proportional to the reduction in the total tax base of Virginia that the separation of West Virginia and the abolition of slavery had produced. Because English bondholders, whom Massey estimated at about one-fourth of the whole number of the state's creditors, had not been responsible for what befell Virginia during the 1860s, they should be entitled to full payment of the principal (less interest during the Civil War), but only from the federal government.

Massey argued that the Funding Act of 1871 had left Virginia responsible for paying the third of the debt assigned to West Virginia, and he predicted that Funder policies would produce disasters. "I confidently believe," he warned, "that if the bondholders ever again get control of the Virginia Legislature, every dollar of the debt of the old State, with all its accumulated and compounded interest, will be converted into new bonds, with tax-receivable coupons. Then, your Legislature, no matter what may be its character, will be compelled to increase taxation sufficiently to pay *full* interest upon the *whole* debt of the old State, and to defray expenses of government and public schools." That would bankrupt Virginians and their state government.

In defending his proposals against Funders' objections that the refinancing he proposed was an unjust repudiation and a dishonor to the state, Massey struck back hard with words that provided one of many clear examples of how the political debate on both sides during the 1870s and 1880s deteriorated into insults and charges of ungentlemanly bad faith. "Some are so weak-minded, or blinded by prejudice," Massey wrote accusingly of his critics, "as to charge that these views savor of *repudiation.* It is a source of regret that there are any who either *cannot,* or *will not* distinguish between an *equitable settlement* of a debt and its *repudiation!* I am sorry for such. They lack either common *perspicacity* or common *honesty.*"[34]

While public debates and legislative bickering increased in intensity and volume during the middle years of the 1870s, neither the Funders nor the Readjusters in the General Assembly made any significant changes in public policy. The legislators passed a few bills designed to increase revenue and to reduce the profitability of paying taxes with coupons. A law enacted in March 1876 placed on local tax collectors the same responsibility that an 1873 law had already imposed on the treasurer, to deduct the value of the tax of 50¢ per $100 market value of the bonds from the value of coupons presented in payment of taxes.[35] Because of the brisk trade in coupons that had been detached from bonds and sold to brokers and to people who wanted to pay taxes with coupons bought at a discount, that law provided the basis for the second important lawsuit to arise and the first case to reach the Supreme Court of the United States (five years later, in 1881) during the long debt controversy.

Governor Kemper tried to put as bright a face as possible on the situation at the beginning of his fourth and final year as governor. He reported in December 1876 that "revenues of the state are sensibly and steadily increasing, while the general expenditures are being correspondingly reduced." Nevertheless, as a principal spokesman for the Funders who was willing to reduce the rate of interest only temporarily, Kemper joined the state's creditors in demanding that "all controversy over the debt shall be settled and put behind us without loss of time." He stated that "facts could be cited to show"—but he did not cite any—"that, in the course of the last ten years, large sums of money which sought investment in Virginia, in enterprises capable of adding greatly to our taxable wealth, were driven off" because of the political controversies and the default on one-third of the interest payments. "In some cases, by reason of the same discovery, promising enterprises actually begun were abandoned and investments wholly or partially made were withdrawn."[36]

As a result of the deep divisions concerning the debt, the general election of 1877 was one of the most unusual in the state's history. By then, nearly all the old, experienced prewar political leaders who had founded the Conservative Party had died or retired from politics. The party's new generation of younger leaders had more eagerly embraced secession and the Confederacy and afterward pursued their political careers with a similarly intense dedication rooted in deeply held convictions.[37] In 1877 the Conservative Party almost split into two factions seeking control of the legislature and the governor's office.

William Mahone, of Petersburg, emerged as the Readjusters' candidate for the gubernatorial nomination. He had been one of the founders and early leaders of the Conservative Party in opposition to radical Republicans and Congressional Reconstruction. He had a distinguished record as a brigadier general in the Confederate army and had had an equally distinguished career as a railroad engineer. Before the war, Mahone had built the line from Norfolk to Petersburg, and after the war, he had acquired control of the railroad from Petersburg to Lynchburg as well as the Virginia and Tennessee Railroad, which linked Lynchburg with other Southern lines at the little border town later renamed Bristol. That formed the basis of what became the Norfolk and Western, but in the process he had let one of his lines default on a large debt, and later in the 1870s he lost control of all his railroads to Northern investors. A short man with a long beard, a strong will, inexhaustible energy, and domineering habits, Mahone gravitated away from his old alliance with the original Conservatives and became the principle spokesman for and eventually the organizing genius of the Readjusters, bringing with him a deep distrust of Northern and international bankers and creditors and their hatred of him.[38]

After Mahone failed on the first ballots to win the nomination for governor at the 1877 Conservative Party state convention, he withdrew from the contest and sat out the campaign. The Funders at the convention eventually rallied behind a man with little political experience and little-known political opinions, Frederick William Mackey Holliday.[39] An unmarried old-fashioned Virginia gentleman of pure patrician outlook and principles, he had been an unsuccessful secessionist candidate for the Virginia Convention in February 1861 and had lost his right arm at the Battle of Cedar Run, when he was an officer in the Confederate army. The disorganized and leaderless Republican Party failed to nominate a slate of candidates, so the Conservative Party ticket ran unopposed, and Holliday, who showed himself to be a fully committed Funder, was elected governor. The Conservative Funders nominated the die-hard Funder and former Confederate general James A. Walker for lieutenant governor, and for attorney general they nominated the incumbent and first state party chair, Raleigh Travers Daniel, who died a few days later.[40] The governor appointed James G. Field to fill the vacancy, and the party later nominated Field for attorney general. Field was also a Confederate veteran who had lost a leg at the Battle of Cedar Run, the battle at which Holliday had lost his arm.[41] Field's opinions on the debt at the time probably were not well known, but he displayed some sympathy for readjustment while attorney general and consequently failed in his attempt to win renomination four years later.

In the 1877 election, Readjusters gained seats in the House of Delegates, but with Bradley T. Johnson, who had recently been elected to the Senate of Virginia, the Funders had one of the principal attorneys for the bondholders in the key position of chair of the Senate Committee on Finance, setting the stage for a renewal of the legislative battles.

A few days after Holliday's inauguration, a member of the House of Delegates fired the first shot when he introduced a resolution that began, "Whereas many of the people of this state are opposed to the execution of the terms of the act of March 31st, [sic] 1871, commonly known as the 'funding bill,' because of a common belief that the passage of said act was procured by bribery, or other means outside legitimate legislative methods: Therefore, Be it resolved, That a special committee of nine be appointed, whose duty it shall be to enquire into, ascertain and report to this house, what improper, corrupt and fraudulent means and appliances, if any, were used in and for procuring the passage of said act." The House sent the resolution to its Committee on Finance for consideration.[42] The

committee never reported back, but the introduction of the resolution revived allegations of corruption against the bondholders and by implication
against the Funders.

A few days after that, a member of the Senate Committee on Finance
presented a thirty-six-page document entitled *Report of the Senate Committee on Finance Relative to the Public Debt, Prepared by Senator Bradley T.
Johnson.* The committee chair's name was part of the title, lest anybody
be left uninformed. The report included a long itemized list of all the outstanding bonds the state had issued, a history of the public debt, and nearly
twenty closely printed pages defending the Funders' beliefs and steward-
ship. Johnson also included a long extract from Alexander Hamilton's 1790
report on the public credit of the United States, in which he had proposed
paying the whole Revolutionary War debt at face value. Johnson dismissed
charges that the Funding Act had been passed as a consequence of corruption and stated that the Virginia government was in better financial condition than Readjusters claimed and, in fact, in better financial condition
than many other states in the country. He also asserted that both manufac-
turing industries and manufactured goods in Virginia were increasing in
value. Echoing Pierpont and Walker and taking a hard line reminiscent of
Kemper and foreshadowing what Holliday later wrote, Johnson declared,
"Repudiation by Virginia of the least part of her duty, would be a blunder
and a crime. There is no such thing as a *little repudiation;* no breach of faith
can be small. The least fracture extends with infinite ramifications through
every part of it, and a pledge once broken can never be restored."[43]

That same year, Johnson also published a scholarly article in the *American Law Review* entitled "Can States Be Compelled to Pay Their Debts?"
In it he wrote accurately, "It has generally been conceded that State debts
rest alone on the faith of the State creating them, and that no remedy exists, under the American system of government, by which the States can
be compelled to perform their contracts." Under the doctrine of sovereign
immunity, which courts recognized throughout the United States, even
though it did not appear in the Constitution of the United States or in the
Virginia Constitution of 1869, a state could not be sued without its consent. (The doctrine did not apply to suits that states filed if they permitted
appeals.) "States cannot," Johnson continued, "it is true, free themselves
from *the obligation* of their debts, except by honest payment; but they can
omit the 'honest payment,' and let the obligation remain. They can pass no
law impairing the obligation of contracts," as he had witnessed in Virginia,

"but they can omit to pass laws to comply with them. They can make nothing but gold and silver a tender for their debts; but they *can* tender a new obligation, reduced in principal and interest, offering to the creditor the alternative of accepting that or nothing. While they cannot avoid their duty, they can and *do* let that duty remain unfulfilled," as he had also witnessed in Virginia.[44] For a bond attorney like Johnson, both forms of failure to fulfill the legal obligation were equally intolerable. For the Readjusters, on the other hand, the legal difference between the two was all-important.

On 22 February 1878 the Readjusters in the assembly passed a Bill Imposing Taxes on Real and Personal Property to Meet the Necessary Expenses of the Government and to Pay the Interest on the Public Debt. Known as House Bill 92 in the legislative journals, it was usually referred to in the newspaper accounts of its progress through the assembly as the Barbour Bill, for its patron, James Barbour, of Culpeper County. A veteran of nearly thirty years in state politics, beginning with service in the Constitutional Convention of 1850–51, Barbour was a member of one of the most influential political families in nineteenth-century Virginia, including a governor of the state who was also a secretary of war and minister to France and another who was a congressman who became an associate justice of the Supreme Court.[45]

The preface to the Barbour Bill stated that the existing 50¢ tax on every $100 assessed value of property was the maximum the people of Virginia could pay. The body of the bill directed that 50 percent of that tax be collected "only in lawful money of the United States" and used "for the exclusive purpose" of paying the operating expenses of the state government; that 20 percent of that tax, also collected only in lawful money of the United States, be expended exclusively on the free public schools; and that 30 percent of that tax, not required to be paid solely in lawful money of the United States, be applied exclusively to payment of interest on the public debt. The bill stated that taxpayers had to pay a minimum of 70 percent of their taxes with money and could use coupons for a maximum of 30 percent. That 30 percent would produce all the money available for paying interest on the debt, even though every tax dollar paid into the treasury with a coupon was a dollar that the treasury could not use to pay that interest.[46] The Barbour Bill was specifically intended to reduce drastically the payment of taxes with coupons and to increase expendable revenue for the public schools. It truly disclosed the priorities of the Readjusters.[47]

During debate in the Senate of Virginia, John Warwick Daniel[48] objected and revealed his core beliefs and those of the most adamant Funders. A Confederate veteran who walked with a pronounced limp from a wound received during the Civil War, he was an attorney who often worked for the railroads, including the Orange and Alexandria, which had competed with Mahone's railroads in the assembly for favorable legislation. Daniel denounced the Barbour Bill as a poorly disguised method of avoiding payment on the interest and principal of the debt. "He said," according to a newspaper report, "he would rather see a bonfire made of every free school in the State, and a bonfire then made of his own home, than that this bill and those that are to follow it should pass."[49] When Readjusters tried to use that report to discredit Daniel more than a year later, he forthrightly wrote that he "believed then, and believe now, that stark repudiation lurked behind" the Barbour Bill. "I said," he quoted himself, "'It were better to burn the schools than sustain them on money taken by force from others; for when the children grow up and realize that they were the wards of repudiation they would blush for their pretended patrons. It were better for the State to burn the schools than pass this bill *and the repudiation measures which, as I believe, were to follow;* and I would rather burn my own house and start life again penniless, houseless, and honest than see her do it.'"[50]

Holliday vetoed the bill. His veto message was even more offensive to the Readjusters and their supporters than Daniel's hyperbolic speech. Holliday objected to the bill for many reasons. "Instead of bringing peace," he predicted, "it is challenging war between the state and the creditors, and keeping alive in bitterness a thing which has already, by its agitation, cost more than its whole sum to the material interests and welfare of this commonwealth." Holliday objected to the bill's provisions as "both unjust and unconstitutional." He correctly labeled the bill a tactic "to deny the tax-paying power of the coupons" that the Supreme Court of Appeals had affirmed in *Antoni v. Wright* in 1872.

Holliday opposed the bill in large part because under its provisions "the legislature is bound to support the free school system at the expense of the state's creditors." He went out of his way to condemn the system of public schools that the Constitution of 1869 authorized and the General Assembly created in 1870. "Our fathers did not need free schools to make them what they were," Holliday lectured loftily in a long attack on the public schools. "Happy this generation could it rival them in those virtues that go to make up the glory of a commonwealth! They would not have tolerated them on the soil of Virginia had they to be established by the denial of their honest debts. . . . Public free schools are not a necessity. The world, for hundreds of years, grew in wealth, culture, and refinement, without them. They are a luxury, adding when skilfully conducted, it may be, to the beauty and power of a state, but to be paid for, like any other luxury, by the people who wish their benefits."[51] Holliday believed that if poor people wanted schools for their children, they should pay for the schools themselves, just as prosperous people had paid for tutors or to send their children to private academies.

The House of Delegates sustained the veto by a vote of 71 to 42, with a large majority in favor of the bill but not quite the two-thirds majority constitutionally required to override it.[52] Holliday won the battle that day but in the process gave his enemies a powerful cache of ammunition to use against him. Much more even than Daniel's rhetorical willingness to see the schools and his own house burned, Holliday's denunciation of public education drew a sharp line between two groups of Virginians: privileged white families like his, who could afford to buy bonds and collect interest on them and also provide an adequate private education for their children; and the majority of all Virginia families, both white and black, who could not. As money for the public schools became increasingly scarce during Holliday's administration, Readjusters repeatedly pointed to his policies and public statements to win support from voters who did not enjoy the privileges and luxuries that he and other prosperous white families enjoyed and to contrast the private interests of foreign bondholders, whom he and the other Funders appeared to favor, with the real interests and immediate needs of ordinary Virginia men, women, and children.[53]

Readjusters angrily assembled in the Capitol a few hours after the clerk read Holliday's veto message in the House of Delegates. Legislators from both houses of the General Assembly met that afternoon and again that night and one after the other condemned the veto and the governor. John Paul, a member of the Senate of Virginia from Rockingham County in the Shenandoah Valley, was one of the rising Readjuster stars who later won election to the United States House of Representatives as a Readjuster. He spoke for them all when, according to a newspaper report, he said, "If any gentleman supposed that this was the defeat of the Re-Adjustment party, he was mistaken. The battle had not really been commenced. They had no idea of surrendering. The people were behind them."[54]

Holliday too spoke as if he had just begun to fight and sent a long special message to the Senate of Virginia a few days later reiterating his opposition to repudiation of any of the state debt. Holliday pointedly told the senators that it was the responsibility of the General Assembly to provide for its payment and payment of the interest, which they had not.[55] On 14 March the assembly responded with a bill that the governor signed even though its preamble in effect poked a legislative finger in his eye. An Act to Provide for the Consolidation of the Public Debt, and the Payment of an Uniform Rate of Interest Thereupon opened as follows: "Whereas the present general assembly was elected with especial reference to a readjustment of the public debt of the state, so that the interest may be punctually paid alike on all classes of it without an increase of the rate or aggregate of taxation . . . and recognizing its duty first to preserve and ensure the continued existence of the state, including the public free school system . . ." The law authorized the governor to exchange bonds issued under the Funding Act of 1871 for new bonds paying 3 percent interest for eighteen years and 4 percent for the next thirty-two years but redeemable after ten years. It specified that the new bonds not be taxed and that none of the new bonds be issued until $15 million in bonds bearing tax-receivable coupons had been returned to the state. It also provided for the issuance of non-interest-bearing certificates for the one-third of the debt again assigned to West Virginia and directed that the plates for printing the new bonds become the property of and under the control of the state government, as if to hint at some corruption in the handling of the plates used to print the earlier bonds.[56]

The Barbour Bill of 1878 and the funding act passed that year demonstrated that a majority of legislators in both houses preferred to pay for the schools rather than pay the bondholders every penny that the Funding Act of 1871 had promised. The two bills also indicated that a majority approved of permanently lowering the rate of interest on the debt but that proposals to reduce the principal did not command a majority. Within a few months, the principal bondholders rejected the funding act of 1878 and in effect dug in their heals to support the most uncompromising Funders against the majority in Virginia, which was then made up of Readjusters and those Funders who endorsed either a short- or a long-term reduction in the rate of interest.

4 THE READJUSTER PARTY

The 1877–78 session of the General Assembly further polarized the politicians and the people of Virginia. The Barbour Bill, Daniel's speech in the Senate, and Holliday's veto brought the public schools to the center of the political debate and clarified the choices voters faced. Men and women throughout Virginia understood what was at stake both for the commercial and business prosperity of Virginia and for the schools and children.

Few of the poorer white people and none of the black people had had access to public schools before the 1860s, and it was obvious that mothers and fathers clearly understood the advantages that the new school system promised for their children. Women provided support for husbands and fathers who opposed the Funders or actively worked for the Readjusters. Moreover, single and widowed women of both races taught in the new public schools and feared that further reductions in the revenue available for public education would cost them their jobs as well as jeopardize the education of their pupils. Men and women who believed that paying the interest and principal were essential to the welfare of Virginia also organized and opposed people who favored readjustment. In the spring of 1878, to give but one example, the editor of a newspaper in Warrenton invited the white women of the town to attend a rally in support of paying the public debt.[1]

There was no election in 1878 in which the two sides could test their strengths against each other. When the assembly reconvened early in December 1878, Governor Holliday reported that he had received a letter from representatives of all the principal London, New York, and Paris banking houses that owned Virginia bonds stating their "very unanimous" objections to the 1878 refinancing act. They proposed a new conference to agree on a new funding proposal for thirty- or forty-year bonds paying 4 percent interest and the creation of a proper new sinking fund for paying the principal.[2] The bondholders' proposal demonstrated that the Readjusters had already won a part of the battle. They had worn down the state's creditors on the question of reducing the interest rate not just for the short term but for the long, which for the future promised to reduce significantly the annual cost to Virginia taxpayers. Even the leading Funders agreed with the most radical Readjusters in opposition to raising taxes to pay the full 6 percent interest.[3]

In Holliday's long annual message recommending that the assembly accept the proposal to negotiate, he stressed the importance of finally reaching a mutually satisfactory solution to the debt problem, which he called "an incubus upon the spirit and a clog upon the movements of Virginia." If he believed that he was being conciliatory by including several pages of strained praise for the concept of a public school system, the condescending tone of his twenty-page message probably made things worse rather than better.[4] Nevertheless, the assembly authorized the governor to invite representatives of the creditors to Richmond to begin negotiations.[5] At that session of the assembly, in the words of agents for the Corporation of Foreign Bondholders and the Funding Association of the United States of America, the Funders "were in very loose order." The Readjusters, on the other hand, "were well organised, and in no uncertainty as to their line of action." The agents condemned the Readjusters as "without principles, perhaps, but they had well-defined aims, which they worked for with persistency and zeal."[6]

Before the talks began, the Readjusters in the assembly pushed through a law to require that tax collectors compile inventories of the revenue they received in coupons and lists of who paid how much. The law also required people paying with coupons to sign them and directed the collectors to return copies of the lists to the auditor of public accounts.[7] The law reflected the Readjusters' desire to ascertain and make public how detrimental to the state's revenue the payment of taxes in coupons was and who benefited from the Funders' policies. Some Funders, though, also opposed the tax-receivable status of coupons, and their numbers evidently increased as the state's budget crisis continued. A Republican Funder and recently appointed United States District Court judge, Robert W. Hughes, was one of them. He colorfully called the coupons "the cut-worm of the revenues,"[8] after the caterpillars of moths that killed crops by gnawing through the bases of their stems. The phrase quickly caught on because every planter, farmer, or keeper of a kitchen garden—that is, a very large majority of all adult Virginians—clearly understood what it meant.

Negotiations began on 30 January 1879 between members of the House and Senate Committees on Finance (James Barbour was chair of the House committee that session) on behalf of the General Assembly, and Hugh McCulloch, president of the Funding Association of the United States of America, and Isaac H. Carrington, an attorney for the Corporation of Foreign Bondholders, representing the American and foreign creditors. During about two weeks of exchanges, they agreed on a new funding plan that the General Assembly passed and the governor signed on 28 March 1879.[9] Despite the initial disorganization of the Funders in the assembly, the new funding act gave them and the bondholders more than it gave the advocates of readjustment.

The law was usually referred to as the McCulloch Act, but Readjusters often called it the Broker's Bill because they believed that the bondholders and coupon brokers benefited from it most.[10] Intended to supplant the Funding Act of 1871 and the failed law of 1878, it authorized the issuance of new registered and coupon bonds to be exchanged for the bonds issued in 1871, the new bonds to run for forty years bearing 3 percent interest for the first ten years, 4 percent for the next twenty years, and 5 percent for the last ten years, payable half-yearly in Richmond, New York, or London, with an option for the state to redeem any or all of them at any time. The bonds soon came to be called "McCulloch bonds" or "ten-forty bonds," reflecting the first interval for the changing rate of interest and their forty-year maturity. The law declared the coupons receivable for taxes at face value and exempted the bonds from taxation. It provided for payment of the unpaid interest then due at fifty cents on the dollar. The act required certain named foreign bondholders to submit at least $8 million worth of securities for exchange before 1 January 1880 or the act would not take full effect.

Like the act of 1871, the new funding act directed the state to issue certificates for the one-third of the principal again assigned to West Virginia. The law levied a 2 percent tax on property to begin in 1885, to be paid into the sinking fund, and authorized the auditor and the treasurer to issue short-term tax-receivable certificates to borrow money to pay the interest any time tax revenue was not adequate for the purpose. Unlike the Funding Act of 1871, the McCulloch Act did not prohibit payment of interest on the existing bonds as a means of coercing creditors to exchange their 1871 bonds for the new bonds.[11]

Some Readjusters in the assembly voted for the McCulloch Bill even though most of its provisions embodied aspects of the 1871 law that Readjusters had condemned, particularly the tax-receivable status of the coupons. The lower initial interest rate may have appealed to them, but the new property tax and the rising interest rate very likely did not. Those Readjusters may have voted for the bill as an improvement on the Funding Act of 1871 without abandoning their desire to replace both with a more drastic plan for refinancing the debt. Funders narrowly prevailed in the legislature and also in the state's courts. In *Williamson v. Massey*, in 1880, the Virginia Supreme Court of Appeals, citing *Antoni v. Wright* and other precedents, upheld the legislature's exemption of the new bonds from taxation and also upheld the requirement that the treasurer accept the coupons at face value for payment of taxes.[12]

While the legislators and the representatives of the bondholders were still negotiating terms of the McCulloch Bill, William Mahone summoned a state convention of all people, irrespective of color, who supported a full-scale readjustment of the debt in order to make preparations for the legislative elections that autumn. Delegates from more than sixty of the state's nearly one hundred counties met in Mozart Hall, one of the large public theaters in Richmond, on 25 and 26 February 1879 and formally created the Readjuster Party. The friendly *Richmond Daily Whig* headlined its long reports of the proceedings "The People's Convention," clearly implying that the Funders did not represent the people of Virginia but only the alien bondholders and coupon brokers.

Two day sessions and one evening session provided opportunities for some of the emerging Readjuster leaders to speak at length. Among them were Frank Simpson Blair, of Wythe County in southwestern Virginia, who was temporary chair of the convention, won election as attorney general two years later, and became a Republican;[13] Abram Fulkerson, of Washington County, also in the southwest, a Democrat who later served in the House of Representatives as a Readjuster but remained a Democrat; John E. Massey, who had published the influential Readjuster pamphlet in 1875; Harrison Holt Riddleberger, of Harrisonburg in the Shenandoah Valley, who had introduced the bills in 1872 to prohibit payment of taxes with coupons and to reduce the annual interest rate from 6 percent to 4 percent; John Paul, also from the Shenandoah Valley, who had declared war on Holliday in 1878; James Barbour, taking time out from the negotiations; and Mahone, who during the opening session made the longest speech.

Several less well known men also spoke and made favorable impressions on the large convention. A man identified in the newspapers as "WM. T. JEFFERSON (COLORED)," of New Kent County, announced that he and the other black delegates, most of whom were Republicans, were delighted to attend "in response to the call which convened the people of Virginia without distinction of color." The report of his remarks quoted him as saying, "As to the debt, we don't want to pay a cent of it. We think we paid our share of it, if it ever was justly chargeable upon us, by long years of servitude. And then, as Virginia has been reconstructed in her territory and in her government, we think that her debt should be reconstructed too." That clever play on words drew a round of applause. Another African American, William H. Brisby,[14] who had voted for the Funding Act of 1871 when he was a member of the House of Delegates, told the convention that the "colored Republicans had formerly been deceived into voting for the Funding Bill, but they were now solid for re-adjustment."[15]

The prominence of African Americans in the founding of the Readjuster Party indicated that an important political realignment had taken place during the battles about the public debt in the 1870s. Conservatives, who during the latter years of Congressional Reconstruction in the 1860s and the early years of the 1870s had sometimes appealed to newly enfranchised black voters to lure them away from the radicalism of the 1860s, had lost them for several reasons. The opposition that most Conservative leaders manifested toward Congressional Reconstruction, their making the poll tax a prerequisite for voting, and the Funders' inadequate provisions for the public schools all offended the state's African American voters, who by the latter years of the 1870s were all, or almost all, Republicans. By inviting those voters into the Readjuster Party, Mahone, who had once been a conspicuous opponent of radical Reconstruction, took the lead in forming a biracial political party that appealed directly to the interests of voters of both races and parties.

The Readjusters argued that Funders would necessarily have to raise taxes on Virginians to pay out-of-state creditors instead of adequately supporting the new public school system, which by then was as popular among most white Virginians as it was among black Virginians. The Readjusters gained support in many of the state's cities as well as in the rural southeastern part of Virginia, which had the highest density and largest number of African Americans, and in the mountains and the southwestern part of the state, which had the lowest density and smallest number of African

Americans. The next battles about the debt were fought out in that new political context, in which the question of the debt and its consequences for the public schools, rather than race, Reconstruction, or old political party identifications, played the most conspicuous part. Readjusters deliberately made their appeal to the state's voters on economic issues and the schools and refrained from emphasizing issues relating to race. The party briefly gained control over the state government and became the most radical reforming party in all of Virginia's history.[16]

The formation of the Readjuster Party and its apparent growing popularity during 1879 truly alarmed the state's creditors. "The Commonwealth of Virginia," the Council of the Corporation of Foreign Bondholders declared in London early in 1880, "has apparently so fallen from the position it once occupied amongst the States of the American Union, as to have made it possible to create there a political and party question, whether just debts, incurred for the development of the country, and the payment of which had been solemnly guaranteed but a few months back should be paid or not." Virginia bondholders complained that they had "made great sacrifices for the benefit of the State" in the form of reduced payments on the interest, and they denounced the Readjusters' proposals as "an astounding breach of good faith."[17] Bondholders elsewhere no doubt agreed.

In the November 1879 legislative election, midway through Holliday's four-year term, Readjusters won substantial majorities in both houses of the General Assembly.[18] The bondholders in London interpreted the election results as a defeat, as "disastrous to the credit of the State. . . . It is obvious that if the supreme authority in the State is determined to set at nought all obligations of faith and honour, and all regard for the acts of its predecessors in the like position, as binding on itself, it not only does its best to ruin those who have trusted that faith, but also to destroy all hope that the State can ever recover its past prosperity, or develop its natural wealth."[19]

As soon as the new assembly began its work in December 1879, the Readjusters used their majorities to achieve some of their political objectives and to strengthen their appeal to all their constituencies before the 1881 election, in which the voters would select the next governor and members of the assembly. Holliday wielded his veto pen, and there were enough Funders in the assembly to sustain his veto of the Readjusters' sweeping bill to refinance the debt at a much lower cost by reducing the amount of the principal to be paid.

The office of governor was a comparatively weak one, though, and Holliday had no means of blocking the Readjusters when early in December 1879, a few days after the new legislature convened, they began making major changes in the state government. Under the state constitution, the assembly without the participation of the governor selected the directors of many of the most important state agencies. The Readjusters replaced nearly all of them. They elected Parson John E. Massey auditor of public accounts, and they replaced the second auditor, the state treasurer, and the secretary of the commonwealth with Readjusters.[20] They later replaced the superintendent of public instruction, William Henry Ruffner, who had founded the state's public school system, with Richard Ratcliffe Farr, who during his first year in office dismissed nearly all the county and city school superintendents in the state and appointed men who looked more favorably on improving schools for both white and black students.[21] The Readjusters began the long, two-step process of repealing the constitutional requirement of paying a poll tax as a prerequisite for voting. And they elected William Mahone to the United States Senate for the term that began on 4 March 1881.[22]

Holliday and the Funders must have known that they were beaten for the time being. The tone of the governor's message to the General Assembly one month after the election was petulant. He announced his opposition to the Readjusters' plan to replace the McCulloch Act with a radically different law by reporting that the 1879 law had proved agreeable to the bondholders, who had exchanged nearly half a million dollars more in bonds than the $8 million required by the McCulloch Act. Holliday also predicted that the state treasury would have a surplus that year, but his long message was largely an arrogant, self-righteous repetition of the essence of his earlier lectures on honor and his veto of the Barbour Bill rather than a persuasive argument about the propriety of paying the debt.[23]

The second auditor confirmed that the bondholders had exchanged bonds valued at more than the requisite amount to put the McCulloch Act into effect,[24] but Massey on one of his first days in office as auditor of public accounts reported that in no year since 1870 had the state collected all the money the state's constitution required for the public schools. State taxes should have yielded more than $4.5 million for the schools during that decade, but the accumulated arrears in the public school fund amounted to more than $1.5 million, and the old Literary Fund, the other source of money constitutionally dedicated to the public schools, was also more than $1.5 million in arrears.[25] Overall, according to calculations made in the 1880s, the state ran an average annual deficit during the 1870s of more than $1 million, while total expenses were only about three times that amount.[26] Both the schools and owners of bonds suffered from the deficits.

Refinancing the debt was the major issue on the Readjusters' legislative agenda during the winter of 1879–80. State senator Harrison Holt Riddleberger introduced A Bill to Reestablish the Public Credit, which both houses of the General Assembly passed on 1 March 1880 . The Riddleberger Bill, as nearly everybody called it, explained its rationale in a long preamble that referred to the party's victory in the recent legislative election and stated that "the people of Virginia have renounced the basis and principles" of the McCulloch Act.

The bill declared that Virginia had no legal or moral responsibility to pay any interest accrued during the Civil War and Congressional Reconstruction because of what the federal government had done to the state during those years. It repudiated one-third of the 1861 principal on the grounds that one-third of the value of taxable property in Virginia—mostly in the form of slaves but also in the form of other taxable property in what became West Virginia—had been destroyed or lost as a result of the war. The bill also reduced the amount due by virtue of what it characterized as the excessive interest paid under the Funding Act of 1871 and recomputed the principal actually owed in 1880 at about $22.9 million. The bill authorized the issuance of new fifty-year bonds paying 3 percent interest to replace all the old bonds; it established a loan office through which people could buy debt certificates for fifty cents on the dollar to help the state pay the old debt; it levied a 2-mill property tax (two-tenths of 1 percent) beginning in 1890 to be paid into the sinking fund for retiring the principal; and it specifically declared that the interest coupons on the new bonds not be receivable for taxes. Its most unusual and unprecedented democratic feature required public approval by referendum in November 1880 before the bill could take effect.[27]

Predictably, Holliday vetoed the bill. The Bill to Reestablish the Public Credit, he began, had "a most captivating title, and ought to arouse in the breast of every citizen of Virginia the profoundest interest," but the essence of his long, blunt veto message was that the public credit did not need to be reestablished; the public debt needed to be paid. He tirelessly and tiresomely lectured the legislators that the bill threatened the public credit on the grounds that most parts of it were unwise, that several parts of it were unconstitutional, and that all of it was unjust to creditors and a violation of the state's faith, which it had pledged every previous time the legislators passed a funding measure.[28] The Readjusters failed to override Holliday's veto,[29] but like his veto of the Barbour Bill, the veto of the Riddleberger Bill stated the Funders' position so well that it could serve as a campaign document for both parties.

Two days after the assembly passed the Riddleberger Bill, it adopted a joint resolution instructing the attorney general to "institute proceedings in the courts" to test the constitutionality of the McCulloch Act; the resolution was passed the next day in both houses of the General Assembly.[30] The annual reports of the state's attorneys general before Rufus Adolphus Ayers took office in January 1886 contain almost no useful information about any of the legal cases relating to the debt and the coupons or the personal or official opinions of the attorneys general on the legal and political issues involved. Attorney General James G. Field did not file any challenges to the McCulloch Act, but he continued, as required by the constitution and the law, to defend the statutes then in force.

One of the first cases he had to try after taking office involved the city sergeant of Richmond and produced a reprise, of sorts, of the 1872 opinion of the Supreme Court of Appeals in *Antoni v. Wright*. The case arose when James Clarke offered to pay a fine to the city sergeant with coupons. The sergeant refused to accept them, so Clarke sought a writ of habeas corpus from the Supreme Court of Appeals to be released for the reason that he had legally paid his fine with the coupons. Judge Joseph Christian[31] delivered the opinion of the court in *Clarke v. Tyler* on 4 April 1878, citing and relying in large part on Wood Bouldin's opinion in *Antoni v. Wright*. Christian wrote that fines people owed to the state or its subdivisions were within the meaning of the words "all taxes, debts, dues and demands due the state" in the Funding Act of 1871 and that the law therefore required the city sergeant to accept the coupons and release Clarke.

Going beyond the law, as almost all the Virginia judges in both state and federal courts did when discussing the public debt, and even going beyond the legal issues involved in the case, Christian inserted his political opinions into the heart of his decision. "A State, like an individual, must be just before it is generous," he wrote when endorsing Daniel's and Holliday's hard lines on debt payment. "No honest man can or will abstract from his creditors what is justly due them in order to give it to his children. No State, in order to educate its citizens, ought to withhold from its just creditors, that which has been pledged, by its honor and plighted faith, to the payment of its just debts." He said that "both obligations must and will be met," but he did not explain how. "The people must be educated, but they must not be educated," Christian concluded with capital letters and as if with a loud voice, "at the price of REPUDIATION AND DISHONOR. Better would be ignorance than enlightenment purchased at such a fearful price."[32]

Waller Redd Staples dissented as he had in *Antoni v. Wright* and for the same reasons he had stated in 1872. He wrote that if the assembly "has surrendered all control of the revenues beyond recall, then, indeed, has government abdicated its functions, and the state stripped itself of one of its attributes of sovereignty."[33] Judges Francis Thomas Anderson and Edward Calohill Burks[34] concurred in the ruling that Christian announced but went on to say that payment of fines with coupons was not a violation of the constitutional requirement to pay fines into the Literary Fund for the support of public education, as Staples maintained, even though the coupons could not then be spent for that purpose. Moreover, even if that part of the law did violate the state constitution, that did not necessarily invalidate the entire act.[35]

The second debt case that Attorney General Field handled, *Hartman v. Greenhow* in 1878, involved Section 117 of the annual revenue act of 1876, which required receivers of taxes to deduct the five-mill tax on the market value of the bonds from the value of coupons submitted for payment of a tax. H. C. G. Hartman, a Richmond taxpayer who had purchased detached coupons from a broker, attempted to pay his tax with them and then sued the tax collector after he deducted the amount of the tax on the bond from the value of the coupon. When the Supreme Court of Appeals heard the arguments of counsel, the attorneys for Hartman argued that to deduct the tax on the bond from the value of the coupon was an impairment of the obligations of contract that the Funding Act of 1871 had created. That had been settled law in Virginia since *Antoni v. Wright* in 1872. The attorney general argued that the deduction corresponded exactly to the deduction that the treasurer had for several years made without legal challenge when people presented coupons to him for redemption. He also argued that neither deduction impaired that obligation. One law merely reduced the amount of interest the coupon holder received, and the other reduced the amount of tax the taxpayer could pay with the coupon. The judges of the Supreme Court of Appeals issued no published opinion on the case, but their clerk recorded that "the judgment of this Court is in favor of the validity of said section of said act and against the right claimed by the petitioner under said article of the constitution of the United States."[36]

The attorney general made essentially the same arguments late in December 1880, after Hartman and his attorneys appealed to the Supreme Court of the United States. Writing for a majority of the court in *Hartman v. Greenhow*, Justice Stephen J. Field declared that the law violated the contracts clause of the Constitution of the United States. He reviewed the federal case law that Bouldin had relied on in 1872 and praised his opinion in the *Antoni* case, which declared that the coupons were a constitutionally protected contract and that they could therefore be used to pay taxes. In this instance, Hartman had purchased the detached coupon with which he paid his tax and was not the original owner of the bond. Field declared that when thus separated, the bond and the detached coupon were separate contracts. He concluded that "surely it is not necessary to argue that an act which requires the holder of one contract to pay the taxes levied upon another contact held by a stranger cannot be sustained. Such an act is not a legitimate exercise of the taxing power; it undertakes to impose upon one the burden which should fall if at all, upon another." Section 117 of the revenue act of 1876 was therefore an unconstitutional impairment of contract.[37]

Hartman v. Greenhow was a victory for the bondholders, the coupon brokers, and the Funders when the Supreme Court handed it down early in 1881. The council of the Corporation of Foreign Bondholders printed portions of the court's opinion in its annual report a few weeks later to reassure the bondholders that the federal courts would protect their rights and the value of their investments. They also knew that they could not count on the political leaders in the Virginia General Assembly. The council perceptively cautioned the investors it represented that "the position of the Bondholders may be weakened, if the Readjusters are able to secure, in the coming State elections, the large Republican negro vote, and to induce a considerable section of the Democratic party to concur with them on the Debt question."[38] In fact, that was almost exactly what happened.

The Readjusters dominated in the year 1881, beginning on 14 March, when about three hundred Republican men, all of them African Americans, met in Petersburg to decide whether to form an alliance with the Readjusters. It was a raucous meeting because many of the men did not want to lose their political identity as Republicans, which they feared might happen if they voted to affiliate with the Readjusters. Mayor William E. Cameron,[39] a white Readjuster whose city government had been notably fair to the city's many black residents, attended the convention and welcomed the delegates. During the opening session, a man dramatically rushed into the convention hall with a telegram and announced that when William Mahone had first taken his seat in the United States Senate that day the new Readjuster senator had voted with the Republicans to organize the Senate that until his arrival had contained equal numbers of Republicans and Democrats. The Republicans in Petersburg cheered the news because it meant that Democrats would not control the Senate and that Mahone, by cooperating with the Republican senators and president, would be well positioned to provide federal jobs to African Americans and other Republicans and build the state's Republican Party into a formidable opposition to the Conservatives and Democrats. For the remainder of the convention, the majority of the Republicans acted as if the Readjusters had already joined the Republican Party rather than as if the Republicans were debating whether to join the Readjuster Party.

The statement of principles they adopted emphasized Republican rather than Readjuster goals. "To the jury, the free schools, and the ballot," it proclaimed, "we look as the highest earnests and the best safeguards of all that is valuable in our citizenship, and it is with the most fervent aspiration that we seek the final obliteration in politics of that color-line which, disastrous to the nation, the State, and all the people, has been especially hurtful to ourselves as a race." But on behalf of themselves and "the colored people of Virginia," the members of the convention endorsed affiliation with the Readjuster Party and proclaimed that the rights of African Americans would be "better secured and preserved by aiding that party in its efforts to achieve and permanently settle the antagonism of races, which has unfortunately affected the prosperity of our State."[40] The dysfunctional Republican Party of Virginia gained a new life as part of a coalition with the Readjusters.[41]

Republicans and Readjusters of both races as well as white Conservatives and Democrats who favored refinancing the debt attended the Readjuster Party state convention early the following June. The convention united them all for the critical November 1881 election of statewide officers and members of the General Assembly. The convention nominated Mayor Cameron for governor; for lieutenant governor, John Francis Lewis, a wartime Unionist from the Shenandoah Valley and briefly the Republican lieutenant governor near the end of Congressional Reconstruction; and for attorney general, Frank Simpson Blair, who had presided over the convention that founded the Readjuster Party in 1879. The convention also endorsed the agenda of the Republicans' Petersburg convention.[42]

The Conservative Party state convention floundered through several ballots and eventually settled somewhat surprisingly on one of the Funders' most bluntly outspoken legislators, John Warwick Daniel, the state senator who had expressed his willingness to burn the public schools rather than spend on them the money he believed should be paid to the state's creditors. For lieutenant governor, the convention nominated James Barbour, sponsor of the Barbour Bill, which Daniel had ferociously denounced. Barbour was unwilling to go along with the Riddleberger Bill, which repudiated part of the principal, and he was also angry at Mahone. Barbour renounced his support of the Readjusters, and even before the Readjusters and the Republicans formed their coalition he reaffirmed his allegiance to the Conservative Party.[43] For attorney general the Conservatives dumped the moderate Readjuster incumbent, James G. Field, and nominated Philip Watkins McKinney, who eight years later won the Democratic Party nomination and the general election to become governor.[44]

The principal issue in the campaign was the debt and its ripple effects, particularly on the schools, not the participation of black men in the Readjuster Party. Readjusters appealed openly to both black and white men regarding the damage that the inability of the state to support the public schools adequately had done to all the state's children. Funders appealed to voters on the grounds that if the state defaulted on even a part of its debt obligations, as the Riddleberger Bill provided, it would become impossible for Virginians to attract enough capital to generate sustained prosperity. Funders declared that both the honor of the state and the state's economic future were at stake. Virginia's voters had a very clear choice in 1881.

Blair, rather than Cameron, became the central figure of the campaign for the Readjusters. He appealed to black and white voters and parents everywhere with the simple argument that the Funders' repeated and failed attempts to pay the high rate of interest on the debt had impoverished the schools. Blair argued that the state's honor, which Funders constantly talked about, would not buy anybody a breakfast and that people needed practical relief from the consequences of the treasury deficit. Funders gleefully ridiculed "Breakfast" Blair and the Readjusters for placing mundane private concerns ahead of the state's obligation to pay its bills and for stating that a poor man's breakfast was more important than the state's honor and credit. Blair tried in vain to turn the advantage back toward himself, but the Funders refused to acknowledge any legitimacy in his point, leaving him no leverage for engaging in debate with them.

The Funders, however, had nothing to offer but ridicule. For nearly ten years they had conspicuously failed to pay the full interest on the debt, and in the process of trying they had allowed appropriations for the public schools to fall to a fraction of what they had been in the beginning. A prominent Readjuster, John Sergeant Wise, son of Henry A. Wise, later ridiculed the Funders in return. "A wag of the period," he wrote, almost certainly referring to himself, "defined a Virginian Debt-payer as one who 'would rather owe you all his life than cheat you out of a cent.'"[45] The voters responded favorably to the Readjuster campaign and elected Readjuster majorities in the assembly and all the statewide Readjuster candidates, placing Cameron in the governor's office.

In spite of the two 1870s constitutional amendments designed to make it more difficult for African American men to register and vote, they evidently registered and voted in increasing numbers at the end of the decade and during the short good times the Readjusters enjoyed at the beginning of the 1880s.[46] Only eight African Americans had won election to the General Assembly in 1877, immediately after the amendments were ratified, but the appeal of the Readjusters among African American voters was such that they helped elect fifteen in 1879 and thirteen in 1881. The number of members of both houses of the assembly had been reduced in the meantime by about 15 percent as an economy measure, so the percentage of African American members rose more than the raw numbers suggest.

When it became evident that the Readjusters welcomed African Americans into the party, black voters exhibited a new eagerness and energy that also produced strong results for Republican presidential candidates. In 1880, the Republican James Garfield received 83,634 votes in Virginia, but Republican nominees received 139,356 in 1884 and 150,399 in 1888. The percentage of men who voted Republican also increased, so that in 1888 Benjamin Harrison lost to Grover Cleveland in Virginia by a margin of only 1,684 out of more than 304,000 votes counted.[47] That was well within the range of fraudulent victory through able manipulation of ballot boxes and tally sheets, at which members of both parties in Virginia excelled.[48]

Republican candidates also did better in statewide races, where the increase in black voting was also notable. In 1881, Cameron defeated Daniel by about 12,000 votes out of more than 211,000 cast, a margin of more than 5 percent. Four years later, when John Sergeant Wise ran as a Readjuster-Republican against the former Confederate general Fitzhugh Lee, the outcome was almost equally close, and when Mahone was the Republican nominee in 1889 he received more than 42 percent of the votes.[49] Considering the unpopularity of the former Readjuster senator among white Virginians by then, that must indicate a continuing large turnout of black Virginians as well as votes of Conservatives and Democrats who through support of the Readjusters became Republicans.

African Americans were essential to the Readjusters' victories in the legislative election in 1879 and the statewide election in 1881, but the Readjusters were never a black-majority party, as Funders alleged, or under the direction of their black supporters, as their enemies charged then and Democrats asserted later. The Readjusters undoubtedly received very strong support from African American men, but white men voted for the Readjusters too, perhaps in larger numbers than black men. The Readjuster Party had an entirely white leadership, and Mahone permitted no African Americans to rise to influential positions in the party. At best, the Readjuster Party treated African Americans as junior partners, which was, to be sure, much better than Conservatives and Funders then treated them or Democrats later treated them.

A majority of the men, both black and white, who voted for the Readjusters were probably farmers, either owners or renters of farms or men who worked in agriculture as hired laborers. Workingmen and artisans in the state's cities and towns also voted for the Readjusters in substantial numbers. By small but reliable majorities, Virginians voted in ways that demonstrated that they believed that the Readjusters better represented their interests and hopes than did the businessmen and professional men for whom the Funders spoke and to whom the Funders primarily appealed. Those men who voted for the Readjusters relied on and believed in the public school system, feared that Funders might raise their taxes to pay interest to people outside the state who owned the bonds, and resented that their tax money could be diverted from supporting the schools to paying the debt. Readjusters ran for office at all levels of the government, not merely in the General Assembly. The electoral ticket for Williamsburg city officials in the May 1881 municipal election listed all the Readjuster candidates and featured a dramatic headline that implicitly condemned the Funders by emphasizing what the Readjusters favored, "Free Schools, Free Ballot, and a Fair Count."[50]

Seven white Readjusters won election to the United States House of Representatives. Robert M. Mayo, Harry Libbey, and Benjamin S. Hooper won election from two of the southeastern congressional districts, where African Americans comprised a majority in most of the counties, but the other two congressional districts in which voters elected Readjusters to Congress were in the mountains of western and southwestern Virginia, where the proportions of African Americans in the population were the state's smallest. John Paul won in the district that included the Shenandoah Valley, and voters in the Ninth Congressional District, in the southwest, elected two Readjusters, Henry Bowen, who ran as a Readjuster, and Abram Fulkerson, who ran as a Democrat. And in one election for a congressman-at-large, the Readjuster John Sergeant Wise, of Richmond, won. Wise and the three Readjusters from the west could not have been elected to Congress without very substantial support from white voters. The Readjusters were never under the control of radical Republicans in Washington or wholly dependent for political success on radical African Americans in Virginia.

Some men who supported the Readjusters and became leaders in the party, such as Frank Blair, had flirted with the Grangers or the Greenback Party, both of which advocated agrarian reforms and currency inflation as a way of increasing the income of farmers. They were not backward-looking opponents of the new national economy based on finance capitalism but well-informed men seeking to change a system that they believed rewarded bankers and railroad executives at the expense of honest commercial agricultural producers. Those white men from nearly every part of the state differed with the lower classes of farmers and workingmen on few issues and had few objections in the beginning to working with or under the leadership of like-minded corporate executives such as the controversial railroad tycoon Billy Mahone.[51]

5 READJUSTMENT, REFORM, AND REACTION

The Readjuster majority elected with the Readjuster governor in 1881 had only one legislative session, not two, during which to achieve its objectives before the next election in 1883 because one of the 1870s constitutional amendments intended in part to reduce the cost of state government changed the frequency of meetings of the General Assembly from annual to biennial.

The members of the new General Assembly convened early in December 1881 and listened to the clerks read a long and testy final message from outgoing Governor Holliday, who repeated all the objections he had stated to Readjuster policies in his vetoes of the Barbour Bill and the Riddleberger Bill.[1] Holliday was disgusted with the success of the Readjusters and their appeals to and reliance on ordinary white and black Virginians. Almost immediately after his term expired he left Virginia—left the country—for several years in search of a place where a man of elite sympathies could comfortably reside surrounded by obedient body servants and free from distasteful democracy.[2]

The Readjuster majorities in the legislature responded quite differently to the new governor's first message, on 6 January 1882. Cameron opened by asking the assembly to adopt something like the 1880 Riddleberger Bill to refinance the debt, noting that money had been diverted to debt service from the fund set aside for supporting the public schools and urging that no such "future invasion" be made on that fund. "I think it would be eminently proper," he went on, opening the full agenda of Readjuster reform, "to grant our colored citizens an institution in which those who have acquired proficiency in common schools may be given the opportunity for broader training." That was the first time an influential white Virginia officeholder advocated creating a college for Virginia's African

Americans. Cameron also asked the assembly to remove a Conservative Party impediment to African American suffrage by repealing the poll tax as a prerequisite for voting.[3]

Riddleberger introduced and the assembly members passed a slightly revised version of his 1880 readjustment bill, and they also passed several other measures to make it more difficult and expensive for people to pay taxes with coupons. (The provisions of the Coupon Killers, as the first of those laws were called, and the controversies and court cases they produced will be treated below.)

Cameron signed the Riddleberger Act on 14 February 1882. Excluding interest from both the Civil War years and from the years of Congressional Reconstruction as well as reducing the amount of principal to adjust for the payment of what it characterized as a too-high rate of interest since 1871, the new law tabulated the total Virginia public debt as of 1 July 1882 at a little more than $21 million, an effective repudiation of about a third of the principal that had been established in the Funding Act of 1871. The law authorized the state government to issue 3 percent fifty-year registered and coupon bonds to that amount and reserved the state an option to redeem the new bonds at any time after 1 July 1900. Owners of the old bonds could exchange them for the new ones at between fifty-three cents and eighty cents on the dollar, depending on when the old bonds (the 1866 bonds issued to pay part of the interest then in arrears, 1871 5 percent bonds, 1871 consols, the peelers, and 1879 ten-forties) had been issued and what rate of interest they had initially paid. The law did not allow the coupons on the new bonds to be receivable for taxes, and it specifically made the printing plates the property of the state's sinking fund. Like the earlier refinancing laws, it authorized a new series of deferred certificates for the one-third of the readjusted principal it again assigned to West Virginia.

The Riddleberger Act levied a 2.25 percent property tax beginning in 1890, payable to the sinking fund, and it prohibited the state from paying any interest on any other bonds after adoption of the law. That final provision terminated the ability of holders of 1871 and 1879 bonds to redeem the coupons and collect interest on their investment, but in light of the court decisions it did not prevent them from paying taxes with the coupons from the old bonds. To that extent, the act did not provide an attractive alternative for all owners of those bonds to exchange them, hence the necessity for the Coupon Killers. The Riddleberger Act of 1882, unlike the

Riddleberger Bill of 1880, did not require approval by popular referendum before taking effect.[4]

The refinancing of the debt drastically reduced the proportion of the state's revenue required to pay the interest from 40–56 percent during the 1870s to 12–25 percent during the 1880s.[5] The Readjusters also completed work on the reform agenda the party had adopted in 1879 and in 1881 when it made common cause with the African American Republicans. During the years of the Readjusters' rise to power, while their leading men argued against privileging creditors over people who depended on the state's government and its public schools, many of the party's leaders embraced a more egalitarian political agenda than any of them had previously expressed or than any Virginia political party had ever supported. Marching in step with non-elite white and black Virginians and as their advocates, the leaders of the Readjuster Party became reformers unlike any in Virginia's history.[6]

During the 1881–82 session of the General Assembly, the Readjusters created the Virginia Normal and Industrial School, the origins of what became Virginia State University, in line with Cameron's suggestion in his first message to the legislators. Located near Petersburg, it was the South's first state-supported college founded for the education of African American public school teachers. The legislators also took the first steps toward gaining control of a small academy for women in Farmville that in 1884 became the State Female Normal School, later Longwood University, the state's first public college for the education of white public school teachers. In an almost complete overhaul of higher education in the state, the Readjusters replaced the members of the boards of visitors of the University of Virginia, the Medical College of Virginia, and the Virginia Agricultural and Mechanical College, which later became the Virginia Polytechnic Institute and State University.[7] The assembly created the first mental hospital for African Americans in Virginia and formally submitted to the voters a constitutional amendment that abolished the poll tax as a prerequisite for voting. The Readjusters also outlawed use of the brutal and humiliating whipping post, a holdover from slavery times, for punishing African Americans.

The Readjusters reduced taxes on farmers and increased taxes on railroads by requiring that tax assessors rather than railroad executives decide how much railroads should pay in taxes on their gross receipts.[8] The Re-

adjusters converted a treasury deficit into a surplus and kept all the prom-
ises they had made during the 1881 campaign. They also elected five new
judges of the Supreme Court of Appeals, to take office when the terms of
all the members elected in 1870 expired at the end of 1882, ensuring that
during the twelve years of those judges' terms the state's highest appellate
court would be much less likely to find any of the Readjusters' legislation
or the refinancing of the debt unconstitutional. Having already sent the
party's leader, William Mahone, to the United States Senate, the assembly
elected H. H. Riddleberger, author of the refinancing bills, to the United
States Senate for the term beginning 4 March 1883.[9]

The assembly session of 1881–82 was the flood tide of the Readjusters.
At the beginning of the 1883–84 session of the assembly, Cameron pointed
proudly to the achievements of the 1881–82 assembly and singled out for
special comment the wholesome consequences for public education. Cameron's remarks stand in stark contrast to Holliday's and exhibit how much
some of the Readjuster leaders had come to differ from the Conservatives
most of them had originally been. "The condition of the public free school
system," Cameron reported, "should engage the active interest of every
citizen of this commonwealth. There is no individual and no element of our
population but should rejoice to know that the state in the past two years
has been able almost to double the facilities for free education."

Cameron explained further, "The executive of the commonwealth
knows no higher duty than to contribute all in his power to furnish the
means for teaching all the people to understand their rights, to know the
limits of their privileges, and to feel and perform the full measure of their
duties. To those whom we have armed with the powers and responsibilities
of citizenship, present or future, a high obligation exists. To call human be-
ings into the front of the battle of life and deny them or obstruct them in
the means which are essential to their intelligent use of freedom would be
as gross an abuse as to call men into real war and fail to put into their hands
the weapons with which to make them soldiers." Himself a former Confederate officer, and many of the legislators having had military service too,
Cameron chose an apt and persuasive figure of speech. "It is to be hoped,"
the governor concluded, "that these views will meet with no opposition in
Virginia, and that all persons of all classes will agree that our best policy, as
our highest duty, dictates the free education of all the children of all classes
of our people."[10]

At the close of the 1882 legislative session the Readjuster members of the assembly issued a long public address to the state's voters and condemned the Funders as Bourbon obstructionists and enemies of all Virginians who did not own bonds. Like reforming Southerners elsewhere, the Readjusters called their opponents Bourbons to brand the Funders as backward, aristocratic obstructionists, as the Bourbon French had been at the time of the French Revolution. The address itemized the achievements of the 1882 assembly session: passage of the Riddleberger Act; submission to the voters for ratification a constitutional amendment to repeal "the odious poll-tax restriction upon suffrage"; "rescuing the public school system—always in peril while Bourbonism was in power"; creation of a college for training African American schoolteachers; reorganization of the state's insane asylums and its school for the deaf and dumb; election of new judges of the Supreme Court of Appeals; reforming the administration of the state's lower courts; streamlining the laws of inheritance; and redistricting the state to increase representation of Readjusters and reduce the number of Bourbons elected to Congress. The address, which almost all the Readjuster executive officers and functionaries, including the second assistant clerks in the assembly and doorkeepers of the Senate and the House of Delegates, signed, also praised President Chester Arthur and advocated a protective tariff as good for American businesses and working people. It was an almost perfect mixture of Readjuster platforms and Republican Party dogma.[11]

The Readjusters and their reconstruction of Virginia's politics attracted national attention, but almost as soon as they achieved their principal objective of refinancing the debt, their larger reforming agenda and the accompanying ideology that developed with it led to their rapid downfall. The increasing acceptance by the party's leaders of African Americans as genuine citizens with full rights of citizenship undermined them more than anything else. While the debt and the schools remained the focal points of political debate during the 1870s, discussions about race and about how much freedom and how many of the rights of citizenship African Americans were entitled to exercise in Virginia were subjects of comparatively less heated discussion than they had been during Congressional Reconstruction. Readjuster policies and public pronouncements of Readjuster leaders, such as Cameron's lecture on public education and advocacy of black voting, changed all that.

Even as the Riddleberger Bill was being debated in the legislature early in 1882, the state's Democratic United States senator, John W. Johnston,

whom Riddleberger succeeded the following year, published a long essay entitled "Repudiation in Virginia" in the February 1882 issue of the
influential national journal the *North American Review*. He summarized
the Funders' legal and constitutional as well as political and financial arguments and attacked the Readjusters from every angle. Johnston concluded
with a call to arms for opponents of the Readjusters to recognize their
enemies as dishonest repudiators and dangerous, radical Republicans.
Johnston invited former Conservatives who had supported refinancing the
debt back to the old party as new Democrats. "The coalition carried the
State," he wrote of the Readjuster-Republican victory in the 1881 election,
"and has produced a breed of bastard Republicans, the progeny of Federal
patronage and repudiation, who have deserted the Democratic party, and
yet say they have not gone to the Republicans. The present effect has been
to give the Republicans increased strength in both houses of Congress."[12]

Riddleberger responded in the same journal in April. In "Bourbonism
in Virginia" he laid out at length the justifications for reducing the Virginia
principal of the debt that he had included in his 1880 and 1882 bills and
attacked the Funders-Conservatives directly for many more reasons than
their insistence on paying the full principal and interest established in the
Funding Act of 1871. "The conservative Democratic party, as it delights
to call itself," Riddleberger sneered, "has been as false in its professions
touching the negro and the elective franchise as it had been concerning the
debt and the schools. By a system of trickery, through disqualifications for
petty offences, and requiring the payment of a head-tax as a prerequisite
to voting, and using every means to prevent its payment, they had virtually disfranchised the negro, and by a system of frauds in the counting and
certifying of returns they had guarded against any accidents resulting from
his casting a vote."

Riddleberger concluded that many Virginians, not just the state's African Americans, understood that Virginia "cannot thrive chained to the
rotting corpse of obsolete ideas" and therefore looked elsewhere than to
the Conservatives and old Democrats for allies. Virginians, he wrote, began
"to realize that a great revolution has swept over America; that with it came
new ideas, change—social, moral, and political; that unless she adapts herself to existing conditions of affairs, she will soon lapse into oblivion and
insignificance even greater than she experienced under Bourbon rule."

Riddleberger boasted about what the Readjusters had done. "Under
Re-adjuster rule," he wrote, Virginia "has aroused herself" and provided

adequate money and support for the public schools. Readjusters had in-creased the number of schools from about 2,500 to more than 5,000, the number of students from 108,074 to 220,736, and the annual school term from three to five months. "The funds diverted" from education to debt payment "have been partially restored," he continued, and the state had created its first public normal institutes for training teachers. "Manhood suffrage has been restored," Riddleberger concluded, "with recognized constitutional qualifications. Population and capital are attracted. Rail-roads are built. New industries spring up. Mines are opened. Manufac-tories are started. Vigor, thrift, and industry are seen everywhere. Virginia is awake and alert. She begins a new career, not only materially, but in thought and action."[13]

Between the publication of Johnston's and Riddleberger's articles, Sen-ator William Mahone made one of the most politically provocative public statements of the entire era. Invited to give the principal address in Bos-ton on the birthday of George Washington in 1882—the invitation itself was a clear recognition of the importance of the changes taking place in Virginia—Mahone sent a long public letter that was widely reprinted or excerpted in Virginia newspapers. "Our people have just declared popular education to be among the most sacred duties and trusts of representative government," he wrote, "and are bravely executing that honorable decree. With valuable and beneficient results we are rapidly guaranteeing a price-less ballot to all entitled to it under the American theory. Conspicuous among the achievements of the advanced thought that places Virginia in full alignment with the highest American civilization is the prompt justice with which she deals with an element of population which has been the fruitful source of passionate disputation. Virginia has closed the long strife, which Mr. Jefferson foresaw and dreaded as he would dread 'the fire-bell at night,' over the status of the colored man. . . . In Virginia he is at last in the full panoply of acknowledged citizenship."[14]

As Riddleberger had done in his "Bourbonism in Virginia," Mahone identified the state's new political culture with "the American theory" and with "the highest American civilization" instead of with traditional Virginia values. Even more than Riddleberger's *North American Review* article that spring or the Readjusters' public address at the end of that year's legislative session, Mahone's declaration was to Johnston's challenge what Holliday's veto of the Barbour Bill had been to the Readjusters before the 1879 gen-eral election. In the 1883 legislative election the reorganized Democratic

Party of Virginia defeated the Readjusters. Midway through the one four-year term of the only Readjuster governor, the Readjusters lost control of both houses of the General Assembly. The main issue then was not the debt or the schools; it was race.

John Strode Barbour,[15] a near relation of the former Readjuster James Barbour, became state chair of the reorganized Democratic Party. Since the 1850s he had been president of the Orange and Alexandria Railroad, which by the 1880s had nearly completed its evolution into the Southern Railway, one of the longest and most consequential railroads in Virginia. Barbour and his railroad interests had repeatedly clashed with Mahone and his during the 1870s, when the two men were both influential support-ers of the Conservative Party and before they became leaders of competing political parties.[16]

Like Barbour and Mahone, most of the leaders of all the major politi-cal parties in post–Civil War Virginia—Conservative, Funder, Readjuster, Democratic, and Republican—were attorneys with close ties to railroad executives and bankers, who shared with each other the general objec-tive of stimulating economic development with commercial and industrial growth, not merely that of reviving the past of the tobacco planters. The politics of financing the debt divided them during the 1870s and drew them apart as their beliefs about race and class in Virginia, which reflected the characteristics and desires of their constituencies, increasingly differed. The evidence, such as in Mahone's 1882 public letter, that Readjusters were embracing an egalitarian political creed with African Americans as fully entitled participants was far too much for opponents of the Readjust-ers and a larger number of white Virginians to swallow.[17]

No prominent white Readjuster actually advocated full equality of the races, but the implications of Mahone's public letter and of the party's poli-cies raised fears that they could. Until after the Republicans in Congress abandoned their commitment later in the nineteenth century to protect Southern African Americans in the exercise of political rights, white South-erners, probably a majority of them, remained deeply fearful that men like Mahone would be able to refashion Republican Parties in other Southern states as radical majorities that relied on black voters and officeholders and would therefore be more or less under the control of radical Northern Republicans and equally radical Southern African Americans. Mahone's letter to the Boston celebration seemed to suggest exactly that future for Virginia.

Mahone appeared to personify the new political ethos in Virginia, but in truth he and a small number of other prominent Readjusters had got far out of step with the majority of white Virginians. The former Confederate general had changed so much since taking part in founding the Conservative Party in the 1860s that during the 1880s he regularly corresponded with African Americans throughout Virginia, some of them poor and barely literate, and treated them with uncommon respect. Most of them, in turn, regarded him as a genuine friend and ally, a sentiment they probably reserved for very few white political leaders.

Mahone's abundant surviving correspondence clearly shows that his attitudes about Virginia's changing society and politics were almost as radical as his political adversaries charged. Preserved in his papers is a remarkable manuscript volume that contains two lists, one of members of Mahone's old Confederate brigade and the other of African American clergymen to whom he wrote asking for support during one of his political campaigns— both lists in one volume with the double-entendre title "Mahone's Brigade."[18] His adversaries, had they known of its existence, would probably have killed to be able to make use of it against him. Billy Mahone had become thoroughly reconstructed as a Readjuster, just as the Readjusters had become the real reconstruction of Virginia politics.

Many white politicians who had agreed with the Readjusters on their plan to refinance the debt bailed out of the coalition soon after they had achieved that objective. They could not go all the way with Mahone and his followers among the ordinary white and black Virginians. It was not just race. To Virginia men and women who remained committed to long and venerable traditions of elite white governance, the large number of ordinary white voters who supported the Readjuster-Republican coalition in 1879 and 1881 was almost equally as alarming as the participation of American Americans. All aspects of the coalition and its 1882 legislative agenda threatened those traditions every bit as much as abolitionists and Free-Soilers had threatened them before the war or as advocates of radical Reconstruction had threatened them immediately after the war.[19]

The brief dramatic rise and fall of the Readjuster Party was an extraordinarily revealing episode in the attempts of Virginians to adapt to the changes that the defeat of the Confederacy and the abolition of slavery required of the people of all the Southern states. In large part, the burden of paying the debt and the popular appeal of the new public school system drove their efforts. The prevalent racism among the state's majority white population fatally undermined the Readjusters' attempts to forge a new coalition of farmers and working-class men of both races that could permanently wrest control of the government out of the hands of the traditional white elites, who had placed their hopes for the future in a continuation of what the Readjusters called "Bourbon" rule.

If the traditional white political leaders of Virginia differed from their counterparts elsewhere, it was in their firm commitment to continuation of elitist government. Their differences with other American political and business leaders on the subject of white supremacy were more of degree than of kind. The Readjusters' reconstruction of Virginia politics and government provided a vivid example of alternative possibilities for the state, perhaps for other Southern states; but the manner in which the party arose and collapsed just as vividly revealed how numerous and formidable were the obstacles that stood in the way of changes that drastic.

For a brief time, though, it looked as if the Readjusters' reconstruction of Virginia might succeed. By repeated small majorities, the state's black and white voters had supported the Readjusters when elections turned on reducing the cost of paying the debt and on providing adequate support for the public schools. Readjusters prepared for the 1883 legislative elections by refining their arguments and energizing their voters on those issues. One particularly creative campaign handout was aimed directly at African American mothers in an obvious attempt to have them persuade their husbands to campaign and vote correctly. Entitled "PUBLIC FREE SCHOOLS!," it listed contrasting figures for every school year from 1877 through 1882, showing smaller appropriations for all schools and for "Colored" schools, as well as smaller numbers of schools and smaller numbers of "Colored Scholars" and "Colored Teachers," under Funder administrations than under the Readjuster administration. The clever designer of the handout actually printed the sums in graduated type sizes to emphasize the differences. Directly below the title in italic boldfaced type is an exhortation that reads, "Let every Mother read, and by the facts which these figures below establish, determine for herself who are the friends of the Children."[20]

The Readjusters had won the political contests with the Funders on the issues of the state debt, taxes, and public schools. The voters repeatedly rejected the Funders' policies and many of the party's candidates. To succeed, therefore, the new Democratic Party disavowed its failed Funder past scarcely a year after the Readjusters' reform assembly adjourned. In preparation for the legislative election in the autumn of 1883, the party's state convention that summer adopted a platform that included this pledge: "The Democratic party accepts as final the recent settlement of the public debt pronounced constitutional by the courts of last resort, State and Federal, and will oppose all agitation of the question, or any disturbance of that settlement by appeal or otherwise."[21]

In 1883 the Democrats made the main issue white supremacy, not the debt, not the schools, not even the state's economic future. They savagely attacked the Readjusters and Mahone as advocates of black rule who not only offered an extension of the worst of radical Congressional Reconstruction but also posed a fatal threat to old Virginia's brand of civilization, which was based on white supremacy and elite government. That helped bring many white advocates of debt reduction into, or back into, the new Democratic Party. A few days before the election, a street brawl in Danville between white and black men seized public attention in large part because Democratic propagandists portrayed the event as a major race riot, the natural consequence of what they labeled a Readjuster plan for African American and Republican domination of the decent white people of the state.[22]

After 1883, no Democratic candidate for governor and few Democratic legislators repeated the blunders of Holliday and Daniel. They all endorsed free public education, even though the commitment of many of them was weak and thus kept appropriations small and left the public schools poorly supported. Appealing to voters on the bases of white supremacy, low taxes, and support (however inadequate) for public schools enabled the Democrats in and after 1885 to win and hold control of the governorship and of both houses of the General Assembly for several generations. They ran against Mahone and his Readjuster-Republican coalition for decades after both were dead.[23]

After winning control of both houses of the General Assembly in November 1883, the Democratic majorities early in the next session of the legislature, before they set out to deconstruct the Readjuster reconstruction, passed a joint resolution accepting the Riddleberger Act as the final settlement of the Virginia debt controversy. Admitting that the Readjusters and the state's voters had won and that the Funders had lost, the Democrats' resolution proclaimed that "the people of Virginia have accepted the act of February fourteenth, eighteen hundred and eight-two, known as the 'Riddleberger Bill,' as the ultimate settlement of the debt of this state; that it is their unalterable purpose that that settlement shall be final, and that any expectation that any settlement of the debt of this state upon any other basis will ever be made or tolerated by the people of Virginia, is absolutely illusory and hopeless."[24]

Much as the Readjusters had done four years earlier, the Democrats, as soon as they won control of the General Assembly in 1883, replaced all the principal state officials, from county superintendents of schools to local judges to the state treasurer, auditor, second auditor, and secretary of the commonwealth. They specifically targeted Attorney General Frank Simpson Blair and accused him of illegally accepting fees from the state treasury to represent Virginia in state and federal courts as part of his job. They also unsuccessfully tried to impeach him and, in *Blair v. Marye,* even forced him to appeal to the Readjuster judges on the Supreme Court of Appeals to direct the auditor of public accounts to issue a warrant that authorized the treasurer to pay his salary.[25]

The Democrats also embarked on a project that took nearly two decades to drive African Americans completely out of politics and public life by making it increasingly difficult and expensive for them to register and vote and for their votes to be properly counted and reported. At a special session of the assembly that met in August 1884, the new Democratic majority passed a new election law over Cameron's veto. Called the Anderson-McCormick Act after its two sponsors, it displaced all election officers in every county and city in the state and authorized the assembly to appoint a new three-member electoral board for each county and city.[26] So long as the law remained in effect (which it did until 1904) and so long thereafter as the Democratic Party held a majority in the assembly (which it did during that span of time and longer), the party could appoint and control all the officers who conducted elections in the state.

Those election officers often looked the other way and sometimes actively connived with party officials who stuffed ballot boxes, intimidated voters, or made African Americans or known white Republicans stand in long lines so that some of them were prevented from voting before the polls closed.[27] And at the first opportunity, the new Democratic majority in the assembly selected John Warwick "I am a Democrat because I am a white man and a Virginian"[28] Daniel to succeed William Mahone in the United States Senate, and they later selected John Strode Barbour to fill the seat Harrison Holt Riddleberger had held.

For the most part, the two 1884 sessions of the General Assembly terminated the contentious period of political debate and legislative maneuvering about the prewar public debt. In the general election of 1885 the Democrats defeated the coalition of Readjusters and Republicans and regained all the statewide offices, leaving Readjusters in control of only the Supreme Court of Appeals. For governor that year the Democrats nominated Fitzhugh Lee, a popular former Confederate general and proud owner of one of the most revered surnames in Virginia. He defeated the former Readjuster congressman John Sergeant Wise, a son of the antebellum governor Henry A. Wise, who along with virtually all other members of the family had abandoned the Conservative Party, which they had come to regard as hopelessly backward-looking. As Henry A. Wise had tried without much success to do as governor during the 1850s, his sons and nephews tried, also without much success, to shape a new Virginia as part of a very different South during the 1870s and 1880s. They had come to believe in the potential of ordinary white Virginians in the post–Civil War South, but even though they all eventually became Republicans, they all remained racists. John S. Wise finally gave up on Virginia and, fearing for his safety, moved to New York, where he practiced law for the remainder of his life.

Among the most important and conspicuous of the defectors from the original Readjuster Party was Parson John E. Massey, who had written and spoken at length in favor of refinancing the debt during the 1870s and had been the Readjuster auditor of public accounts in 1880. In part because of differences with Mahone and resentment at being passed over for governor in 1881, Massey broke with the Readjusters soon thereafter. In 1885 he won the Democratic Party nomination for lieutenant governor and was elected.[29] His later opposition to full funding of public schools for African Americans while he was superintendent of public instruction strongly suggests that the Readjusters' attitudes about African Americans were an important motivation for him to quit the party.[30]

The 1885 statewide election appeared to be a smashing defeat for the Readjusters and their reforms, but the Democrats won the state by a margin of less than 5 percent of the vote.[31] The importance of the Democratic victory was not in its margin but in its effect. The election killed the Readjuster Party but left the Republican Party, with its energized African American voters and its enlarged number of white voters, still very much alive. The possibility that the coalition of lower-class voters of both races could regain a majority in local, legislative, statewide, and federal elections in turn further energized the new Democratic Party in pursuit of its elitist and white-supremacy agenda.

6 THE COUPON KILLERS

Before the single four-year term of Governor William E. Cameron concluded on the first day of 1886, the Readjuster Party was dead. Its defeat and demise and the speedy triumph of the Democrats still left unsettled all the questions relating to West Virginia's presumed responsibility for part of the old debt. Legal conflicts replaced political conflicts and threw into the courts a long series of cases that arose from the oldest of the problems the Funding Act of 1871 had created, how to suppress the payment of taxes with coupons. The new controversies about the coupons did not pit Readjusters against Funders or even Democrats against Republicans. Instead, they arrayed legislators, lawyers, and judges on either side of a simple question with what turned out to be extraordinarily complex legal complications: could the General Assembly eliminate or reduce to insignificance the payment of taxes with 1871 and 1879 coupons?

All the many laws the assembly passed for that purpose were not equally important, but consecutively they present a narrative of the evolution of public policies intended to benefit some Virginians and to obstruct or burden other Virginians who wished to use coupons to pay taxes. Ultimately, the laws took direct aim at the bondholders and brokers, who made profits buying coupons at a discount for sale to Virginia taxpayers. And although all the many lawsuits those laws brought about were not equally important, together they contain another narrative of the events that ultimately forced an end to the legislation and litigation and to the whole of the long Virginia debt controversy.

When the Readjuster majority passed the Riddleberger Act and the party's reform measures at the 1881–82 General Assembly session, the legislators also passed several bills intended to stop payment of taxes with coupons. The first two of the laws became known almost from the date of their passage as Coupon Killers.[1] Those laws and subsequent legislation that assembly members adopted even long after the disappearance of the Readjuster Party led to the largest gush of lawsuits in both state and federal courts and to several important decisions in the Supreme Court of the United States. That was in part, but only in part, because some of the laws were sloppily written or contained provisions that appeared to contradict provisions in other of the laws.[2]

The preamble to the act of 14 January 1882, Coupon Killer No. 1, stated that because "bonds purporting to be the bonds of this commonwealth" issued under the funding acts of 1871 and 1879 were in existence "without authority of law," perhaps because counterfeited or improperly recirculated after being exchanged, it was necessary for the assembly to protect the rights of bondholders, enforce the legal contracts between them and the state, and prevent frauds being perpetrated on the state in the collection of revenue.[3] That statement of purpose appeared to give legal clothing to the body of the law that required proof of authenticity of coupons before they could be used to pay taxes and also to divert prying judicial eyes from the practical effects of the law. Ordinarily, judges did not look beyond the wording of a statute to ascertain legislative intent and guide their interpretation.

The legislators included that language in the law even though the state treasurer and the second auditor, who were both Readjusters, explicitly informed the assembly that they had never seen any counterfeit or forged coupons.[4] The Readjuster attorney general reported in 1883 that many of the coupons submitted for payment of taxes "were forged, and counterfeits, or had been before redeemed by the Commonwealth."[5] A few men who worked in the treasurer's and the second auditor's offices later deposed that spurious coupons existed,[6] and in 1887 the Readjuster judges on the Supreme Court of Appeals accepted that they did,[7] but a Republican federal judge stated flatly in 1886 that "none had ever been known to exist, and none have ever been found."[8] It is possible that some people described as forged or spurious the coupons that had been clipped from 1871 peeler bonds, which were not tax receivable under the act of 1872.

Coupon Killer No. 1 required that men and women who wished to pay taxes with coupons also had to pay their taxes at the same time "in coin, legal tender notes, or national bank bills" but stated that the tax collector could take coupons clipped from the 1871 bonds—bonds and coupons issued under the funding act of 1879 were inadvertently not mentioned in the body of the statute—and give a receipt for them pending the outcome of a jury trial, which the taxpayer could request to ascertain whether the coupons offered in payment of taxes were genuine. The new law required that if a taxpayer sought a writ of mandamus from the Supreme Court of Appeals to require the collector to accept the coupons in payment of taxes, as Andrew Antoni had done in 1872, the tax collector must respond that he was willing to accept the coupons in payment of taxes if they were judged genuine. If the trial jury then declared the coupons authentic, then the collector must accept the coupons, mark the tax bill as paid, and return the money. The act's final section declared it in force from the time of its passage. The editor of the monthly *Virginia Law Journal* later declared that that was "for the purpose of obstructing the reception of the coupons during the existence of the then Court of Appeals." The judges' terms were to expire later in the year, when they were all to be replaced with the judges that the Readjusters in the assembly had elected.[9]

The second law, Coupon Killer No. 2, signed on 26 January 1882, took effect on 1 December of that year, when the new judges of the Supreme Court of Appeals took office. Without any explanatory preamble, it abolished most of the legal options that had been available to people attempting to force acceptance of coupons in payment of taxes. It required that "the several tax collectors of this commonwealth shall receive in discharge of taxes, license taxes, and other dues, gold, silver, United States treasury notes, national bank currency, and nothing else." The law imposed a fine on tax collectors who illegally received coupons in payment of taxes and required that taxpayers who wished to pay with coupons could surrender them to the collector but still had to pay with money under protest. They then had thirty days to go to trial to prove their right to pay with coupons. The most important language in the law abolished Antoni's old remedy of an appeal for a writ of mandamus: "There shall be no other remedy in any case of the collection of revenue, or the attempt to collect revenue illegally, or the attempt to collect revenue in funds only . . . and no writ for the prevention of any revenue claim, or to hinder or delay the collection of the same, shall in anywise issue, either injunction, supersedeas, mandamus, prohibition, or any other writ or process whatever." That made it almost impossible for anyone to pay any tax with coupons unless he or she was willing to file suit for a jury trial and pay the expenses of the trial if unsuccessful. The law made that process more expensive and specified that in the event of a judgment in favor of a tax collector, the taxpayer had to pay a five-dollar attorney's fee to the collector.[10]

Later in the same session, the assembly adopted an amendment to Coupon Killer No. 1, which also went into effect immediately. It declared that "no writ of mandamus, prohibition, or any other summary process whatever, shall issue in any case of the collection, or attempt to collect revenue, or to compel the collecting officers to receive anything in payment of taxes other than as provided" in Coupon Killer No. 2.[11] That immediately removed all other options than the trials the two Coupon Killers required for people who wished to pay taxes with coupons between passage of the amendment on 7 April 1882 and 1 December of that year, or after that date when Coupon Killer No. 2 took effect. The 1882 assembly also added a new anti-coupon section to the annual law for assessing and collecting state taxes. It stipulated that all professional license fees, also referred to in some sections of the code as license taxes, be paid only with "lawful money of the United States" and not with coupons.[12]

The close similarity of the jury trial provisions of the two Coupon Killers quickly led to confusion, in part because of uncertainty whether the second replaced the first on its operative date in December and effectively repealed it without explicitly stating as much. The stage was set for litigation. Andrew Antoni, who had been the plaintiff in the 1872 challenge to the law that prohibited payment of taxes with coupons, was the plaintiff in the lead case that challenged the constitutionality of Coupon Killer No. 1. He filed suit against the Richmond city tax collector, Samuel C. Greenhow, in the first of many of what became known as the Virginia Coupon Cases. On 27 April 1882 the Conservative judges of the Supreme Court of Appeals ruled in *Antoni v. Greenhow*, but without issuing a published opinion because the members were evenly divided in number,[13] "that the judgment of this court is in favor of the validity of said act." Anticipating an appeal, the judges had the clerk add to the record of their decision, "In making this certificate, this court, in the event a writ of error is granted by the Supreme Court of the United States, ventures to express the opinion that a speedy hearing of this case in that court is imperatively required by the best interests and welfare of the people of Virginia."[14]

When in March 1883 the Supreme Court of the United States handed down its ruling in *Antoni v. Greenhow*, Chief Justice Morrison R. Waite noted that the judges could not inquire into the motives of the legislature.

The preamble to Coupon Killer No. 1 had its intended effect in allowing the assertion of the existence of spurious bonds and coupons to cover
the necessity for trials to establish that coupons submitted for payment of
taxes were genuine. The chief justice therefore framed the point of law
in question thus: "The right of the coupon holder is to have his coupon
received for taxes when offered. The question here is not as to that right,
but as to the remedy the holder has for its enforcement when denied. At
the time the coupon was issued, there was a remedy by mandamus from
the Supreme Court of Appeals to compel the tax collector to take the coupon and cancel the tax. This implied a suit, with process, pleadings, issues,
trial, and judgment." For a majority of the Supreme Court, Waite ruled
that because Coupon Killer No. 1 required a court proceeding with all its
attendant procedural protections of the rights of the parties involved prior
to forcing a collector to accept the coupons, the law did not violate the
rights of the taxpayer to enforce the constitutionally protected contract the
coupons embodied. The taxpayer merely had to pursue a different but entirely adequate equivalent remedy at law to require acceptance of coupons
in payment of taxes.[15]

Associate Justice Stephen J. Field dissented vehemently. He believed
that the law obviously and deliberately made it difficult or impossible for
holders of coupons to pay taxes with them, and for that reason he deemed
it an unconstitutional impairment of the legal contract between the state
and the coupon holder. Field also dismissed the law's rationale stated in
the preamble for requiring the jury trial and specifically cited the official
printed statements of the state treasurer and the second auditor that they
had seen no forged or counterfeit coupons or bonds. He also denied that
the expensive legal process provided for in Coupon Killer No. 1 was re-
motely comparable to the simple mandamus procedure on which Antoni
had previously relied and that it was so difficult and expensive a procedure
as to constitute "a most palpable and flagrant impairment of the obligation
of contract." Field concluded, "No legislation more destructive of all value
to the contract is conceivable unless it should absolutely and in terms repudiate the coupon as a contract at all. It is practical repudiation."[16]

Associate Justice John Marshall Harlan also dissented, and in equally
strong words. "To my mind," he wrote, "it is so entirely clear that the
change in the remedies has impaired both the obligation and the value of
the contract that I almost despair of making it clearer by argument or il-
lustration." The financial cost to the coupon holder of attempting to force

receipt of coupons in payment of taxes in the manner the law prescribed made it "almost absolutely certain that his attorney's fee and the costs for each jury trial will be several times greater than the amount of the coupons involved. The result, then, is that he will lose more by presenting his coupons in payment of his taxes than by making an absolute gift of them to the commonwealth."[17]

Field and Harlan were certainly correct in their assessments of the practical and financial burdens that Coupon Killer No. 1 placed on men and women who wished to pay their taxes with coupons. They were also correct in believing that that was precisely why the legislators had drafted and passed the law, which is why they concluded that it was an unconstitutional impairment of the contract rights of the coupon holders. Indeed, even before passage of the Coupon Killers and other anti-coupon laws, the bond attorney William L. Royall wrote that the expense of challenging a Virginia law all the way through the state and federal courts was so great that ordinary people for ordinary purposes could not afford to defend their legal rights that way. "The costs of prosecuting a suit through the Circuit Court of the State, the Supreme Court of Appeals of the State, and the Supreme Court of the United States," he calculated, "will aggregate in the average from two to five hundred dollars. These must all be borne by the party who is finally unsuccessful in the Supreme Court of the United States."[18]

The Supreme Court's decision in *Antoni v. Greenhow* sustained the ruling of the Supreme Court of Appeals and affirmed the constitutionality of Coupon Killer No. 1. In his opinion for the majority, the chief justice stated that it was unnecessary to take notice of the amendment to Coupon Killer No. 1 that abolished mandamus proceedings because Antoni's case had arisen and was already in the process of adjudication prior to passage of the amendment.[19] He also entirely avoided and therefore left unanswered the main question that Field and Harlan raised, whether the law in its operation, not merely in its substitution of one legal procedure for another, significantly impaired the coupon owners' right to pay taxes with coupons. The differences between the chief justice's opinion and the two dissents were sharp. The majority grounded its opinion on whether the substitution of one legal process for another was acceptable procedure insofar as the legal rights of one taxpayer were concerned. The dissenters grounded their objections on the practical consequences of the major change in public policy for all the people the law affected.

Litigation continued in Virginia's city and county courts and in the Supreme Court of Appeals. Attorneys and judges also disagreed about the intent and meaning of the two Coupon Killers and their relationship to and effect on each other. Owners of the 1871 and 1879 coupon bonds also had no incentive to exchange them for Riddleberger bonds because both they and the bond brokers could make profits in the market for tax-receivable coupons.

The editor of the *Virginia Law Journal* wrote that almost immediately after the Virginia Supreme Court of Appeals upheld Coupon Killer No. 1, taxpayers filed "thirty or forty cases" in the Richmond Court of Hustings to prove the authenticity of the 1871 coupons they had submitted for payment of taxes.[20] H. M. Smith Jr., also of Richmond, submitted coupons from 1879 McCulloch bonds in payment of his taxes. Late in November 1882, on one of his last days on the Supreme Court of Appeals, Judge Francis T. Anderson for a unanimous court upheld a verdict of the Richmond Court of Hustings that Smith's offer of McCulloch bond coupons was exempt from the requirements of Coupon Killer No. 1 that he first prove the authenticity of the coupons through a jury trial. Even though the preamble to the law clearly asserted the existence of spurious 1871 and 1879 coupons and bonds, the body of the law requiring the trial specifically mentioned only coupons issued under the Funding Act of 1871 and made no reference to coupons issued under the act of 1879. For the court, Anderson stated that the preamble of the law was not an integral or essential part of the statute and need not be referred to unless the meaning of the body of the law was doubtful and the language of the preamble might help clarify it. The operative section of the law was quite clear; therefore Coupon Killer No. 1 did not apply to any of the coupons from the 1879 McCulloch, or ten-forty, bonds.[21]

The Supreme Court of Appeals also refused in 1882, but without comment, to hear an appeal from the same court about the new clause in the tax law that required payment of business or professional license taxes with lawful money only. In *Commonwealth v. Taylor* it let stand the lower court's judgment that the applicant for a business or professional license could pay the tax with genuine coupons.[22] Those decisions left Virginia men and women who owed taxes and were holders of or applicants for business and professional licenses able to pay their taxes and to obtain new licenses or renew old licenses with 1879 coupons and with judicially authenticated 1871 coupons. In the mid-1880s, people in Virginia could buy detached coupons for about 40 percent of their face value, meaning a 60 percent savings on a Virginian's tax bill, and brokers in London could buy them at about 30 percent, giving them an opportunity to earn a nice profit when they sold them to taxpayers in Virginia.[23] The state treasury was the big loser.

The provisions of the Coupon Killers also affected taxpayers resident outside of Virginia. The Baltimore and Ohio Railroad was a corporation chartered in Maryland but owning a substantial amount of track and numerous buildings, locomotives, and rolling stock in Virginia. It sought relief from the effects of Coupon Killer No. 1 in federal court in the spring of 1883. The corporation being deemed, as other chartered companies were, an artificial person capable of defending its interests in court, and having its headquarters in Maryland rather than in Virginia, took advantage of Article III, Section 2, of the Constitution of the United States, which granted jurisdiction to federal courts in cases between citizens (or, by extension, artificial persons) of different states.

The railroad paid $6,411 in taxes on its property in Augusta County with 1871 coupons that its officers had purchased from a broker or bond agent but did not also pay in money at the same time, as Coupon Killer No. 1 required. The tax collector consequently seized and after sixty days prepared to sell some of the railroad's property in that county to satisfy what he declared was an unpaid tax bill plus a penalty for nonpayment. The railroad sought an injunction from the United States Circuit Court for the Western District of Virginia to prohibit the sale. On 15 May 1883 Judge Hugh Lenox Bond issued the injunction, citing the previous month's Supreme Court decision in *Antoni v. Greenhow* that Coupon Killer No. 1 required collectors to accept payment with authenticated 1871 coupons. The judge concluded in *Baltimore & Ohio Railroad Co. v. Allen* that the railroad had legally paid its tax with coupons and "would have to pay it again" in money because the railroad had "no adequate remedy at law" under any other Virginia statutes. Bond issued the injunction to prohibit the tax collector from proceeding with the sale.[24]

In a very long dissenting opinion, Judge Robert W. Hughes objected that the suit was in reality a suit against the state of Virginia and its public policies and not against one of its public officials in the particular person of a county tax collector. The Eleventh Amendment to the Constitution of the United States prohibited federal courts from hearing cases that citizens of one state filed against the government of another state. Hughes also went well beyond the specific issues of the case and declared that Coupon Killer No. 1 and Coupon Killer No. 2 were both in effect and that the second provided an alternative method of enforcing the coupon holders' contracts with the state.[25] Hughes did not believe, as some Virginia attorneys understood, that Coupon Killer No. 2 in effect repealed or for all practical purposes superseded No. 1.[26]

Hughes published his dissent as a separate pamphlet with the title *The Coupon and Tax Question;* part of its long subtitle indicated that it was the official decision of the federal court.[27] The editor of the *Virginia Law Journal* later wrote about Hughes's dissent as if it were the opinion of the court, which no doubt misinformed some attorneys and very likely complicated considerations of the legalities involved. The editor also wrote, as if there were a direct cause and effect, that immediately after Hughes published his dissent, numerous taxpayers filed suit and proved the authenticity of "thousands of dollars in coupons verified by the evidence of experts." Presumably, the "experts" were people who testified that they had personally witnessed the clipping of the coupons from the bonds.[28]

Later in 1883, Attorney General Frank Simpson Blair appealed a judgment against a tax collector in the circuit court in Lynchburg that permitted twenty-three men and business firms in that city to pay their taxes with coupons from McCulloch bonds. Blair evidently hoped that the new Readjuster judges of the Virginia Supreme Court of Appeals would declare that their Conservative predecessors had been wrong in *Commonwealth v. H. M. Smith Jr.* when they dismissed the relevance of the explanatory preamble of Coupon Killer No. 1. The attorney general asked them to rule that the law required that coupons from 1879 McCulloch bonds be treated the same as coupons from 1871 bonds and be subjected to a trial to ascertain their authenticity before a tax collector could be forced to receive them. Late in November 1883, without dissent, the judges in *Commonwealth v. Guggenheimer* rejected Blair's argument and affirmed that the former judges had correctly settled the question concerning the meaning of Coupon Killer No. 1. Moreover, because the defendants had submitted their coupons in payment of their taxes before Coupon Killer No. 2 went into effect, nothing in that law could override the specific language of No. 1 in their case.[29]

For the whole court, Judge Benjamin Watkins Lacy, who had been the Readjuster speaker of the House of Delegates during the session prior to the one that adopted the two Coupon Killers, went beyond the mere reliance on *Commonwealth v. H. M. Smith Jr.* and explained that the judges could not construe the words of the two laws "so as to defeat the act of the legislature in any respect." The language of Coupon Killer No. 1, he wrote, "as it was completed and approved, is the expression of the legislative will. . . . And we may add, that the two acts being considered together, and having been passed by the same legislature within the same month, the difference between them cannot be considered as accidental, but must be accepted as the deliberate result of the legislative will."[30] That appeared to confirm that Hughes was correct in his view that Coupon Killer No. 2 did not repeal or replace Coupon Killer No. 1. The following year the Democratic majority in the General Assembly appropriated $336.05 to compensate the treasurer of the city of Lynchburg for his losses as the unsuccessful defendant in the case.[31]

The lawsuits of 1883 increased rather than settled the confusion about the Coupon Killers. Early in the assembly session of 1883–84, the Senate of Virginia formally asked the auditor of public accounts to explain why Coupon Killer No. 2 had "not been enforced, and why it is that in the face of that act, proceedings under the act approved the 14th day of January, 1882, known as Coupon-Killer No. 1, are being recognized by him." To which the auditor replied that he and the governor had employed counsel to defend the state's public officials in suits that attorneys brought under No. 1. Relying in part on Hughes's May 1883 dissenting opinion, he maintained that the two Coupon Killers were "in nowise, as assumed" in the Senate's resolution, "in antagonism to each other; nor has the latter in any sense repealed the former . . . that the last act was merely in aid of the first; that it reinforced the first, but did not repeal it."[32]

The year 1884 therefore began with almost all the legal issues relating to the coupons still very much unsettled. Payment of taxes with coupons in spite of the anti-coupon laws continued to vex the courts, perplex the taxpayers, and starve the treasury of money. In the new political and legal environments, with the old divisive political issues finally resolved, some Democratic state officials showed that they were determined to be just as relentless enemies of tax-receivable coupons as their Readjuster predecessors had been.

For the creditors, things had gone from very bad to much worse following the overthrow of the Readjusters, which should have made things better. In London early in 1884 the Virginia Committee of the Council of the Corporation of Foreign Bondholders deplored the ill effects on bondholders of the Riddleberger Act and the Readjusters' anti-coupon laws, which the corporation's officers and counsel had been fighting "unremittingly" for two years. The committee's members were even more disappointed that after defeating the Readjusters, the Democrats had endorsed their policies. Democratic legislators' acceptance of the Riddleberger Act in December 1883 was, "so to speak, re-enactment of a Bill, which amounts virtually to the repudiation of the Debt" and "deals a death-blow to the hopes of the Bondholders, so far, at least, as the power of the Legislature of Virginia is concerned."[33] Bondholders in New York and elsewhere agreed with the men in London. The only means they still had to protect their investments was to continue challenging the anti-coupon laws in court.

Just as importantly and much to the discomfort of state officials in Richmond, the court decisions and doubts also delayed and actually threatened to obstruct refinancing the debt as the Riddleberger Act of 1882 authorized. When the new assembly convened in December 1883, Governor Cameron reported that a delay in the printing of the new bonds (following reassignment of the printing contract to a more politically sympathetic printer),[34] combined with the legal uncertainties, had to that date (about twenty-two months after passage of the Riddleberger Act) prevented all but about 6 percent of the Riddleberger bonds from being issued. That left nearly all the bonds issued under the Funding Act of 1871 and the McCulloch Act of 1879 still outstanding and their coupons still available for sale and purchase on the open market and for payment of taxes. The governor also reported that the omission of mention of the 1879 coupons in the operative clause of Coupon Killer No. 1 defeated much of the purpose of that act, leaving the state forced to rely on the legally untested "act of January 26, 1882, commonly known as coupon-killer No. 2." The governor asked the assembly to provide for hiring additional counsel to defend public officials and the interests of the state in the numerous court cases filed after adoption of the two Coupon Killers.

"Remaining with the general assembly," Cameron advised the new Democratic majority in somewhat awkward language, "is the duty or the privilege of making to live or letting to die the scheme of funding known as the Riddleberger act." Writing more directly, he concluded, "It is as true now as it has always been, that readjustment, to be successful, must be coercive; and that every ultimate power residing under the constitution of the commonwealth of Virginia must be exhausted to protect her from excessive and unjust claims."[35]

The litigation about the anti-coupon laws threw the responsibility for salvaging the Riddleberger Act and preserving the state's budget from renewed deficits onto the new Democratic General Assembly. In March 1884 the assembly required that the second auditor create a new Tax-Receivable Coupon Bond Sinking Fund. The law directed him to deposit in it all coupons from bonds issued under the acts of 1871 and 1879 that the state received for payment of taxes and to compile an exact record of the numbers and dates of all coupons and the numbers of the bonds from which they had been clipped. The law also required him to compute the difference between the amount of interest that had been payable on each coupon when it was issued and what would have been due on a Riddleberger bond so that the difference could later be deducted from the principal due on the matured bond.[36] That threat of a future reduction in the return on the matured bonds did not suppress the active profitable market in coupons.

In 1884 the Democratic assembly added new sections to the annual revenue law to require that school taxes be collected in lawful money only and that the money and records be kept in separate accounts.[37] Those sections closely resembled the provisions of the Readjusters' Barbour Bill of 1878. The assembly added another new section to the annual revenue law to obstruct the business of coupon brokers. It required that every person who sold a tax-receivable coupon in Virginia pay an annual license fee of one thousand dollars on every place of business the broker maintained in the state. It also levied a 20 percent tax on the value of all the coupons sold.[38]

Early in 1884 the Supreme Court of the United States issued an important jurisdictional ruling in *Smith v. Greenhow*. Richmond city treasurer Samuel Greenhow had entered a taxpayer's place of business in May 1883 and seized and removed a table, a bookcase, and the books in that case, valued in the whole at about one hundred dollars. Greenhow seized the property because the owner of the business had paid his property taxes with McCulloch coupons but had not also paid with money as Coupon Killer No. 2 required. Alleging damages to his property and business at six thousand dollars, Smith sued Greenhow in the United States Circuit Court for the Eastern District of Virginia to require him to return the seized property and pay damages. The court dismissed the case for the reason that it presented no issues that were within the jurisdiction of the federal courts. Smith appealed that ruling to the Supreme Court of the United States, which without dissent reversed the circuit court and declared that the right of Smith to pay taxes with his 1879 coupons was a right that the impairment-of-contracts clause in the Constitution of the United States protected.

The federal Act to Determine the Jurisdiction of the Circuit Courts of the United States, and to Regulate the Removal of Causes from the State Courts, and for Other Purposes—also known as the Judiciary Act of 1875 and as the Jurisdiction and Removal Act of 1875—had granted federal courts jurisdiction in cases involving rights that the Constitution of the United States protected as well as in suits for damages in those cases if the amount involved exceeded five hundred dollars. Consequently, *Smith v. Greenhow* presented what became known then and thereafter as a legitimate federal question.[39] That meant that more coupon cases were going to be tried in federal court, as well as in state courts. The General Assembly authorized the auditor of public accounts to employ counsel to protect the interests of the state and defend a tax collector in another case then pending in federal court concerning the authority of the treasurer of the city of Richmond to seize the property of a woman who had paid her taxes with coupons but not also with lawful money.[40]

In February 1884 the Supreme Court of Appeals also ruled on a jurisdictional matter. It was the first of two lawsuits that illustrated how easily an attorney might overlook one of any of several legal or procedural technicalities and sink his client's case. Laymen probably understood the two cases as illustrating that apparently inconsequential technicalities could deny justice to Virginia citizens.

In July 1883 John C. Williams had presented nineteen coupons worth a total of $249 in payment of a license tax in the city of Richmond. A jury determined that the coupons were genuine, following which the collector formerly would have accepted them, marked the tax bill paid, and authorized issuance of the license. Williams instead presented the coupons at the state treasury for exchange into money in order to pay the tax with that money, which as far as he was concerned was the same as paying with the coupons. The acting state treasurer noticed that the list of coupons authenticated in court omitted one of the $3 coupons. He therefore refused to pay Williams anything, even the $246 balance. Williams's attorney filed suit in the hustings court of the city for a writ of mandamus to compel the treasurer to pay him. Through his attorneys, the treasurer objected that by statute the case should have been prosecuted in the circuit court of the city, that the court of hustings had no jurisdiction, and that therefore the entire proceeding was illegal and of no effect. In *Taylor v. Williams* the Supreme Court of Appeals agreed. The judges also ruled that because Williams had not first obtained a warrant from the auditor of public accounts authorizing the treasurer to pay him, the treasurer could not have refunded the money anyway. The court ordered Williams to pay court costs and left him stuck with either $246 or $249 worth of legally authenticated coupons but still without a paid license to do business.[41]

In consequence, the assembly passed a law adding two new provisions to Coupon Killer No. 2. One directed that when a jury declared that coupons offered for payment of taxes were genuine, the tax collector should send them to the office of the auditor of public accounts to begin the process of payment. The other prohibited any person from suing a tax collector "for levying upon the property of any tax-payer"—that is, seizing and selling property for nonpayment of taxes—if the taxpayer had paid taxes with coupons but had refused to pay in gold, silver, or lawful paper money.[42]

The other coupon case that involved a question of judicial procedure arose in 1885. After the treasurer of the city of Lynchburg, V. G. Dunnington, lost a case in the city's corporation court under the amended Coupon Killer No. 2, he appealed the judgment of $526.05 against him. Attorney General Frank Simpson Blair won for him a judgment in the Virginia Supreme Court of Appeals that the taxpayer's attorney had filed the suit improperly under an available court procedure other than the one specified in the law.[43] "It is no answer to this objection," Judge Benjamin Watkins Lacy wrote for a majority of the court in *Dunnington v. Ford,* "to say that one way was as good as the other, or that the form adopted to commence the proceedings was a substantial compliance with the law, or more convenient to the suitor. . . . It avails nothing in this case—the suit is not brought as required by law."[44] The fine points of legal procedure at issue in Dunnington's and Williams's cases were aspects of the coupon litigation that mystified laymen and confirmed many of their suspicions that the lawyers, legislators, and judges were merely devious defenders of particular special interests and seekers after loopholes rather than advocates of genuine justice.

So, too, did the provisions of some of the laws. In the spring of 1884 two wholesale grocers in the city of Richmond paid their license taxes with money and also with mature 1871 coupons in order later to be able, through the process of a trial, to prove the authenticity of the coupons and to require the acceptance of the coupons and the return of the money. After the city treasurer refused to accept the coupons, the two grocers applied to the United States Circuit Court for the Eastern District of Virginia for a writ of mandamus to direct the treasurer to accept the coupons. Early in May, Judge Robert W. Hughes declined to entertain the suit. Referring to the two Coupon Killers that had abolished mandamus proceedings for that purpose in the state courts, he noted in *Harvey and Another v. Commonwealth* that the Judiciary Act of 1875 required federal courts to follow as closely as possible the laws and legal processes in the state where the case arose. Because the state courts could not issue a writ of mandamus in that case, his federal court could not do so either.[45]

Hughes nevertheless wrote again, and wrote at length, about "the merits of the case" and the distinctions some of the attorneys and legislators sought to make between taxes levied for the purpose of raising revenue and taxes levied for regulatory purposes or for professional or business licenses. It was an important point because payment of license fees with coupons posed the same legal questions as payment of taxes with coupons when the license fees were defined as taxes. "No refinements in lexicography," Hughes began, "nor hypercriticisms upon the purport of words or phrases, can make such a charge anything else but a tax." He went on to explain, "There are taxes *per capita* levied upon persons exercising the privilege of residence in a state. There are taxes *ad valorem* levied upon persons exercising the privilege of holding property in the state. There are license taxes levied upon persons exercising the privilege of carrying on the business of merchants, or manufacturers, or other callings. They are all essentially the same in their fundamental nature; they are a charge imposed by the state for the exercise of privileges, as a compensation to herself for the protection which she affords by her laws alike to persons, to property, and to honest occupation. It is useless to say that such a charge is only a tax, when levied for the purpose of revenue; for there are such things as prohibitory taxes, the object of which is the opposite of revenue, which are taxes nevertheless." (The 1884 law imposing a license tax of one thousand dollars on the offices of coupon sellers and taxing the coupons they sold was one such tax intended to be prohibitory.) "It is unavailing to refine upon such a subject," Hughes concluded. "It is offensive, if not insulting, to the common sense of every candid citizen to pretend that the charge which the state may see fit to impose on merchants for the privilege of carrying on their business is anything else than the commonplace thing which practical men call a tax."[46]

Old Funders and agents and attorneys for men and women who owned coupon bonds continued to fight for their beliefs and for the interests of their clients, just as old Readjusters, many new Democrats, and people who wished to prevent the use of coupons for payment of taxes, fees, fines, and licenses continued to seek means to reach their objectives. The cases they filed and the points of law they raised often involved large amounts of money in addition to the legal rights and principles they sought to enforce or exercise. The cases kept Attorney General Blair busy. In addition to appearing in circuit courts in several cities and counties, he also represented the state's officials in trials in federal courts in Norfolk and Harrisonburg as well as in the Supreme Court in Washington, D.C.[47]

In 1884 Judge Thomas Stanley Atkins, of the Richmond Court of Hustings, declared unconstitutional the sections of the revenue law adopted that year that placed a tax of one thousand dollars on the offices of sellers of coupons and charged the broker a tax of 20 percent of the face value of the coupons they sold. In *Commonwealth v. Maury* he cited several federal precedents showing that a tax on a business transaction involving an article of commerce was in reality a tax on the article. From that he deduced and therefore declared that the license tax on the sale of coupons was an impermissible tax on the coupons because the tax reduced the value of the coupons, which impaired the contract between the state and the owner of the coupons.[48] That was the first, not the last, case of its kind in the attack on the coupons. The Supreme Court of the United States later had to rule on that subject too, but in the meantime tax collectors and courts elsewhere in the state may not have known about the ruling of the judge of the local Richmond court, or if they did, they probably believed that they were not compelled to abide by it. The practical effect of that decision was probably very limited.

In August 1884, during a special session of the General Assembly, the new Democratic auditor of public accounts, Morton Marye, reported to the Senate of Virginia that when the bonds of 1871 were printed, the word *dues* had inadvertently been omitted from the language the Funding Act required be printed on each coupon declaring that matured coupons were to be receivable for "all taxes, debts, dues and demands due the state." Marye appended legal advice he had solicited from Wyndham R. Meredith, a Richmond attorney who specialized in bond litigation. "It would seem," Meredith concluded, "that these evidences of indebtedness are null and void," and he urged the General Assembly to act to restore legal validity to the coupons.[49] If Marye and Meredith hoped their reports would prompt the legislature or the courts to clarify the legal status of the coupons and declare finally whether payment of taxes and fines with coupons was constitutional, they were mistaken.

Some state officials administered the Riddleberger Act to produce the results they desired. Section 5(a) of the law directed that when holders of the 1871 bonds submitted them or coupons from them to the sinking fund in exchange for new Riddleberger bonds dated 1 July 1882, they would receive new bonds with a face value of 53 percent of the value of the old bonds. If the old bonds still had attached coupons that had matured since the most recent half-yearly interest payment, those coupons were to be valued dollar for dollar in the exchange. In April 1884, the New York investor John P. Faure (or his agent acting for him, which was legally the same thing) presented 150 detached thirty-dollar coupons, all of which had matured after 1 July 1882, to be exchanged for new Riddleberger bonds dollar for dollar. Officers of the sinking fund refused to exchange them at all, as if the law actually prohibited funding all detached coupons after 1 July 1882 or even prohibited funding them at the rate of fifty-three cents on the dollar because they had matured after that date.

Faure applied to Judge Hughes for a writ of mandamus from the federal court to compel the sinking fund to exchange the coupons for Riddleberger bonds dollar for dollar. On 11 August 1884 the judge granted the writ and explained, "It is competent for the legislature, within some reasonable time, to declare by statute that, after a future date, unpaid and past due coupons detached from consol bonds shall not be funded dollar for dollar . . . but it is certainly premature in the commissioners of the sinking fund, who are not a legislature,—who are but a branch of the executive charged with ministerial powers exclusively only,—to perpetrate a measure of legislation, in the form of an arbitrary rule of funding, which, they admit, may involve a difference of millions of dollars in the rights of the state's creditors." Hughes also repeated his condemnation of the tax-receivable coupons as "cut-worms of the revenue."[50]

As a consequence of that court decision, the Democratic majority in the General Assembly, which was meeting in a special session at the time, amended the Riddleberger Act. It directed that thereafter all bonds and coupons were to be funded at the rates of exchange specified in the Riddleberger Act as if they had been exchanged on the effective date of the statute, 1 July 1882, which meant that past-due coupons could not later be funded dollar for dollar. That was a partial after-the-fact justification of the sinking-fund commissioners' office policies, but only a partial one, because the sinking fund still had to exchange those coupons at the rate of fifty-three cents on the dollar.[51]

A second amendment to the Riddleberger Act, which the assembly adopted later in the special session, in November, stopped interest payments on some coupons after 1 January 1885 and on others after 1 January 1888. The amendment also required that when old bonds were exchanged for new bonds after 1 January 1885, the treasurer should remove coupons from the new bonds bearing maturity dates prior to the date of actual issue. That prohibited people from paying taxes with them or coming back later and demanding payment of interest on coupons that had reached their dates of maturity before the bonds were even issued. The law also required the Commissioners of the Sinking Fund thereafter to pay fifty cents on the dollar for coupons from McCulloch bonds. The new law was called the Wickham Amendment after its sponsor, Williams Carter Wickham, a former Confederate general and then a Republican member of the Senate of Virginia.[52]

Within a few days of Hughes's 11 August opinion in the *Faure* case, fourteen people filed new, similar suits in his court, and he then issued a revised opinion with a further explanation to settle all the cases in the same way. The failure of the state's attorney general to appear at the hastily called meeting of the federal court led Hughes to presume that the state acquiesced in his original opinion and did not contest the fourteen new suits. His acting as he did provoked controversy, to which his revised, or supplementary, opinion, which he published in the *Richmond State* on 2 September 1884, contributed in no small degree.

In his second opinion in *Faure v. Sinking Fund Commissioners,* Hughes explained at great length that the evident intent of the Riddleberger Act had been to draw in the outstanding coupon bonds to be exchanged for new Riddleberger bonds so as to save money in the long run. The Riddleberger Act, he wrote with characteristic bluntness and typical wordy awkwardness, "was accepted by the public conscience of Virginia; both the political parties, which embrace her voters, having adopted it as a finality in State finance. To so construe or change that act as to leave tax-receivable coupons

. . . unprovided for, to vex the Treasury, to encumber the courts, and to fly-blow the reputation of the State in the monetary centres of the world, is practical—may I not say intentional—repudiation. The result must be that these coupons will come into the courts for litigation—most of them into this court. The evil of such a policy is, that it not only prevents the funding of tax-receivable coupons, but it creates distrust, not to say disgust, in creditors as to the good faith of the State, and tends to prevent the funding of the consol and ten-forty bonds themselves. It thus cuts up by the roots the scheme of funding, and makes the $30,000,000 of tax-receivable coupons contingently maturing in the future a certain prospective debt, to be dealt with by the courts."[53]

In that opinion even more than in the first, Hughes's political and personal beliefs about the political issues were on conspicuous display. His critics charged that both his personal beliefs and his own political history as a Funder early in the 1870s and as the 1873 Republican candidate for governor had destroyed his pretense to disinterested judicial objectivity. That gave the highly opinionated and outspokenly partisan chair of the Commissioners of the Sinking Fund an opening to damn Hughes for both rulings, for the manner in which he issued them, and for being a pliant tool of William Mahone and the hated Republicans in Washington.[54]

The chair was Frank G. Ruffin, who had been a vigorous advocate for refinancing the debt but was also a consistently and belligerently partisan Democrat. He had recently published two pamphlets attacking Mahone for his 1880s alliance with Northern Republicans, who he charged had ruined Virginia during the 1860s.[55] Ruffin condemned both of Hughes's decisions in the *Faure* case with a twenty-four-page pamphlet printed in November and placed, as somebody told Hughes, on the desk of every member of the General Assembly, which was still meeting in special session. Ruffin disputed Hughes's interpretation of the law and wrote that as a well-known Funder, the judge had protected the interests of the bond-holders rather than the interests of Virginians.[56] Hughes, in turn, published a pamphlet to reply to Ruffin,[57] who at the end of the year replied with a rebuttal to Hughes's rebuttal.[58] Both men used intemperate language, misstated dates and matters of fact, and argued inconclusively about whether the state's attorney general had received proper notice of the second hearing of the case. Hughes and Ruffin each aggravated the other's followers but accomplished little else. It was an unseemly but not atypical exchange for the time. It was lucky for both men that that was as bad as it got. Their language could have led to a duel, and Hughes had experience in that line. Back in 1869, when Hughes was the editor of a Republican newspaper, he had fought a duel with William E. Cameron, who was then editor of a Conservative newspaper. The future federal judge shot and wounded the future governor.[59]

7 THE COUPON CASES

The Supreme Court of the United States declared Coupon Killer No. 2 unconstitutional on 20 April 1885. For the next two years, with renewed budget deficits threatening the state, the General Assembly passed more laws to try to prevent payment of taxes with coupons, and people filed more lawsuits relating to the enforcement and challenging the constitutionality of the original anti-coupon laws and the new ones as well. Organized bondholders mobilized to force acceptance of coupons on the state's tax collectors and to prevent the Riddleberger Act from succeeding.

The several lawsuits that led to the Supreme Court's invalidation of Coupon Killer No. 2 began when people tried to pay taxes with coupons rather than with money; tax collectors refused to accept the coupons, and local officials seized and sold the taxpayers' property for nonpayment of taxes. The taxpayers then sued for recovery of their property and for damages. Together the cases were known as the Virginia Coupon Cases and were often referenced in legal citations that way. Because William L. Royall, the Virginia agent and legal counsel for the Virginia Committee of the Council of the Corporation of Foreign Bondholders, was the lead attorney in the suits to force acceptance of the coupons, his patrons in London referred to the lawsuits as "Mr. Royall's cases."[1]

Justice Stanley Matthews for a bare five-to-four majority of the Supreme Court stated the reasons for striking down Coupon Killer No. 2 in the lead case, *Poindexter v. Greenhow*, an appeal from the hustings court of the city of Richmond. The city's treasurer, Samuel C. Greenhow, had refused to accept coupons from 1871 bonds in payment of Thomas Poindexter's taxes. Because Poindexter had not simultaneously also paid with lawful money, Greenhow had seized Poindexter's property to the equivalent value of the taxes due. Matthews ruled that Coupon Killer No. 2 was a clear impairment of the constitutionally protected contract. He cited numerous legal precedents to the effect that an offer, or tender, of lawful money to pay a tax constituted payment of the tax; repeated that Virginia's law and courts as well as federal courts had defined the coupons as a lawful medium for payment of taxes; and concluded, therefore, that the treasurer had acted without legal authority when he seized property for nonpayment of taxes. Matthews dismissed the arguments of Greenhow's attorneys that the tax-receivable character of the coupons made them, in effect, bills of credit, which the Constitution of the United States explicitly prohibited the states from issuing. He also rejected the argument that the treasurer was merely a stand-in for the state and that the case was in reality an impermissible suit against the state to which the state had not agreed to be a party.[2]

Immediately thereafter, in handing down decisions in several other cases the same five-to-four majority relied on the authority of *Poindexter v. Greenhow* on the main point of the unconstitutionality of Coupon Killer No. 2. In *White v. Greenhow*, the court directed the United States Circuit Court for the Eastern District of Virginia to adjudicate another, almost identical case against Greenhow, who had seized three thousand dollars' worth of property for nonpayment of taxes. The value of the property seized in violation of the taxpayer's constitutionally protected right had far exceeded the five-hundred-dollar minimum required to grant federal courts jurisdiction under the Judiciary Act of 1875.[3]

Chaffin v. Taylor was a very similar case that reached the Supreme Court by a different appellate path. It arose after the treasurer of Henrico County seized property from a taxpayer who offered coupons in payment of his taxes but refused to offer money at the same time. The taxpayer sued the treasurer in the circuit court of the county to recover the property. He lost and appealed to the Virginia Supreme Court of Appeals, which refused to hear the appeal because the decision of the circuit court had been "plainly right" according to Coupon Killer No. 2.[4] The Supreme Court of the United States reversed the decision for the reasons stated in *Poindexter v. Greenhow*,[5] and it refused to reconsider when the treasurer sought to force the issue again the following year.[6] And in *Allen v. Baltimore and Ohio Railroad Company*, an appeal from the 1883 decision of the federal court, the Supreme Court affirmed the decision of the federal judge in granting an injunction to prevent the county treasurer from selling the railroad's property because the railroad had offered to pay—and therefore had in fact lawfully paid—its taxes with 1871 coupons.[7]

In *Carter v. Greenhow* and in *Pleasants v. Greenhow*, however, the Supreme Court sustained decisions of the federal court for the Eastern District of Virginia to dismiss suits under circumstances very similar to Poindexter's and White's on the grounds that the Judiciary Act of 1875 did not provide those taxpayers a legal remedy in federal court for recovery of the property because the amounts involved were less than $500.[8] And in the final case decided that day, *Marye v. Parsons*, the Supreme Court ordered that the United States Circuit Court for the Eastern District of Virginia dismiss a suit that Edwin Parsons, a citizen of New York, had filed alleging that the laws of Virginia had rendered essentially worthless his $28,010 stock of mature 1871 coupons. Parsons complained that without assurances that tax collectors would receive the coupons in payment of taxes, he could not profitably sell them to Virginia taxpayers. His attorneys argued that that destroyed the coupons' value and thereby impaired the contract they embodied. The Supreme Court ruled that because the New York broker did not owe taxes in Virginia, he did not have standing to sue. Any tax collector's anticipated future refusal to accept his coupons in payment of taxes that other people owed was no violation of his ability to enforce a contract that he did not in reality have with the Commonwealth of Virginia.[9]

The Supreme Court decided all seven Virginia Coupon Cases by the same five-to-four majority. Justice Joseph P. Bradley, on behalf of himself, the chief justice, and two other members of the court, dissented on the grounds that all the suits were in substance suits against the state and its public laws and not against the public officials of the state named in the suits. Under the widely acknowledged doctrine of sovereign immunity, because the government of Virginia had not given its citizens permission to sue it in state court, they therefore could not sue the state in federal court; and the Eleventh Amendment prohibited any federal court from hearing the cases of the Baltimore and Ohio Railroad and of Parsons. "In our judgment," Bradley concluded, "none of these suits can be maintained, for the reason that they are, in substance and effect, suits against the State of Virginia. We have not thought it necessary or proper to make any remarks on the moral aspects of the case. If Virginia or any other state has the prerogative of exemption from judicial prosecution, and of determining her own public policy with regard to the mode of redeeming her obligations, it is not for this Court, when considering the question of her constitutional rights, to pass any judgment upon the propriety of her conduct on the one side or on the other."[10] That final comment suggests that the four-man minority may have believed that Coupon Killer No. 2 was not morally defensible even though it was constitutional.

Later in the spring of 1885 the Supreme Court decided one additional Virginia coupon case. *Moore v. Greenhow* arose when the treasurer of the city of Richmond refused to accept matured coupons in payment of a license tax from a traveling wholesaler—a sample merchant, in the language of the time. The salesman applied to the circuit court of the city for a writ of mandamus to require the treasurer to accept the coupons. The treasurer refused, so the sample merchant appealed to Virginia's Supreme Court of Appeals. The judges declined to require the circuit court to issue the writ, whereupon the merchant appealed to the Supreme Court of the United States. For the court, Matthews overruled the two Virginia courts on the basis of the precedent established in *Antoni v. Greenhow,* which required the treasurer to receive the coupons in payment of the license tax. Justices Stephen J. Field and John Marshall Harlan filed a brief concurring opinion indicating that they stood by the principles stated in their dissents in *Antoni v. Greenhow* but nevertheless joined in the decision of the court in *Moore v. Greenhow.*[11]

Waller Redd Staples assisted Attorney General James G. Field in arguing all the Virginia Coupon Cases before the Supreme Court of the United States, for which the General Assembly paid him $1,250.[12] Staples had dissented in the very first coupon case to reach the state's appellate court, and after his term as a judge expired, he became a hired counsel in opposition to the tax-receivable coupons.

Nowhere in his 1885 opinion for the court in *Poindexter v. Greenhow* did Matthews have or make occasion to note the very close similarity of the trial provisions in the two Coupon Killers or to suggest that the provisions he believed clearly made No. 2 unconstitutional also meant, or could also mean, that No. 1 was unconstitutional for the same reasons in spite of the Supreme Court's earlier decision that in other respects No. 1 was constitutional. Curiously, attorneys for owners of bonds and coupons filed few suits in federal court to have Coupon Killer No. 1 declared unconstitutional for the same reasons that the Supreme Court had declared Coupon Killer No. 2 unconstitutional. The few suits they filed with that objective failed.

In one of those few suits, *Jones v. Commonwealth of Virginia,* in December 1885, Judge Robert W. Hughes in the United States Circuit Court for the Eastern District of Virginia rejected appeals in four cases from the hustings court of the city of Richmond and another from the hustings court of the city of Norfolk. The plaintiffs had asked that the federal court order that at the jury trials to ascertain the authenticity of coupons and whether they could be accepted in payment of taxes the juries also determine the constitutionality of Coupon Killer No. 1. Hughes ruled that even though the federal question of the impairment of obligations of contract was involved, the state law specifically authorized the trials only to ascertain whether coupons submitted for payment of taxes were genuine or could be received for payment of taxes, and therefore the federal court had no authority to require jury trials in city courts of hustings to pass on the constitutionality of the law.[13]

In the other case, on 12 April 1886, Chief Justice Morrison R. Waite for a unanimous Supreme Court of the United States in *Stewart v. Virginia* sustained a ruling of the federal court for the Eastern District of Virginia remanding to the Circuit Court of Henrico County the trial under Coupon Killer No. 1 of the authenticity of $3,807 worth of coupons submitted in payment of taxes. The ruling was sustained on the grounds that the trial under a state law had been merely for the purpose of ascertaining whether the coupons could be received for taxes and therefore did not involve a federal question that could or should be heard in federal court.[14]

Soon after the Supreme Court issued its decisions in the Coupon Cases in the spring of 1885, William L. Royall traveled to London to consult with his employers and allies. Owners of Virginia bonds had agreed with him that they should continue to pursue legal relief in the federal courts, where they had had some success even though state officials refused to abide by the courts' decisions, and to use the state's courts, in which they had had little success, against the state. Royall had written back in 1878 and Justice John Marshall Harlan had stated in *Antoni v. Greenhow* in 1883 that legal costs to a taxpayer could exceed the amount of tax he or she wished to pay with coupons;[15] but Royall's litigation had also demonstrated that the legal expenses to the state could exceed the amount of tax it collected through prosecutions under Coupon Killer No. 1. The bondholders therefore agreed to continue trying to force acceptance of coupons for taxes through suits in state courts, not in hopes of winning law cases but in hopes of "mulcting the State" and eventually making it accept coupons as a better alternative than repudiating the obligations the funding acts of 1871 and 1879 had created when they made the coupons tax-receivable.[16]

By the time of Royall's visit to London, the English bondholders had begun concerted action to render the Riddleberger Act ineffective. The Corporation of Foreign Bondholders began taking possession of 1871 and 1879 bonds under agreement with their owners to cooperate in flooding Virginia with coupons and to prevent any further exchanges of the old bonds for Riddleberger bonds. So long as most of the Riddleberger bonds remained unissued, the bondholders could try to force coupons on the state or entice the assembly to adopt a new funding act that fully restored the tax-receivable character of the coupons. Without some such change in Virginia policy or law, the value of the 1871 and 1879 bonds remained low, and it was not in the interest of the bondholders to chance raising the market value of the Riddleberger bonds, which did not have tax-receivable coupons and also paid a lower rate of interest.[17]

Late in 1885 Judge Robert W. Hughes issued two notable opinions in the United States Circuit Court for the Eastern District of Virginia. The first, *Gorman v. Sinking Fund Commissioners,* concerned the August 1884 amendment to the Riddleberger Act, which required that 1871 coupons could not be exchanged dollar for dollar for new Riddleberger bonds. Hughes ruled that the law could not be construed to operate retroactively on coupons that had matured prior to the date of the amendment but were not submitted for exchange until after that date. As a consequence of Hughes's decision, at that late date a citizen of New York was not entitled to have his old 1871 coupons funded in Riddleberger bonds dollar for dollar. At the same time, Hughes also accepted the constitutionality of the November 1884 Wickham Amendment, which imposed as of 1 January 1885 a reduced rate of exchange for funding 1871 coupons; set at fifty cents on the dollar the exchange rate for McCulloch bond coupons; stopped payment of interest on several series of matured coupons at specified dates; and required the treasurer to remove from Riddleberger bonds before issuing them all the coupons with maturity dates prior to the actual date of issue.[18]

In *Norfolk Trust Co. v. Marye* Hughes ruled that the state treasurer had acted in violation of Coupon Killer No. 1 when he refused to accept 1871 and 1879 coupons in payment of back taxes. The law required him to accept them in payment of taxes if genuine or to accept 1871 coupons provisionally along with full payment in lawful money pending a jury trial to ascertain their authenticity. In keeping with *Poindexter v. Greenhow* but in contrast to his dissenting opinion in the 1883 case *Baltimore & Ohio Railroad Co. v. Allen,* Hughes also ruled that the case was not in fact against the state but against a public official of the state. He declared that his court possessed authority to require the state's treasurer, Morton Marye, to accept the coupons because the amount at issue was greater than five hundred dollars and involved a federal question, the impairment of the coupon owner's contract.[19]

Early in 1886 the Virginia Supreme Court of Appeals and the Supreme Court of the United States ruled on some of the anti-coupon laws the Democratic majorities in the General Assembly had adopted. In *Greenhow v. Vashon,* which the Supreme Court of Appeals decided on 14 January, the Readjuster judges upheld the requirement that school taxes be collected only in lawful money and not in coupons and that the school tax money be segregated from other revenue. For himself and three of the four other judges, Robert Alexander Richardson endorsed nearly every conclusion that Waller Redd Staples had stated in his 1872 dissent in *Antoni v. Wright* and apparently refrained with reluctance from overturning that decision. Like Staples, Richardson denied that the coupons were contracts. He declared that the 1884 requirement for the separate collection of school taxes was not only consistent with Article VIII, Section 8, of the Constitution of 1869 but actually a prudent requirement to enforce that section so as to raise money that the state could spend on the schools. The consistency between the constitutional requirement and the act under consideration, Richardson wrote, "is a thing so plain that there is not the least tendency to obscurity, except by a multiplication of words." He then multiplied his own words: "It goes without saying, it speaks for itself; it is plain to the naked eye of common sense; there can be no two opinions about it; the enactment of those two sections was not only warranted, but was positively commanded by that highest authority for legislation, the organic law of the State."[20]

The use of coupons to pay professional license fees came before the Supreme Court of the United States in January 1886, when two attorneys appealed to halt what they argued were unconstitutional prosecutions for practicing law without a license. An attorney from Richmond and one from Fauquier County had tendered 1871 coupons and some money in payment of their license taxes and the associated registration fees, but in both instances the local government had refused to issue a renewed license to practice law for the reason that payment with coupons was not legal payment. Local commonwealth's attorneys prosecuted the attorneys for practicing law without a license. The Richmond attorney was none other than William L. Royall. He and William H. Sands, of Fauquier County, sought relief from the Supreme Court. On 1 February 1886 the court ruled unanimously in the two cases *Royall v. Virginia* and *Sands v. Edmunds* that a tender of payment of the license tax with coupons was the legal equivalent of payment, that the local officials had therefore illegally refused to issue the licenses, and that consequently the two attorneys could not be lawfully prosecuted for practicing law when not in possession of illegally withheld licenses.[21]

The Supreme Court heard four other Virginia coupon cases during the same session, all of which involved questions of jurisdiction and in two of which Royall was a principal. In *Barry v. Edmunds*, which also arose in Fauquier County, the Supreme Court determined that even though the taxpayer, Robert P. Barry, owed much less than five hundred dollars in taxes, which was the legal minimum for a federal court to take jurisdiction, he could sue in federal court for recovery of damages done to his property and reputation if the collector had seized his property under circumstances that could justify a greater award than the sum originally at issue. At the sale of the seized property, county officers had publicly denounced Barry as an evader of taxes and tried to destroy his credit with the public. "The dignity and value of the right assailed," Justice Matthews wrote for the unanimous Supreme Court, "and the power and authority of the source from which the assault proceeds, are elements to be considered in the computation of damages if they are to be not only compensation for the direct loss inflicted, but a remedy and prevention for the greater wrong and injury involved in the apprehension of its repetition."[22] When the Supreme Court's reporter printed the decision, he included a long section from the arguments and evidence that Barry's attorneys had presented. The attorneys had asserted that Virginia's Democratic Party, being in control of the General Assembly and of most of the local offices, had used all the party's public officials to prevent payment of taxes with coupons, including harassing and prosecuting people who refused to cooperate or who continued to try to exercise the constitutionally protected rights that the federal courts ruled they possessed.

In two rulings both styled *Ex Parte Royall,* which the Supreme Court issued on 1 March 1886, Royall failed to obtain writs of habeas corpus to release him from the custody of the Richmond city jailor while awaiting trial on a charge of selling a tax-receivable coupon without having paid the license fee of one thousand dollars. Royall initially petitioned the federal circuit court and argued that because the courts had declared that the laws under which he had been charged and would soon be prosecuted were un-constitutional impairments of contract, the federal judge had jurisdiction to issue the writ to release him from jail. The judge refused to issue the writ, so Royall appealed his decision to the Supreme Court and simultane-ously petitioned that court to issue the writ of habeas corpus. In the first case, the Supreme Court unanimously ruled that the federal judge not only had jurisdiction but also had discretion and that the judge had acted law-fully within that discretion in declining to issue a writ prior to the trial.[23] In the second case, the Supreme Court declined to issue the writ itself.[24] Nei-ther decision prevented either court from issuing a writ of habeas corpus at any time later. Noted legal scholars have called Royall's case "a landmark in federal jurisdiction" in that it marked "the beginning of restrictive judicial interpretation of the Habeas Corpus Act of 1867" and thereafter limited use of the broadly worded law in cases relating to political issues.[25]

Following a year in which the Supreme Court had declared some of the anti-coupon laws unconstitutional, early in 1886 the General Assembly passed several new laws to make it even more difficult for people to prove in court that their 1871 coupons were genuine and therefore receivable for taxes. The laws added new burdens to the requirement for proof of authenticity of the 1879 coupons and in effect amended Coupon Killer No. 1. The form of the bonds suggested the nature of the new laws. When the state treasurer initially issued the bonds, he had authenticated them by personally signing each bond. Official registers and other documents in the treasurer's and second auditor's offices had recorded each bond's number and date of issue and the name of the person who first acquired it. None of the individual coupons attached to the bonds contained an authenticat-ing autograph signature. Instead, each bore the printed number of the bond to which it was attached, its date of maturity, the amount of interest it earned at maturity under the act of issue, the text indicating that it was tax-receivable, and the treasurer's printed name.

The first in the series of new laws was an amendment to the section of the code of Virginia that dealt with proving the authenticity of documents in court and did not even mention bonds or coupons. It placed the whole burden of proof on the person who wished to verify that a printed docu-ment was genuine or not fraudulent. The law "further provided, that expert evidence shall not be received to prove the genuineness of any paper or instrument made by machinery, or in any other manner" than by the actual, personal handwriting of the person who had issued or authenticated the original document. In the case of coupons, that meant the treasurer's signature on the original bond from which the coupon may have already been clipped, but it prohibited introduction of testimony about the authenticity of the printing or even the act of clipping that could prove that a particular coupon had once been attached to a particular, authentic bond.[26] The Virginia Committee of the Council of the Corporation of Foreign Bondholders in its annual report for 1888 declared bluntly, "The ingenuity of this device is only equalled by its dishonesty."[27]

The second law required that "in the trial of any issue involving the genuineness of a coupon . . . the defendant may demand the production of the bond; and thereupon it shall be the duty of the plaintiff to produce such bond, with proof that the coupon was actually cut therefrom."[28] If the taxpayer had purchased a detached coupon or for some other reason did not then have the bond, he or she could not present it to the court and consequently could not win the case. If found constitutional, those two laws would make it virtually impossible for men and women who purchased detached coupons from the bond brokers to prove that the coupons were genuine and legally tax-receivable.

Another law adopted in that same session of the assembly declared it a felony punishable by two to ten years in the state penitentiary and a fine of up to five hundred dollars for "every person who, with intent to defraud, falsely makes, forges, counterfeits, alters, or passes or attempts to pass, utter, publish, sell or use any bond, coupon, obligation or security of the state of Virginia." Attempting to submit coupons of doubtful authenticity in payment of taxes could therefore under some circumstances become a criminal offense.[29] An act of 27 February 1886 established a one-year grace period beginning on 1 July of that year in which people could file suits to prove the authenticity of coupons that had matured before that date and thereafter prohibited any new suits from being filed more than one year after the date of maturity printed on any coupon.[30] An amendment to the law concerning the payment of business and professional license taxes required that all payments be made in "coin, legal tender notes, or national bank bills"; if in coupons from either 1871 or 1879 bonds, the coupons first had to be proved authentic under the provisions of Coupon Killer No. 1 as amended.[31] But the first two acts of the 1886 assembly session in effect had amended Coupon Killer No. 1 in such a way as to make it practically impossible to prove that the coupons were genuine.

The assembly also established a board made up of the attorney general, the secretary of the commonwealth, the auditor of public accounts, the second auditor, and the state treasurer and empowered it to award compensation to tax collectors who lost cases when people sued them to force acceptance of coupons for payment of taxes or to recover damages if the officials had seized and sold their property for nonpayment.[32] The new Democratic state attorney general, Rufus Adolphus Ayers, who took office on 1 January 1886, later testified that the assembly had passed the law as a direct consequence of the Supreme Court's April 1885 decision in *Poindexter v. Greenhow,* which had declared Coupon Killer No. 2 unconstitutional.[33] Soon after passage of the new law, the auditor of public accounts issued instructions to all the state's tax collectors and directed them to seize and sell at public auction property on which taxes had not been paid with lawful money, assuring the collectors that they would not be losers as a result of doing so.[34]

And on 1 March 1886 the assembly defined and outlawed the old offense of barratry—attorneys commencing lawsuits for their own purposes or emolument—and provided for punishing attorneys convicted of the felony with disbarment for life. The assembly's action was aimed at such bond attorneys as William L. Royall, who had long been engaged in defending bondholders and owners of coupons and was himself then a principal in some of the lawsuits. In fact, he had purchased and sold one coupon in order to be prosecuted under the licensing act so that he could challenge the constitutionality of that law; and he had offered coupons in partial payment for renewal of his law license in order to challenge the law requiring payment of license taxes in money only. The new law did not mention coupons or any of the recent court cases, but the index to the acts of the 1885–86 session of the General Assembly included a cross-reference to the act on barratry from the entry on filing legal petitions, which initiating a coupon case required; Joseph P. Bradley, an associate justice of the Supreme Court of the United States, perhaps relying in part on a catalog of anti-coupon legislation that Royall or some other Virginia attorney provided to the court, later listed the act among the assembly's attempts to obstruct payment of taxes with coupons; and the Virginia Committee of the Council of the Corporation of Foreign Bondholders reported on the law to its members but described the offense as champerty, a closely related practice in which attorneys associated with their clients and in effect became illegally interested parties to a suit.[35]

The new laws enacted in 1886 faced legal challenges almost as soon as the assembly passed them. Acting under the auditor's instructions, tax collectors began to seize and sell property for nonpayment of taxes, and local prosecutors took taxpayers to court, or aggrieved taxpayers sued to recover their property. The Virginia Supreme Court of Appeals issued its first opinions on those cases in December and the following January.

On 9 December 1886 in three cases, *Cornwall v. Commonwealth, Newton v. Commonwealth,* and *Burruss v. Commonwealth,* the judges by votes of 4 to 0 and with one judge absent ruled in favor of the constitutionality of the law requiring the presentation in court of the bond from which a coupon had been clipped at a trial to ascertain the authenticity of a coupon submitted for payment of taxes. The judges declared that the act did not violate the impairment-of-contracts clause of the Constitution of the United States, because it had nothing to do with contracts; it had to do with admissible evidence. Moreover, the judges declared those lawsuits to be cases improperly brought against the state.[36]

On 11 January 1887, in *Commonwealth v. Weller & Sons,* also by a vote of 4 to 0 and with the same judge absent, the judges upheld the laws prohibiting expert testimony in trials of coupons and requiring presentation of the bond from which a coupon had been removed. Judge Benjamin Watkins Lacy wrote that the law requiring presentation of the bond in court "does not in any way affect the obligation of the contract. . . . The rule prescribed is one which affects the mode of procedure only, and is in accordance with the principles of the common law. It is a fundamental principle that the best evidence is required, of which the case is susceptible, and it is one of the most important of the rules of evidence." The signed genuine bond being the best evidence, it had to be produced to prove the authenticity of the coupon, even though under the other new laws no other evidence was allowed to establish that the coupon had once been attached to it.[37] On 13 January 1887 in a one-sentence ruling that relied on *Commonwealth v. Weller & Sons,* the judges settled fifty-eight similar cases that had been appealed to it.[38]

One week later, in *Commonwealth v. Jones,* the Supreme Court of Appeals ruled that a sample merchant who had submitted coupons in payment of his license tax and registration fee could not pursue his trade pending issuance of the license or because the city officials had refused to issue the license. The judges tried to distinguish the sample merchant's appeal from the Supreme Court's decisions in *Royall v. Virginia* the previous year. Judge Robert Alexander Richardson declared untenable the merchant's assertion that his case and Royall's were so much alike that his case had to be settled the same way. "The language of the court," Richardson wrote condescendingly of the Supreme Court's decision, "is not fairly susceptible of any such construction as contended for. The highest judicial tribunal in the land could never, by the language employed, have intended to make a roving peddler of goods by sample the arbiter of the constitution and laws of this State." Richardson also wrote positively but in contradiction of what some other judges had written, "No fact—certainly none connected with the history of the Virginia State debt—is better established than that there are spurious bonds of the State out, some of which have been presented and claimed as valid, and their invalidity incontestably established. It is idle to attempt to 'whistle down the wind' the existence of such spurious bonds, and the absolute necessity of protection against them."[39]

In February 1887, in *Commonwealth v. Maury,* Richardson and the same judges sustained the constitutionality of the section of the revenue law that required payment of an annual license tax of one thousand dollars on all establishments where men sold Virginia coupons as well as the 20 percent tax on the value of the coupons sold. The license tax, Richardson wrote, was not in any way a violation of the contract rights of owners of bonds or coupons, nor was the tax on the sale of the coupons, although effectively a tax on the coupon, a violation of a contract right. "In a word, then," he wrote, echoing what Waller Redd Staples had written in dissent in *Antoni v. Wright* in 1872, "the power of taxation is a part of the legislative sovereignty of the State. It existed when the bonds and coupons were issued, they having, in fact, been issued subject to this power of taxation, which was not in any way released or surrendered by their issuance, and being the *lex temporis*"—that is, the law of the land—"is part and parcel of the bond and coupon contract. If this power of taxation was not expressly reserved, it matters not."[40]

In October 1886, while those cases were working their way to the Supreme Court of Appeals, Judges Hugh Lenox Bond and Robert W. Hughes presided together over two jury trials in the United States Circuit Court for the Eastern District of Virginia. In each, a married couple sought compensation and damages from a county tax collector who had seized and sold their property after they offered coupons in payment of taxes. In the first case, *Willis and Wife v. Miller,* the tax collector of Rappahannock County had seized and sold three horses, one colt, ten cattle, eighty-five sheep, a wagon, and a buggy after the Willises had offered coupons in payment of

the $123 tax due on their farm but had not paid the portion of the tax dedi-
cated to the schools with lawful money. They sued him in federal court for
$10,000. Bond instructed the members of the jury that under the Constitu-
tion of the United States the coupons were tax-receivable for all purposes
and that the jury had to find for the Willises if the evidence proved that the
collector had seized their property knowing that the law under which he
acted had been declared unconstitutional. The jury so found but awarded
them only $150 in damages, nothing like the $10,000 they asked for but
perhaps enough to cover the value of the animals and vehicles seized and
sold.[41] In the other trial, *Strickler and Wife v. Yager,* the taxpayers had paid
their Page County school tax in lawful money but tendered coupons for the
balance of the tax due on their real estate. At the auction of their seized
property, they purchased it for $9. Under the same instructions that Bond
had issued to the jury in the Willis case, the jury awarded the Stricklers $9
in damages.[42]

In the statement of facts printed with the official report of the two trials is an unattributed, frustrated judicial observation that Bond, being the
senior jurist, probably wrote. The judge complained that "it appeared from
the two trials which had been held that a jury of Virginians proposed to let
it be known that they would not protect their fellow-citizens from willful
trespasses committed upon them, when those fellow-citizens relied upon
the constitutional laws of the United States only for that protection; and, if
the jury chose to take this position, the court was powerless to assure the
citizen any redress."[43] In making the small awards for damages, the jury
in each case had done the very minimum allowed and in effect sustained
as far as possible the execution of the state's anti-coupon laws. The jurors,
much like the legislators and other public officials, had done their small
part in trying to kill the coupons too.

Early in 1887, when the Supreme Court of Appeals was handing down
its decisions on the 1886 laws, William L. Royall was back in court. On 1
May 1886 he had offered the Richmond city treasurer, Samuel C. Greenhow, a fifteen-dollar coupon from an 1871 bond and ten dollars in lawful
money to renew his license to practice law plus seventy-five cents in silver
coin for the associated registration fee. Greenhow had refused to accept
both the coupon and the money and cited the law requiring that all such
licenses and fees be paid in lawful money only. The Richmond Court of
Hustings had fined Royall fifty dollars and costs for the misdemeanor of
practicing law without a license. He appealed to the Virginia Supreme

Court of Appeals, which on 25 February 1887 ruled that the hustings court had been "plainly right" and denied Royall a hearing.[44] He therefore appealed to the Supreme Court of the United States. On 28 March 1887 Chief Justice Morrison R. Waite reversed that ruling in *Royall v. Virginia.* Writing for the whole court and rather tersely, Waite concluded that this case could not be "distinguished in principle" from Royall's 1886 case, in which the Supreme Court had ruled that the state official's refusal to accept the coupons was an unconstitutional impairment of the contract the coupon embodied. During the proceedings on the new case, the state had acknowledged that the coupon "bore on its face the contract of the State of Virginia that it should be received in payment of all taxes, debts, and demands due the state." To the Supreme Court, that demonstrated that Royall's offer of the coupon was "a good tender" and therefore lawful payment of the license tax. The chief justice concluded that that "brings this case within the ruling by this Court in the other."[45]

Royall later applied to the Supreme Court of Appeals for reimbursement of his costs in successfully appealing its ruling to the Supreme Court of the United States and in clearing his case in the court of hustings, but the court in *Ex Parte William L. Royall* dismissed his petition for compensation.[46]

8   THE COUPON CRUSHER

Early in 1886, Virginia's new Democratic governor, the former Confederate general Fitzhugh Lee,[1] fresh from his victory over the Readjuster-Republican coalition in the 1885 general election, reported to the General Assembly that the state's "financial condition, already sufficiently embarrassed, will it is feared be still further complicated" as a consequence of the Supreme Court of the United States having declared unconstitutional several of the General Assembly's laws designed to thwart payment of taxes with coupons. Moreover, juries in several of the state's cities and counties had ruled coupons authentic in spite of the surviving laws intended to make it impossible to prove that they were.[2] Lee blamed the attorneys for the Corporation of Foreign Bondholders and recommended that the assembly appoint commissioners to explain to the bondholders in the strongest and plainest language possible that the legislature would never retreat from the terms of the Riddleberger Act or tolerate the payment of taxes with 1871 or 1879 coupons and that the bondholders must cease promoting the litigation, which undermined the state's attempt to drive the coupons out of circulation and threatened its solvency.[3]

The state's financial situation grew worse during the first years of Lee's administration. Coupons continued to pour into the treasury, and the state actually reduced some taxes even as it assumed expensive new responsibilities for caring for disabled veterans of the Confederate army and navy. The laws designed to reduce or halt payment of taxes with coupons had been somewhat effective before being invalidated, so in 1886 the assembly passed the laws that placed legal barriers in the way of people who tried to prove coupons genuine in court. People had paid more than $1 million in taxes with coupons in 1880 and more than $725,000 in 1882, but following passage of the Coupon Killers that year the sum plunged to less than

$50,000. It rose in 1884 to about $173,000 but then dropped back to about $50,000 in the two years thereafter.[4] The whole of the annual state budget in the mid-1880s was a little more than $2 million, and the coupons therefore remained a very serious problem.

When Lee summoned a special session of the assembly in the spring of 1887 to receive the report of a committee to revise the code of Virginia, he informed the legislators that during the second half of 1886, in spite of the anti-coupon laws, "in fifty-five counties and twelve cities of the commonwealth, upwards of three thousand persons have tendered coupons for their taxes and licenses, to the amount of $105,258.11."[5] That is, in about half the state's localities for only half the year people paid about 5 percent of the state's anticipated annual revenue with coupons. Prorated for the whole state for the whole year, coupons might rise to as much as 20 percent of the revenue. That threatened to renew the debilitating deficits of the 1870s. The legislators decided to replace the invalidated anti-coupon laws with new ones, but at that very time the Corporation of Foreign Bondholders intervened with a proposal to open negotiations to try to resolve the differences.

The differences had grown greater and the conflicts more personal and intense. The bondholders and their council continued litigation to force the state to accept the coupons for taxes, and it also denounced the government of Virginia for acting in bad faith. William L. Royall, in particular, infuriated Virginia government officials every chance he got in implementing the policies of the corporation. Not only did he continue to assist taxpayers with their suits to pay taxes with coupons but he tried to sue the state board that the assembly had established to compensate local officials who lost cases after attempting to seize and sell taxpayers' property. He even tried to sue one of the grand juries that indicted him and threatened to sue any grand jury in the state that took action against him.[6] In 1889 bondholders arranged for publication of a new edition of Bradley T. Johnson's 1878 report on the public debt, which had denounced all reductions of interest or principal as immoral and illegal repudiation.[7]

But even though Royall and the bondholders had won every important federal case they filed against the anti-coupon laws, state officials continued to find ways to evade the effects of the courts' rulings. The investors collected no interest on their bonds, salvaged very little in the sale of coupons to taxpayers, and saw the value of their bonds remain low. In spite of the forced optimism of the words in the council's annual reports, they were not making progress, so in September 1886 owners of Virginia bonds met in London and decided to try to reach an agreement with the state government.[8]

In the spring of 1887, soon after the special session met in mid-March, representatives of the council traveled to Richmond bearing their proposal to open new negotiations "to conclude arrangements with the State of Virginia or others in relation to the said bonds and coupons on any terms, and to carry the same into effect by presenting the same bonds and coupons to the proper authority, and exchanging them for other securities or otherwise."[9] The vague proposal suggested that a completely new funding plan involving an exchange of old coupon bonds for new bonds could be negotiated that would withdraw some or all of the coupons from circulation or perhaps replace all the existing bonds with a new issue of bonds on which the state could and would pay all the interest. Lee advised the assembly to appoint commissioners to meet with the bondholders, and the assembly complied. Negotiations began in mid-May but soon broke down because of serious disagreements between the legislators and the representatives of the bondholders about the portion of the state's revenue that should be devoted to the public schools and the portion that was realistically available for paying interest on the debt.[10]

As the negotiators were floundering toward an impasse, the members of the assembly acted on a new plan for attacking the tax-receivable character of the coupons. As William L. Royall later wrote somewhat laconically and inaccurately, "The use of coupons was spreading rapidly, and it became evident that the State would be forced to pay her debt unless something could be done to stop the use of coupons. Thereupon the wise men of Virginia put their heads together and devised an Act of Assembly which, for ingenious cunning to pervert the law and justice, has no parallel in the annals of legislation."[11]

Lee suggested, the assembly passed, and on 12 May 1887 he signed a law to circumvent the problems that arose after the federal courts had declared that a taxpayer's offer of genuine coupons in payment of a tax was legally equivalent to the payment of the tax and that therefore the state's tax collectors could not then seize and sell the taxpayer's property for nonpayment. "Let us change the position," Lee suggested to the legislators, "and let the commonwealth take the initiative. This can be done by instituting suit to recover the taxes, and giving the tax-payer a day in court to prove his coupons to be genuine and make good his tender."[12]

It is not clear who was the originator of what was quickly dubbed the Coupon Crusher.[13] In effect, but without explicitly stating the fact, it defined the offer of coupons for payment of taxes as default of payment. Under Coupon Killer No. 1 and the remaining laws still in force, coupons were not tax-receivable until proved genuine, which could be done only after a taxpayer surrendered them to the tax collector. The new law required county and city attorneys for the commonwealth to file suit in the local circuit court to collect in money the tax a taxpayer proposed to pay with coupons. The law empowered the attorney general to act on behalf of the state treasurer in like circumstances. It established a legal presumption that all coupons were of doubtful authenticity, again placed the whole burden of proving the genuineness of the coupons on the taxpayer, and left in place—in fact, relied on—the two acts of 1886 that prohibited expert testimony as to the genuineness of the coupons and that authorized plaintiffs, in this instance prosecuting attorneys, to require defendants, in this instance taxpayers, to present in court the original bonds from which the coupons had been clipped. If, in spite of the multiple obstacles, a taxpayer prevailed against the state in the lawsuit, the taxpayer had to pay court costs and a fee of ten dollars to the commonwealth's attorney.[14]

Royall and the bondholders knew that they had no realistic hope of succeeding in a suit against the Coupon Crusher in a state court, so they looked to the federal courts. Acting for James P. Cooper, an English agent of the Corporation of Foreign Bondholders then temporarily resident in Virginia, and several other men who had purchased coupons from English bondholders and sold them to Virginia taxpayers, Royall filed suit in federal court to stop enforcement of the Coupon Crusher and challenge its constitutionality.[15] He asked the court to issue an injunction to prohibit the state treasurer, the attorney general, and every local treasurer and commonwealth's attorney in Virginia from prosecuting taxpayers under the new law until its unconstitutionality could be established. On 6 June 1887 Judge Hugh Lenox Bond issued a temporary injunction in *James P. Cooper, et al. v. Morton Marye, et al.* and scheduled a hearing on the constitutionality of the Coupon Crusher for the following October.[16]

On the very next day after Bond issued the temporary injunction, Attorney General Rufus Adolphus Ayers[17] deliberately violated it to bring the question of the constitutionality of the law before the Supreme Court of the United States as quickly as possible. He publicly refused to dismiss or to stop process on a suit he had already begun on behalf of the state treasurer against the Baltimore and Ohio Railroad Company; and he served notice that he would also proceed under the law against the Wheeler and Wilson Sewing Machine Company. The commonwealth's attorneys for Loudoun County and Fauquier County also began prosecutions under the act, making all three of them vulnerable to contempt-of-court citations for violating the injunction.[18]

On 8 October 1887 Bond found each of them in contempt of court, fined the attorney general five hundred dollars, fined each of the commonwealth's attorneys one hundred dollars, and ordered all three of them jailed until each should "purge himself of his contempt" by paying the fine and dismissing the lawsuits.[19] Ayers and the others refused because, as Ayers argued, the federal court "had no jurisdiction whatever to award the injunction" and therefore no lawful authority to jail them for violating it.[20] He and the other two men then appealed their contempt citations to the Supreme Court of the United States by petitioning for writs of habeas corpus to release them from unlawful confinement. The Supreme Court allowed each to post a bond of one thousand dollars and be released pending its decision in the case.[21]

The justices heard oral arguments in the case styled *In Re Ayers* on 14 and 15 November 1887 and issued their decision on 5 December. The question before them was not the constitutionality of the Coupon Crusher, as Royall had intended and Ayers had hoped, but jurisdiction, whether the federal circuit court had legal authority to issue the injunction. Royall argued that only the specific state officials named in the case were parties to the suit, not the Commonwealth of Virginia. Bond's injunction forbade the state's officials from acting; it did not forbid the state government from doing anything. Therefore, Royall argued, because the state was not a party to the suit, the federal court had jurisdiction in the suit between citizens of the state and citizens of a foreign country.[22]

The issue that the Supreme Court had to decide was whether the suits against certain named public officials of Virginia were suits against them individually or in reality suits against the state government and its public law. Under the doctrine of sovereign immunity, a state government could not be sued in any court without its consent, and if the suits Royall filed were against the state, the Eleventh Amendment also denied jurisdiction to all federal courts. Justice Stanley Matthews, who had written several opinions in cases related to the Virginia debt, including the 1885 Coupon Cases, issued a twenty-two-page opinion for the Supreme Court. He concluded that Ayers was correct, that the federal court lacked jurisdiction to issue the injunction, and that therefore the men should be released from the contempt citation. His reasoning was that although the named defendants were all public officials of the Commonwealth of Virginia, none of them had any personal interest in the outcome of the suits they had filed. They had acted as the state government's only agents to enforce the new law. Indeed, the suits they had filed against taxpayers were in the name of the state and not in their own names. Matthews concluded that the suit was against the state. He also wrote that Royall's clients were merely owners of coupons but not taxpayers and consequently had no standing to sue because they had no contracts with the state that enforcement of the act of 1887 could impair; consequently there was no federal question at issue. Matthews declared that the suit Royall had filed on his clients' behalf was one that no federal court could entertain for any reason.[23]

Justice Stephen J. Field filed a brief opinion concurring in the judgment but noting that he had dissented from the majority's opinion in one of the cases Matthews cited to support his opinion. Field also commented on the real reason behind the application for the writs of habeas corpus, the series of anti-coupon laws the General Assembly had enacted. "The numerous devices to which the state has resorted in order to escape from her obligations under the forms of law may, it is true, seriously embarrass the coupon holder in the assertion of his claims," he wrote critically but with due deference to the constitutional powers and responsibilities of the state's legislature, "but that is not a sufficient reason for denying to the state the right to prosecute her demands for taxes in her own courts. If the obstacles to the maintenance of the claims of the coupon holder, presented by the state legislation, are repugnant to the Constitution and laws of the United States, we cannot assume in advance that they will be sustained by the courts of Virginia when the coupons tendered are produced in the suits mentioned, and for that reason deny to her a hearing there upon her own demands."[24]

Justice John Marshall Harlan dissented, stating that the Supreme Court's own precedents required it to identify the parties to a litigation as the persons named therein and not presume that because the defendants were Virginia state officials the state was therefore the real defendant. "A contrary view," Harlan concluded, "enables the state to use her immunity from suit to effect what the Constitution of the United States forbids her from doing—namely to enact statutes impairing the obligation of her contract. If an officer of the state can take shelter behind such immunity while he proceeds with the execution of a void enactment to the injury of the citizen's rights of contract, it would look as if that provision which declares that the Constitution of the United States shall be the supreme law of the land . . . had lost most, if not all, of its value in respect to contracts which a state makes with individuals."[25]

In Re Ayers settled the jurisdictional question then before the Supreme Court in that one case. Neither it nor any of the other coupon cases in which attorneys argued that suits should be regarded as suits against the state rather than suits against individual public officials clearly established how to distinguish one class of suits from the other. The Supreme Court had been almost evenly divided on that question in *Poindexter v. Greenhow* in 1885, and the Ayers case in 1887 furnished no clear guidelines for the future. The Supreme Court's issuance of the writ of habeas corpus freeing Attorney General Ayers and the two commonwealth's attorneys left the Coupon Crusher fully in force. It also left in force several additional anti-coupon laws that the special session of the assembly passed in May 1887 and that had not been challenged. One of them made it a misdemeanor for any state official to "receive (except for identification and verification) any paper or instrument purporting to be a coupon, detached from a bond of this State, for any taxes, debts, dues, or demands due the State, until the same shall have been verified in the mode prescribed by law."[26] Another amended and reenacted the section of the revenue act that placed a license tax of one thousand dollars on every office of every coupon seller (reducing the amount to five hundred for offices in cities or counties having fewer than ten thousand inhabitants) and a 20 percent tax on the value of the coupons they sold, but it also stipulated for the first time that no such licensed person could sell coupons to any other than taxpaying residents of the licensing city or county.[27] A third new law made it a felony punishable by up to five years in the state penitentiary for any dealer in coupons to sell or resubmit a detached coupon that some other person had already submitted for payment of taxes,[28] indicating that the brokers had been making multiple attempts in different jurisdictions to force acceptance of their supplies of detached coupons. A fourth law required tax collectors to keep detailed records of all detached coupons submitted for payment of taxes and made it a misdemeanor punishable by a fine of up to one hundred dollars and a penitentiary term of up to one year for any person who knowingly submitted for payment of taxes a coupon that had

previously been submitted.[29] The assembly also adopted a brief joint resolution on 14 May requiring the second auditor to obtain from the printer
and destroy the printing plates for the Riddleberger bonds and coupons as
well as all printed bonds and coupons then remaining in the possession of
the printer.[30] It passed another on 24 May authorizing the hiring of counsel
to assist the attorney general in defending tax collectors who were sued
after seizing and selling the property of people who had tried to pay taxes
with coupons.[31]

The Supreme Court handed down its decision in the Ayers case on 5
December 1887. Two days later Governor Lee opened the regular session
of the General Assembly with the news pleasing to him that for the time being the Coupon Crusher and the other laws adopted in the spring were still
in full force. In spite of the failure of the negotiations with representatives
of the Corporation of Foreign Bondholders in May, Lee was optimistic in
December that a mutually satisfactory solution to all the problems relating
to the bonds and coupons could still be reached. Revenue was up because
the Coupon Crusher reduced tax payments with coupons. Lee informed
the legislators that "the number of coupons coming into the Treasury in
proportion to the cash revenues upon which the State depends to carry on
the Government, is not yet crippling her schools or her eleemosynary and
educational institutions, or blocking the wheels of her State government."
Moreover, Lee predicted that the state could afford to pay the interest
on the Riddleberger Bonds "without increasing the taxes of her citizens."
Under those circumstances and perceiving that some of the bondholders
and legislators still appeared willing to negotiate, he recommended that
the assembly suspend "for a reasonable time, the institution of all legal
proceedings under the act of May 12, 1887," the Coupon Crusher, as a
demonstration of goodwill, which might persuade the bondholders to renew negotiations.[32]

Second Auditor Hugh G. Ruffin—the former secretary of the Commissioners of the Sinking Fund who had engaged in the pamphlet war with
Federal Judge Robert W. Hughes and had condemned William Mahone
and his Republican allies—was less optimistic than the governor about the
budget. Ruffin predicted that the state might run a small deficit that year
because too many residents of Virginia were still able to pay some taxes
with coupons.[33] During the 1887–88 legislative session, the senators and
delegates debated bills to amend acts relating to coupons and the debt

but adopted no measures of consequence, and they declined to suspend prosecutions under the Coupon Crusher in hopes of luring the bondholders back to the negotiating table.

Many of the English bondholders, though, were averse to new negotiations. The Council of the Corporation of Foreign Bondholders redoubled its efforts to prevent exchanges of 1871 and 1879 bonds for Riddleberger bonds and to continue the coupon litigation. The Virginia Committee warned other bondholders "that their only chance for preserving their property is to continue the present fight with their tax-receivable Coupons; if they ever surrender the security of these Coupons they may as well make up their minds to lose both principal and interest."[34] Early in 1890 the committee went so far as to publish a long report on the fiscal condition of the Virginia state government to demonstrate that Governor Lee had deliberately misled his constituents and the public when publishing data about the state's revenue that appeared to prove the state's inability to pay more interest than it did or that the state could survive if forced to take coupons in payment of taxes.[35] That might be regarded as a new low point in relations between the state government and the English creditors following 1882, when the Readjusters passed the Riddleberger Act and the Coupon Killers.

During 1888 and 1889, while the legislators and bondholders dug in their heals, each evidently waited for the other to act first, and both watched as another series of lawsuits challenging the constitutionality of the anti-coupon laws began to work their way through the state and federal courts. The federal court for the Eastern District of Virginia had ten coupon cases on its docket in 1889, and the federal court for the Western District of Virginia had eighteen, most of them against tax collectors who had seized and sold or attempted to sell property of people who had paid taxes with coupons.[36]

On 5 December 1888 the Virginia Supreme Court of Appeals ruled in *McGahey v. Commonwealth* that the Coupon Crusher, the laws that prohibited the introduction of expert testimony to prove the genuineness of detached coupons and allowed prosecutors to demand that defendants produce the bond from which coupons had been detached, did not impair any constitutionally protected contracts between the state and owners of the coupons. The judges declared that the laws merely provided judicial methods and clear rules of evidence for proving the genuineness of coupons submitted for payment of taxes.[37] The judges in effect augmented that decision in three subsequent cases. In March 1889, in *Commonwealth v. Hurt,* they ruled that when a taxpayer presented a coupon for verification and payment of taxes and also produced the bond from which it had been detached, the prosecutor could require that the genuineness of the bond also be verified.[38] In September of that year, in *Smith v. Clark,* they in effect reconfirmed the constitutionality of the Coupon Crusher in ruling on a case mistakenly filed under that act in a city corporation court and not, as the law required, in the circuit court.[39] And in March 1890 they ruled in *Mallan Bros. v. Bransford* that a taxpayer who had tendered coupons in payment of taxes and had also under protest paid with money, as Coupon Killer No. 1 required, could not sue the tax collector for recovery of the money after the tax collector had deposited the money in the state treasury.[40]

Governor Fitzhugh Lee had taken office at the beginning of 1886 with hopes of finally resolving all the financial, political, and legal problems the debt controversy had created, and in 1887 he recommended adoption of the Coupon Crusher to end the controversy's most difficult problem. He was disappointed on all counts by the end of his four-year term. When he delivered his last message to the General Assembly on 4 December 1889, Lee reluctantly reported that he could see no immediate prospect of new fruitful negotiations with the bondholders and no hope of actually crushing the coupons. During the fiscal year ending 30 September 1889, he informed the assembly sadly, Virginians had succeeded, in spite of all the legal barriers, in paying $214,580 in taxes with coupons, a too-small reduction from the previous fiscal year's $258,938 and much more than in the years immediately before he had become governor.

Lee again blamed the owners of old bonds for not exchanging them for Riddleberger bonds and condemned them, along with the bankers and some taxpayers, for continuing "their persistent use of coupons for the payments of taxes," which prolonged and increased the difficulties. "Whilst the forced receipt of these coupons instead of money for the taxes of the State has been a source of great annoyance to the officers charged with the collection of her revenues," Lee pointed out, the creditors may have damaged their own interests in the process, because "it has in some measure diminished the ability of the State to pay ultimately the same creditors, and has resulted in no immediate benefit to them, because the net sum realized from the sale of these coupons to tax-payers, after deducting the cost of litigation to them, is almost nothing."[41] Like all of his post–Civil War predecessors, Lee left office at the end of the month disappointed at having been unable to bring to an end the controversies arising from the state debt.

A few days after Lee retired from the governor's office, members of the House of Delegates requested from the second auditor an estimate of how much the November 1884 Wickham Amendment to the Riddleberger Act had driven down the market price of coupons and how much money the state had saved and would later save by its operations. The Wickham Amendment had prohibited exchange of old coupons after set dates and required that thereafter coupons must be exchanged within one year of their date of maturity. Ruffin reported that the market price of coupons was down to about 20 percent of face value, but he could not ascribe that directly to the amendment. He also reported that the inability of people to exchange the old coupons might save the state and cost the bondholders nearly $11.5 million between then and the maturity date on the bonds.[42] If the report suggested a new method of taking coupons out of circulation, the legislators did not adopt any new measures on the subject. Perhaps they hoped that the creditors would look at the numbers and cease their resistance. Members of the General Assembly also knew that the Supreme Court of the United States had scheduled oral arguments on several more Virginia coupon cases for the spring, which may have inclined the legislators to await the results before adopting any more anti-coupon laws.

The new Democratic governor, Philip Watkins McKinney,[43] entered office on the first day of January 1890 as firmly committed as Cameron and Lee had been to the 1882 Riddleberger Act. A few days after he was sworn in, he had an unexpected opportunity to say so. Even though relations between the state and the bondholders were worse than seriously strained, the chair of the Council of the Corporation of Foreign Bondholders wrote the governor offering on behalf of the council and the English Committee of Virginian Bondholders to meet with representatives of the state government to agree on the general outlines of a new debt settlement before reopening formal negotiations. No doubt basing his overture on the council's estimations of Virginia revenue, he wrote that the "points in divergence" that had led to the failure of the 1887 negotiations had not been "so great as to preclude, as the council ventures to hope, the adjustment of the questions at issue, especially bearing in view the increase in taxable values and the consequent increase of available revenue."[44]

McKinney forwarded the letter to the General Assembly with a message that in its first sentences expressed strong skepticism about the invitation but then changed its tone. "We have offered them, under the Riddleberger bill, terms as liberal as the financial condition of the State will allow," McKinney wrote. "That bill has been approved repeatedly by each political party in the State, in its conventions, and ratified by the people at the polls." McKinney nevertheless saw a possibility of solving the main problem by withdrawing from circulation a large number of the 1871 and 1879 bonds and their tax-receivable coupons. He suggested that "if the bondholders propose different terms, not materially increasing the principal or interest" that the Riddleberger Act had established, "it would be well to require, as an indispensable condition of considering any such proposition, that it should embrace a *bona fide* tender of so large a proportion of the consol and ten-forty bonds as to guarantee a settlement of the whole debt if it should be accepted."[45]

On 5 March 1890 the General Assembly created a commission to receive and evaluate proposals for revising the funding of the state debt and agree to suitable ones, requiring the creditors to post a $1 million good-faith bond in advance. The assembly named Governor McKinney chair of the commission, which also included the lieutenant governor, the speaker of the house, the chair of the Senate's Committee on Finance and Banks, the chair of the House's Committee on Finance, and one other member of the House of Delegates.[46] That set in train the last major refinancing of the portion of the old debt that Virginia still acknowledged owing, but for the time being it again left unprovided for the one-third that the General Assembly had assigned to West Virginia back in 1871.

Before the debt commission and representatives of the bondholders opened new negotiations, the Supreme Court unanimously invalidated most of the Virginia anti-coupon laws. On 19 May 1890 the judges declared in *McGahey v. Virginia*, in *Bryan v. Virginia*, and in *Cooper v. Virginia*, all decided together, that the coupons were contracts between the state and the owners of the coupons and that "the obligation of contract is impaired, in the sense of the Constitution, by any act which prevents its enforcement or which materially abridges the remedy for enforcing it which existed at the time it was contracted, and does not supply an alternative remedy equally adequate and efficacious." For the court, Justice Joseph P. Bradley explained that the law that prohibited expert testimony to establish the genuineness of detached coupons so much interfered with and burdened the taxpayer's right to pay taxes with coupons that it was an unconstitutional impairment of the obligations of contract; that the law that allowed the state to require the production in court of a bond from which a coupon had been detached was for the same reason an unconstitutional impairment of the obligations of contract; and that the prosecution provided for in the Coupon Crusher, although it was not an issue in any of the cases, might also be an unconstitutional impairment of the obligations of contract.[47]

In *Ellett v. Virginia,* which the Supreme Court considered and decided at the same time, the justices ruled that court costs taxpayers incurred in defending themselves and their right to pay with coupons under the Coupon Crusher could be paid in coupons because they were to be paid to the state and not to the prosecutor.[48] In *Cuthbert v. Virginia,* the court ruled that the "enormous license fee of $1,000" that the assembly had imposed on sellers of detached coupons effectively destroyed the market value of the coupons and was therefore an unconstitutional impairment of the obligations of contract.[49] In *Ex Parte Brown,* the court ruled that the law (by then incorporated in the Code of 1887 as Section 415) prohibiting use of coupons older than one year was an unconstitutional impairment of the obligations of contract.[50]

On the other hand, in *Hucles v. Childrey* the Supreme Court ruled at the same time that the Virginia law requiring payment in lawful money rather than in coupons for a license to sell alcohol was acceptable under the contracts clause because its purpose was in part regulatory.[51] And in *Vashon v. Greenhow,* on an appeal from the 1886 decision of the Supreme Court of Appeals, the Supreme Court ruled that the section of the revenue law adopted on 15 March 1884, requiring payment of school taxes with lawful money, was in compliance with and in fact required by the state constitution to raise money that could be spent on the schools.[52]

At the end of the Supreme Court's long decision on those cases, Bradley appended an exasperated comment. "It is certainly to be wished," he wrote, "that some arrangement may be adopted which will be satisfactory to all the parties concerned, and relieve the courts, as well as the Commonwealth of Virginia, whose name and history recall so many interesting associations, from all further exhibitions of a controversy that has become a vexation and a regret."[53]

9 THE OLCOTT ACT OF 1892

After the Supreme Court declared most of the state's anti-coupon laws unconstitutional in 1890, the final acts in the saga of the Virginia debt controversy began. William L. Royall later claimed sole personal credit through the numerous lawsuits he filed in state and federal courts for eventually forcing Virginia to renegotiate the debt settlement yet again and pass still another—the final—funding bill.[1] He probably exaggerated his personal importance. His legal challenges to the coupons had invalidated most of the anti-coupon legislation but left remnants of the 1882 Coupon Killer No. 1 and the 1887 Coupon Crusher in force. His first attack on Coupon Killer No. 1 and his two attacks on the Coupon Crusher had failed. *In Re Ayers* in 1887 became a jurisdictional case unrelated to the constitutionality of the Coupon Crusher, and the Supreme Court merely commented on but evaded the question of its constitutionality in *McGahey v. Virginia* in 1890. Moreover, the creditors made their preliminary overture to the state, and the General Assembly created the Virginia Debt Commission before, rather than after, the Supreme Court invalidated the anti-coupon laws. Nevertheless, Royall's role was so prominent that Attorney General R. Taylor Scott wrote in his annual report late in 1891, "*Truce* was declared between *Mr. Royall,* counsel for the '*English bondholders,*' and myself, pending the effort to adjust the 'public debt,' but contention and strife continues over coupons *in the cities,* especially between tax-paying citizens and the Commonwealth."[2]

Taxpayers continued to demand and often win trials to verify the authenticity of coupons or to sue for damages after attempting to pay with coupons and then having their property seized and sold for non-payment. Late in 1892 the attorney general included in his annual report an impatient comment on the continuing litigation and public dissatisfaction.

"Some of *our own people, especially taxpayers in the cities,*" Scott wrote, "continue to tender coupons, and complain grievously of *'the jury statute,'*"—the Coupon Killer—"its expense and burdens, but fail to apply the remedy always at hand—*let the coupon severely alone.* Then, and not until then, will the Commonwealth be at peace, and, as is her sovereign right, control the funds in her treasury."[3]

The Supreme Court's stated wish that the whole business should be finally settled operated as intended, as an invitation impossible to decline for people like Governor Philip Watkins McKinney, who initially had appeared reluctant to enter new talks with the bondholders, as well as for the principal bondholders, who had gained little or nothing as a result of the *McGahey* case. Following that decision, nobody had anything to win by continuing the judicial contests, but everybody had something to lose by not agreeing to a mutually satisfactory final settlement. The state could not get rid of the coupons, which threatened the treasury with renewed deficits and even made it difficult to pay the interest; the owners of the bonds could not sell the coupons for a reasonable profit because they were down to about 20 percent of their face value; and both parties continued to spend money in litigation that returned them nothing.

The only remaining winners were the coupon brokers, but some of them also stood to lose. Edwin Parsons, the New Yorker who had lost one of the Virginia Coupon Cases in 1885, had continued to purchase detached 1871 and 1879 coupons and contracted with Virginia taxpayers to pay their taxes with the coupons. He made money on the difference between the price he paid for the coupons and the price he charged taxpayers for paying their taxes. In 1894, while in possession of about fifty thousand dollars' worth of matured coupons, Parsons sought an order from the federal court to force the treasurers of Petersburg, Richmond, and Norfolk to accept the coupons. Judge Charles Henry Simonton, of South Carolina, presiding in the absence of ailing Judge Robert W. Hughes, ruled in *Edwin Parsons v. C. A. Slaughter, C. H. Phillips, and W. W. Hunter* that Parsons did not have standing because he was not a Virginia taxpayer and therefore had nothing to lose when the treasurers refused to accept coupons he had purchased for paying other people's taxes. The judge dismissed the case.[4]

The state and the bondholders had fought to a standstill. Following the Supreme Court's *McGahey* decision, a group of New York financiers had organized a six-member committee to act in the interests of the bondholders and seek a final, mutually acceptable settlement. The chair was

Frederic P. Olcott, a New York banker, Democrat, and former comptroller of that state. The Council of the Corporation of Foreign Bondholders yielded leadership to Olcott's committee and no doubt against the wishes of some of the English creditors temporarily suspended sponsorship of litigation against the anti-coupon laws. The New York bankers were willing to settle for a new financing plan that would resume interest payments and secure eventual payment of the principal the Riddleberger Act had promised to pay. That too disappointed at least some of the English bondholders, but it brought about a final settlement.[5]

In April 1891 Olcott's committee wrote to McKinney offering to open fresh negotiations with the debt commission. Early in June and again in November, the committee submitted proposals designed to complete what the Riddleberger Act of 1882 had begun but what the legal complications about the tax-receivable coupons had prevented, namely, replace all the outstanding 1871 and 1879 bonds with new bonds on which Virginia could and would pay both the interest and the principal and also put a stop to the payment of taxes with coupons. Under the leadership of the Corporation of Foreign Bondholders, so few creditors had exchanged their old bonds for the 1882 bonds that a large majority of the Riddleberger bonds remained in the treasurer's office in Richmond, unissued, as late as 1892. According to calculations published in the debt commission's final report, up to 1891 "only about $4,300,000 of the bonds bearing the troublesome tax-paying coupons have been retired under the Riddleberger Act."[6]

The English creditors had defeated the operations of the Readjusters' refinancing of the debt, but a decade after its passage the creditors finally accepted most of its terms. The debt commission agreed to the proposal that the Olcott committee presented in November and that former president Grover Cleveland and other influential political and financial leaders helped contrive. Governor McKinney heartily endorsed the agreement when he submitted it to the General Assembly on 14 January 1892. "Though the Riddleberger bill was passed ten years ago," he reported, "the debt is still unsettled, and a disagreeable litigation, distressing to the State and unprofitable to the creditors, has been going on, increasing in bitterness and extent each year. It has sorely vexed our people and consumed our revenues; and the State, like a culprit, has been dragged before the courts of the Commonwealth and the inferior and supreme courts of the United States."[7]

The state's American creditors and an appreciable number of its English creditors had been worn down to the point that they reluctantly accepted the much-reduced principal and rate of interest the Riddleberger Act had imposed in 1882, much as the state's Democrats in 1883 had given up on defeating that readjustment of the debt. The creditors even accepted a further reduction in the interest rate for a short time in order to bring about a new settlement. On behalf of the creditors, the Olcott committee promised to obtain and deposit with the state $23 million in 1871 and 1879 bonds in exchange for $19 million in new hundred-year bonds paying 2 percent interest for the first ten years and 3 percent for ninety to cover the balance of the indebtedness that the Riddleberger Act of 1882 had authorized, computed at nineteen twenty-eighths of the principal established at that time. With most or all of the old coupon bonds safely in the offices of the sinking fund, the problem of tax-receivable coupons would at last be crushed. It was true that the state would pay the bondholders more interest during the hundred-year term of the new bonds than on the fifty-year Riddleberger bonds, but the initial annual cost to the state would be less. McKinney estimated that tax revenue was adequate to allow the state to pay the full interest on the new bonds. The proposed settlement could save Virginia more than $91,000 annually during the first decade, which would permit the state to purchase some of its own debt and thereby further reduce the amount of money required to pay the increased rate on the remnant thereafter.[8] The bondholders gained too. They were confident that they would receive interest payments again and that the principal would eventually be paid, and they could reasonably anticipate that the market value of the bonds would increase in the meantime.

McKinney told the General Assembly with satisfaction that because the bondholders "have sent to us their agents with their proposition, and we have accepted it, and are prepared to comply with the terms of the settlement on our part, the odium of repudiation does not rest on us, and when charged against Virginia is false and slanderous." Moreover, "the coupon vendor will find no sale for his depreciated currency among our patriotic tax-payers, and the coupon will become as worthless as the shinplaster of a past generation,"[9] referring to the essentially valueless paper currency that had been called by that derisory name earlier in the nineteenth century. In boasting that the Olcott committee had proposed terms of settlement to Virginia that absolved the state of any responsibility for repudiation of part of the state's debt, McKinney deliberately ignored the partial repudiations that the assembly had made in the 1870s, when it reduced interest rates several times, and again in 1882, when it reduced the interest rate again and also significantly reduced the amount of principal to be paid. But by 1892 the creditors were finally willing to swallow the losses they could not hope to recover in order to salvage the remainder.

The members of the General Assembly were eager to agree to the Olcott committee's proposal. Within a week of receiving McKinney's long letter of endorsement, together with the much longer official report of the debt commission, which contained the texts of all the correspondence and negotiation documents, the Senate of Virginia by a vote of 33 to 0 and the House of Delegates by an unrecorded voice vote endorsed the agreement.[10] Both houses speedily passed what contemporaries dubbed the Olcott Act, and McKinney signed it on 20 February 1892. Perhaps because of the skillful legal draftsmanship of the Olcott committee's attorneys and banking experts, the text of the law exhibited none of the inadvertent internal inconsistencies or omissions that had characterized some of the earlier funding bills and anti-coupon laws.

The law made the Olcott committee responsible for obtaining and depositing with the state $23 million in bonds issued under the funding acts of 1871 and 1879 and for distributing the new hundred-year bonds—soon to be called "century bonds"—to the owners of the old bonds. At the time of the exchange, the state would issue $19 million in new hundred-year bonds paying 2 percent interest for ten years and then 3 percent interest for ninety years. The law exempted some Virginia bonds that the U.S. government and some of the state's colleges and universities then owned, and it specifically prohibited any funding of the one-third of the original principal that Virginia had insisted since 1871 was West Virginia's proper portion. As in the past, the state issued new deferred certificates stating that West Virginia's portion would be provided for after the conclusion of an agreement between the two states.

The new bonds replaced the 1871 and 1879 bonds at the same rates of exchange established in the Riddleberger Act of 1882. The state retained an option to redeem any part or all of the bonds after fifteen years. The law exempted the new bonds from taxation and did not permit the coupons to be used to pay taxes, but it allowed taxpayers who still had old coupons that had previously been tendered in payment of taxes to use them as lawful payment of taxes for a limited time. It also included clear procedures for exchanging the old bonds and registering the new. The law declared the printing plates for the new bonds to be the property of the state, and it repealed the Riddleberger Act and the amendments to it adopted in August and November 1884.[11]

The state and its creditors being, at last, jointly committed to the success of a practical new plan for paying the interest and principal of the old debt and putting a stop to the payment of too large a part of the state's taxes with coupons, the Olcott committee did its part, and the state prepared to do its part.[12] The resolution of the problems with the coupons and the negotiation of the new debt settlement coincided with and was probably in part a consequence of a period of increased prosperity in Virginia that significantly improved the condition of the state treasury. When McKinney made his last report to the General Assembly in December 1893, shortly before the conclusion of his term, he boasted, "I am gratified to be able to say that our financial condition is better than it has been for many years, and it is steadily improving. Our revenue is now ample to meet the regular expenses of the government, sustain the asylums, aid institutions of learning, and continue the present liberal appropriations to the public free schools, pay the interest on the public debt, and provide for our Confederate veterans." During his four years in office, the state's revenue had increased by almost half a million dollars, about 20 percent. Moreover, McKinney went on, "The State debt has been settled to the satisfaction of our creditors," and more than $24.5 million in old bonds—well in excess of the required $23 million—had been exchanged and more could be if the assembly would amend the law to allow a little more time. He so recommended, and he also advised the assembly to authorize the commissioners of the sinking fund to purchase as many state bonds as possible "so that there shall be no increase in the amount to be paid in meeting the 3 per cent. interest when it falls due."[13]

On 31 January 1894 the assembly amended the Olcott Act to allow the extra time for exchanging bonds as McKinney had suggested,[14] and on 12 February it authorized the sinking fund to purchase state bonds issued under the Riddleberger and Olcott Acts to withdraw them from circulation and make it unnecessary to pay interest on them.[15] On 21 February the assembly repealed all the laws requiring and governing the trials that the Coupon Killers, the Coupon Crusher, and the other anti-coupon legislation required for determining whether coupons submitted for payment of taxes were genuine.[16]

One more case—the final one—in the long sequence of important court cases relating to Virginia coupons arose shortly after the General Assembly adopted the Olcott Act but well before it repealed the anti-coupon laws. In 1892 two men and two business firms in Norfolk presented matured 1871 and 1879 coupons to the city in payment of their real estate taxes (but not the school tax) and also paid the full amount of the tax then due in money and demanded a jury trial, as Coupon Killer No. 1 required, to determine whether the coupons were genuine. The jury ruled that the coupons were tax-receivable, but the local commonwealth's attorney, with the assistance of the attorney general, appealed the decision to the Supreme Court of Appeals. On 15 March 1894, with one dissent (but no dissenting opinion), Judge Robert Alexander Richardson delivered the court's opinion in *Commonwealth v. McCullough* and overturned Judge Wood Bouldin's 1872 opinion in *Antoni v. Wright*. The court declared that the provisions of the funding acts of 1871 and 1879 making the coupons tax-receivable for all purposes violated Article VIII, Sections 7 and 8, of the Constitution of 1869.

Richardson rested his argument in part on the rationale of Waller Redd Staples's dissent in *Antoni* but primarily on the authority of the 1886 opinion of the Supreme Court of Appeals in *Greenhow v. Vashon* and the 1890 opinions of the Supreme Court of the United States in *Vashon v. Greenhow* and in *Hucles v. Childrey,* decided along with *McGahey v. Virginia.* In those cases, the state's and the country's highest appellate courts had determined that the state's constitution required, or permitted the General Assembly to require, payment of school taxes and liquor license fees in lawful money only. Richardson concluded that the provisions in the two funding acts that made coupons receivable for all taxes were inconsistent with those rulings and therefore unconstitutional.

Twenty-two years after Bouldin's opinion and Staples's dissent, the Supreme Court of Appeals adopted the rationale of Staples's dissent as the law of Virginia: the tax-receivable coupon provisions of the funding acts of 1871 and 1879 violated the state constitution; the exchange of old bonds for new under those laws did not create a valid contract of which the coupons were a part, inasmuch as nothing of value had then changed hands, so there was no constitutionally protected contract that the assembly could not modify; the General Assembly had no constitutional authority to pass a law or create a contract that prohibited a later assembly from repealing or changing it; and the state constitution required that taxes paid to support the public schools be paid in lawful money only.

In recalling how the first of the funding acts had been passed, Richardson, like the other Virginia judges before him, wrote a long and impassioned paragraph about the impoverished and vulnerable condition of the state after what he charged the U.S. government had done to it during the Civil War and Congressional Reconstruction. The people who had proposed and passed the Funding Act of 1871, he wrote, had taken unfair advantage of Virginia and forced the coupon provision—he repeated the popular phrase, "cut worm of the treasury"—on the unsuspecting citizens of the state. If it had not been for "the unfortunate decision by this court in *Antoni v. Wright*," Richardson suggested, "there never could have been any difficulty in the way of a just and equitable adjustment between the State and her creditors," deliberately ignoring or minimizing the importance and complexity of the many political and legal issues that had independently complicated and upset the state's attempts to get out of having to pay part of its debt. And even though "the indebtedness of Virginia has at last been justly, equitably, and satisfactorily settled by the State and her creditors," he wrote, " a small minority of such creditors who hold bonds and coupons, past due and to become due, amounting to about $2,300,000, obstinately hold out and refuse to accept the liberal terms of said settlement, and, with seeming remorseless vindictiveness, continue to harrass the State by a perpetual clamor for the stipulated 'pound of flesh'" in the form of a demand that the state accept their coupons for payment of taxes. That was a decidedly unjudicial and injudicious way for the judge to refer to some of the parties in the case before him.[17]

Richardson concluded his opinion by relying on what he stated were incontestable historical facts. "It should be remembered," he wrote, "that it was the first legislature of Virginia after her restoration to statehood that passed the funding act of 1871"—it was the second session of that assembly. "It was the bounden duty of that body to set apart and protect the school fund which had been solemnly dedicated by the constitution for the benefit of all the people of the commonwealth; but instead of performing the duty thus imposed, that body neglected to do so, and undertook to pledge that fund, with all other taxes, to the payment of coupons. No act more flagrantly illegal was ever perpetrated by any legislative body." Although what Richardson then wrote was not in every respect entirely accurate, it was consistent with how the Funding Act of 1871 was often characterized then and thereafter in political discourse, and that characterization eventually passed into the state's folklore and historical consciousness. "It is as well understood as any historical fact of the times," he concluded, "though not as readily susceptible of complete proof, that the funding act of 1871 was a huge fraud palmed upon the State in her poverty and distress. We are fully sensible of the fact that these things ordinarily should find no place in judicial opinions, but, as a part of the history of this long vexed subject, they may serve somewhat the purpose of vindicating the old commonwealth from the many aspersions attempted to be cast upon her good name."[18]

The principal taxpayer in the case, A. A. McCullough (no relation to Hugh McCulloch, for whom the 1879 funding act was named), and his attorneys appealed Richardson's decision to the Supreme Court of the United States. After a very long delay during which attempts of other people to pay taxes with coupons fell off noticeably,[19] the justices finally heard oral arguments on two days in February 1898 and issued their decision in *McCullouch v. Virginia* on 5 December of that year. Associate Justice David A. Brewer prefaced his opinion with an understatement. "Perhaps no litigation has been more severely contested," he wrote, "or has presented more intricate and troublesome questions, than that which has arisen under the coupon legislation of Virginia. That legislation has been prolific of many cases, both in the state and federal courts, not a few of which finally came to this Court." The decision of the Supreme Court of Appeals in the McCullough case, though, invalidating a key provision of the original Funding Act of 1871, presented an entirely new set of bothersome questions. "Now," Brewer continued, "at the end of 27 years from the passage of the act, we are asked to hold that this guaranty of value, so fortified as it has been, was never of any validity, that the decisions to that effect are of no force, and that all the transactions which have been based thereon rested upon nothing. Such a result is so startling that it at least compels more than ordinary consideration."[20]

Brewer and the other members of the Supreme Court refused to retreat a single step from the court's previous rulings that within the meaning of the Constitution of the United States the coupons were protected contracts that the state could not impair. They also reaffirmed that even though the Supreme Court ordinarily deferred to a state's highest appellate court in interpreting a state's constitution and statutes, the impairment of obligations of contract was an exception to the rule. The Supreme Court in *Vashon v. Greenhow* and in *Hucles v. Childrey* had found valid grounds for the state to require payment of school taxes and liquor license taxes with money and not with coupons, but that did not furnish an excuse for retroactively declaring parts of the original funding act unconstitutional. To do so, Brewer explained, "ignores the difference between the statute and the contract. . . . The statute precedes the contract. Its scope and meaning must be determined before any question will arise as to the validity of the contract which it authorizes." Consequently, "if there were, as it seems there were, certain special taxes and dues which, under the existing provisions of the state constitution, could not be affected by legislative action, the statute is to be read as though it in terms excluded them from its operation."[21]

The court had heard a long argument from the state's counsel that the Supreme Court did not have jurisdiction to hear the appeal because this was in fact no impairment-of-contracts case; all that was at issue was the Virginia court's interpretation of the 1871 and 1879 acts under the Constitution of 1869, not any of the subsequent laws or court cases involving the coupons or anti-coupon laws. Brewer acknowledged that Richardson's opinion "only incidentally refers to statutes passed subsequent to the act of 1871," but that law "gave effect to the subsequent statutes, and it has been repeatedly held by this Court that, in reviewing the judgment of the courts of a state" in such circumstances, the Supreme Court was "not limited to a mere consideration of the language used in the opinion, but may examine and determine what is the real substance and effect of the decision." Brewer concluded that if the judges ignored all the statutes and court cases of the intervening years, that "would be a clear evasion of the duty" that the Supreme Court had to settle the legal issues of the lawsuit before it.[22]

Brewer dismissed an argument that because the 1894 General Assembly had repealed most of the anti-coupon laws after the Supreme Court of Appeals declared the coupon provisions of the two funding acts unconstitutional, there was therefore no longer any legal grounds for the suit or the appeal. He also dismissed the related argument that the local and state officials whom McCullough had sued in 1892 no longer had any legal responsibility to act and McCullough was therefore attempting to sue the state without its consent. On all counts, the Supreme Court overturned the decision of the Virginia Supreme Court of Appeals and rejected the arguments of the state's counsel. Brewer reaffirmed that the coupon clauses of the Funding Act of 1871 and the McCulloch Act of 1879 were constitutional and that the coupons were constitutionally protected contracts between Virginia and the owners of the coupons.[23]

Associate Justice Rufus W. Peckham dissented on a purely jurisdictional issue. Appointed to the Supreme Court after all the earlier coupon cases had been decided, he believed that no federal question had been involved in the trial or appeal in the state courts and that therefore the Supreme Court of the United States had no jurisdiction to review or reverse the Virginia court's ruling. "This Court," he declared, "is not entrusted with the duty of supervising all decisions of state courts to the end that we may see to it that such decisions are never inconsistent, contradictory, or conflicting. We supervise those decisions only when a federal question arises."[24]

Peckham had a point, but it was a limited one and ignored what the important changes in the state's public law had meant to Virginia's taxpayers and its bondholders. The Readjuster judges of the Virginia Supreme Court of Appeals had issued rulings on contract and coupon cases that were inconsistent with decisions that their Conservative predecessors had issued. Some of those decisions were also inconsistent with decisions of the Supreme Court of the United States on the important federal question whether the coupons from 1871 and 1879 bonds were constitutionally protected contracts. In that, however, the Readjuster judges did not behave very differently from the Democrats in the General Assembly, who had enacted many more laws to obstruct payment of taxes with coupons than the few the Readjusters had passed. The Democrats clearly designed their laws to empower the state's public officials to sabotage what the Supreme Court declared were the constitutionally protected rights of coupon owners and to evade obeying the court's rulings. State and local prosecutors, tax collectors, treasurers, and other officials had got away with enforcing the laws in spite of rulings of the Supreme Court of the United States. Peckham ignored most of the historical context and the consequences of the decision from which he dissented.

The attorney general of Virginia at the time of the Supreme Court's *McCullough* decision, Andrew Jackson Montague, acknowledged that the state lost on every point. With respect to the 1871 and 1879 coupon bonds, he reported sadly that "no remedy seems to be left the State save to refuse to pay the principal of the bonds at maturity, upon such terms as she may demand; for when the maturity of these bonds is reached, the matter will then be entirely within the control of the State as to the principal."[25] Nobody could sue the state without its consent to compel payment of the principal. However, by then the Olcott Act appeared to be operating very much to Virginia's advantage, and it withdrew most of the bonds with tax-receivable coupons from circulation. Governor J. Hoge Tyler dismissed as an insignificant problem the small residue of outstanding bonds with tax-receivable coupons. In large part because of the Olcott settlement, the state's new century bonds had become, as the governor put it, "popular as an investment and have increased in market value. Our own people are already large holders of these bonds and will, I think, in a short time absorb the debt."[26]

Soon after adoption of the Olcott Act in 1892, and long before the *McCullough* decision in 1898, the Olcott committee and the General Assembly, acting in a spirit of relieved cooperation, agreed to make a few small modifications to the 1892 law in order to allow extra time for people to exchange old bonds for new bonds and to permit the holders of some coupons to pay taxes with them for a short interval.[27] The Olcott settlement worked and brought an end to all the political divisions concerning the debt, accusations of repudiation or bad faith, and major lawsuits over coupons. Payment of taxes with coupons had dropped to less than one thousand dollars annually by the early years of the twentieth century.[28] The state's purchase of its own bonds also enabled it to keep interest payments and contributions to the sinking fund well within the state's ability to pay in spite of the severe national economic depression that began in the year after the assembly adopted the Olcott Act. At the end of December 1901, when the interest rate was scheduled to rise from 2 percent to 3 percent, the governor reported that the market value of the state's bonds had recently risen from about 70 percent of face value to par.[29] And in that circumstance the long-suffering owners of the bonds could sell them for much more than they could ever have hoped to obtain before passage of the Olcott Act.

Almost every governor's message to the General Assembly from the mid-1860s through the early 1890s contained long lamentations about the problems the public debt created, but following implementation of the Olcott Act the issue disappeared from political debate and also from public view. Governors thereafter seldom ever mentioned the debt at all unless to express satisfaction with the rate at which the state was purchasing and retiring the bonds and thereby reducing the outstanding principal and payments on the interest. In 1906, four years before the Olcott Act required that a portion of the state's property tax receipts be annually paid into the sinking fund to retire the principal, the assembly increased the fund's annual appropriation for purchasing bonds from $42,000 to $74,000 to accelerate the retirement of the debt.[30]

In 1936 the General Assembly adopted the last funding act. It authorized the sinking fund to issue new bonds up to the amount of $11.75 million at the lowest available rate of interest in order to purchase all the outstanding Riddleberger and Olcott bonds.[31] That enabled the state to retire the last of the debt with a payment of about four hundred thousand dollars in 1944.[32] The closing of the books on the old antebellum debt attracted almost no notice. The decades of raucous political controversies, financial headaches, and prolonged litigation were all two or three generations in the past. The final payments were so anticlimactic and involved such a relatively small sum of money that they did not remind very many people of all the tumults and difficulties that the many problems arising from trying to pay off the antebellum debt had once produced. And by then the other problem, the share of the old debt that Virginia had always insisted West Virginia should pay, had also been resolved to Virginia's advantage.

10 UNFINISHED BUSINESS

The 1893–94 session of the General Assembly, which repealed all the anti-coupon laws to smooth the way for payment of the state debt under the Olcott Act, also acted on two issues left over from the Democrats' destruction of the Readjuster Party and one other concerning the debt.

Early in January 1894, fifty-one weeks before the twelve-year terms of all five Readjuster judges on the Virginia Supreme Court of Appeals expired, the General Assembly elected five well-known Democrats to take their places at the end of the year. After the new judges took office in January 1895, the Richmond Bar Association threw a lavish banquet "as a compliment to the new Supreme Court of Appeals." More than two hundred of the region's leading social and legal luminaries attended and listened to a long oration about the glories of the state's legal elite, beginning with an encomium for the Readjusters' predecessors. "Of this able court," all but two of whom had by then died, recalled John Randolph Tucker, the former attorney general of the Confederate state of Virginia, "the record of their decisions conveys an estimate which makes them worthy of their honored predecessors. Their praise is voiced by the profession for learning, ability, and integrity." He deliberately chose to say nothing about the recent Readjuster judges and in effect deleted those judges, that court, and twelve years of jurisprudence from Virginia's legal history.[1]

The second thing the assembly did in 1894 was make changes to the state's election laws. The 1884 Anderson-McCormick election law had worked to the advantage of the Democrats by suppressing the number of African Americans elected to public office. Eight African Americans served in the General Assembly in 1884, but only six won seats in the assembly in 1885, seven in 1887, and in 1889 only four. They were the last black legislators in Virginia until 1968, and by the end of the 1890s very few

African Americans still held local offices anywhere in the state. Republicans in Congress had by then largely given up trying to force Southern states to abide by either the letter or the spirit of the Fifteenth Amendment, allowing white men in Virginia and most other Southern states to exclude most African Americans from politics. Such measures as the Anderson-McCormick Act had worked as intended.

In other respects, however, the Anderson-McCormick Act had not worked as well as intended. Republican candidates continued to receive more than 40 percent of the vote in most gubernatorial and presidential elections. So long as Republicans remained that strong, the threat to white supremacy and elite government that the Readjuster-Republican coalition had posed could revive. Violence, fraud, cheating, and other undemocratic actions became so notorious that in 1894 the assembly again reformed voting practices.

Ever since the introduction of voting by ballot in Virginia in the 1860s, candidates or political parties had distributed to voters ballots with candidates' names printed on them—sometimes a separate ballot for each office, sometimes a party ticket with all the party's candidates for an electoral district. The so-called Walton Act, adopted in 1894, changed the method of voting and introduced the secret, or Australian, ballot to Virginia for the first time. That deprived poll workers and others of the ability to switch ballots or fold several ballots together and stuff ballot boxes with them. After passage of the Walton Act, the state provided ballots with all candidates' names printed on them and required voters to draw a line "though three-fourths of the length of the name" of every candidate that the voter wanted to vote against.[2] That created a new form of corruption, because it left Democratic vote counters a wide leeway to decide that a Republican voter had not drawn a long enough line through the name of a Democratic candidate or that a Democratic voter had drawn a long enough line through the name of a Republican candidate. The Walton Act did nothing to reduce the other forms of corruption, such as bribing or threatening voters.[3]

The new law further reduced the number of African American voters, who were almost all Republicans, more than it did the number of white voters, because African Americans were proportionally more likely to be illiterate than white men and therefore unable to mark ballots as they wished. Illiteracy remained high for both races, but it was higher for African Americans because of the state's and many of the localities' discriminatory pinch-penny appropriations for the public schools.

The third step the assembly took in 1894 revived an important component of the debt controversy that had remained dormant for more than two decades. The legislators debated how to try to obtain some payment from West Virginia for the portion of the antebellum debt that Virginia had always maintained was that state's responsibility.[4] The new governor, Charles T. O'Ferrall,[5] intervened in the debates two days before the assembly session concluded and reminded the legislators that the certificates Virginia had issued with each round of bonds—the so-called Virginia Deferred Certificates, the name indicating that West Virginia's part of the debt would be paid after the two states had agreed on West Virginia's proper portion—became part of Virginia's contract with its creditors. He requested that the assembly name commissioners to open negotiations with West Virginia to obtain payment for the creditors.

"It is an obligation which perhaps cannot be enforced," O'Ferrall admitted, "but it is nevertheless a moral obligation" that Virginia "cannot in honor to herself disregard." Because Virginia had issued the certificates representing one-third of the debt of the old state of Virginia, the new state of Virginia might be held partly responsible for securing payment of that debt for the certificate holders. "A compliance with the contract and the keeping faith with her creditors, I think," the governor continued, "should prompt Virginia, now that she has settled her part of the debt, to go forward and effect an adjustment with her late co-contractor and now her sister State, and turn over to the creditors, let it be little or much, whatever she may receive, in full exoneration of all obligations, statutory or moral, which may rest upon her."[6]

The legislators created a new seven-member Virginia Debt Commission composed of three members of each house and one member appointed by the governor. The assembly "authorized and directed" the commissioners "to negotiate with the state of West Virginia a settlement and adjustment of the proportion of the public debt of the original state of Virginia proper to be borne by West Virginia." It prohibited the commissioners from opening negotiations until "the holders of a majority in amount of said certificates" approved, and it made any agreement the commissioners reached with West Virginia subject to the future approval or disapproval of the General Assembly.[7]

Much as the Olcott committee had acted as an agent for the state's creditors at the beginning of the 1890s, officers of the First National Bank of New York began taking the certificates on deposit under letters of agreement with the owners that authorized the bankers to negotiate on their behalf for payment of the debt. By December 1894 they had gained control of certificates worth nearly $10 million and notified the commission. The commission members concluded an agreement with the bankers to cooperate with them in seeking payment from West Virginia. The agreement stipulated that the bankers and owners of the certificates "will accept the amount as ascertained by the Commission to be paid by the State of West Virginia in full settlement of their claims."[8]

On 7 January 1895 O'Ferrall wrote to the governor of West Virginia, William A. McCorkle, to inform him of the agreement between the commission and the bankers. O'Ferrall explained that "there was no disposition whatever upon the part of Virginia to interfere with the prerogative of the Executive and Legislature of West Virginia to deal with the question as to them may seem proper. Virginia has simply endeavored to remove the difficulties which appear to have been in the way, and to place it within the power of West Virginia to make a satisfactory adjustment. . . . Now, submitting the whole matter, and expressing the hope that this question which has so long been a subject of discussion and a source of more or less embarrassment to both States, will be speedily determined and finally settled."[9]

The Virginia commissioners then invited the Legislature of West Virginia to appoint commissioners to negotiate with them,[10] but West Virginians had long since shed any residue of embarrassment about the antebellum debt. In fact, they had good reasons to resent references in the financial literature to the Virginia Deferred Certificates as West Virginia's public debt, and they blamed the actions of the Virginians that had created that misunderstanding and consequent misrepresentation.[11] The Corporation of Foreign Bondholders had begun characterizing the deferred certificates as West Virginia debt as early as 1879 and by 1889 declared the unfunded certificates to be a default by the government of West Virginia.[12] By a brief and frosty joint resolution the West Virginia Legislature refused to negotiate.[13]

The commission's report to the next session of the Virginia General Assembly in January 1896 was gloomy in tone and contained no recommendations for what to do next.[14] The following year the West Virginia Legislature declared in even stronger terms that "West Virginia does not owe one cent of the so called 'Virginia debt,' and that this Legislature is opposed to any negotiations on that subject."[15] The members of the Virginia Debt Commission, lacking any new ideas or opportunities for acting, did not even meet during the next four years.[16] In the meantime, though, another group of New York bankers under the leadership of John Crosby Brown, chair of the board of Brown Brothers & Company, formed a new committee in 1898 to act on behalf of the certificate holders. On 5 February 1900 Brown informed the Virginia Debt Commission that his committee had secured certificates worth more than $8 million and that the owners had authorized the committee to cooperate with the commission in seeking payment.[17]

The members of the Virginia Debt Commission recommended to the General Assembly of Virginia that "some officials or public functionaries of the State should be empowered by the General Assembly to take such action or institute such proceedings as may appear to be necessary to protect the State's interest." They proposed joint legal action on behalf of the state and the owners of the certificates if at least two-thirds of the 1871 certificates (excepting those the state continued to hold) and "at least a majority of all the other certificates" could be deposited under the commission's control "with the guarantee on the part of the holders of the certificates" that they would accept whatever they could jointly obtain from West Virginia "in full settlement of the one-third of the debt of the original State of Virginia, which has not been assumed by the present State of Virginia."[18]

The General Assembly authorized the Virginia Debt Commission and the attorney general to act in cooperation with representatives of the certificate holders to "institute such proceedings on behalf of the state as may in the judgment of said commission and attorney-general be needful and proper to protect the interest of the state and bring about and carry into effect a settlement."[19] The West Virginians again refused to negotiate, and the state's legislature declared bluntly that it "declines and refuses to take any action in regard to what is known as the Virginia Debt, or Virginia Deferred Certificates," and that "the State of West Virginia is in no way obligated for the payment of any portion of the said debt, or certificates."[20] The Virginia commissioners continued to press for a settlement and on 2 September 1902 appointed the state's new attorney general, William A. Anderson,[21] counsel to the commission.[22] Two weeks later they revised and renewed the agreement with Brown's committee.[23] The West Virginia Legislature at its next session in January 1903 reaffirmed in unequivocal language that the state did not "owe any part of the so-called Virginia debt" and that "this Legislature is opposed to any negotiations whatsoever on that subject."[24]

Two years later, though, perhaps as a consequence of the threat of a lawsuit, the Senate of West Virginia agreed to hear what the Virginia Debt Commission had to say.[25] On 1 February 1905 the commission member Randolph Harrison addressed the legislators at length. He recounted the creation of the debt; the actions of the West Virginia conventions, of the General Assembly of the Restored Government of Virginia, and of Congress when admitting West Virginia to the Union; and the provisions of the West Virginia Constitution of 1863, by which the new state had assumed a responsibility to pay its proper portion of the debt of the original state. After reciting the early failed attempts at negotiations, Harrison urged the state senators to accept the legal and moral responsibility that the Virginia commissioners believed West Virginia had to pay the original state's creditors. The commissioners had calculated that the value of the outstanding Virginia Deferred Certificates issued under the authority of the various Virginia funding acts was then almost $15.5 million.[26]

Harrison's appeal to the senators had no effect. The West Virginia Legislature again refused to acknowledge that the state had any responsibility to pay any part of the debt or to negotiate with the Virginia Debt Commission.[27] That appeared to leave Virginia with no other option but to sue West Virginia to force that state to pay the owners of the certificates and thereby extinguish any residual claim against Virginia that they might assert. Early in 1904, though, the Supreme Court of the United States had issued a decision in a case that exhibited some of the same characteristics of the claim that Virginia and the owners of the Virginia Deferred Certificates had against West Virginia, and the aftermath of that decision appeared to place Virginia in jeopardy.

That case also involved state bonds. North Carolina had issued bonds to subsidize construction of a railroad, much as Virginia had issued bonds to purchase stock in and subsidize construction of railroads. In dealing with its own debt problems after the Civil War, North Carolina had defaulted on payment of those bonds. Some owners of the bonds had deeded them to the state of South Dakota, which had then sued North Carolina for payment. The legal and constitutional issues in that case were not all relevant to the Virginia–West Virginia debt, but in *South Dakota v. North Carolina* the Supreme Court by a majority of 5 to 4 ruled in favor of the South Dakota claim for payment of the North Carolina bonds it owned. That decision established that the court's original jurisdiction in suits between states included suits for payment of such a debt as the antebellum North Carolina bonds represented.[28]

What were the implications for Virginia and West Virginia? Could that decision make Virginia liable on its own or jointly with West Virginia for paying the part of the old debt that the deferred certificates represented? The Virginia Debt Commission and the Brown committee had repeatedly renewed their agreement to cooperate in seeking payment from West Virginia, but a few owners of deferred certificates had retained their certificates and not been party to the agreements. The *South Dakota v. North Carolina* decision could provide an alternative way for them to force payment. Some of the certificate holders appeared to be contemplating deeding some of their certificates to South Dakota or perhaps to some other state so that it could sue Virginia and / or West Virginia to compel each or both to pay the principal and interest. A successful suit against either state or both could provide a method by which the owners of the certificates could force either state or both states to pay the debt through a third state's treasury. As it turned out, South Dakota never tried to collect on the North Carolina bonds, but the mere possibility that it could aid the owners of Virginia Deferred Certificates might raise the prices of the certificates on the open market and allow the owners to sell them for a profit. The case could also provide a precedent by which the certificate holders could demand that the states pay them directly.

Attorney General Anderson consequently concluded in the autumn of 1905, "This matter has assumed an acute, and, from some points of view, a grave aspect." More than "six-sevenths of each and every class of all the deferred Virginia certificates" were by then under the joint control of the commission and the committee or were promised under conditions that authorized the commission on behalf of Virginia to sue West Virginia for payment. Under the agreements in effect, the Brown committee promised to pay all the costs of the lawsuit because the owners of the certificates would be "the chief beneficiaries." The certificate owners had also agreed "to accept such adjudication against West Virginia" as a full and final settlement of their claims and "thereupon release Virginia from any liability on account of said certificates, except as trustee." Anderson promised that just as soon as 90 percent of the certificates were securely under the joint control of the commission and committee, he would file suit against West Virginia on behalf of Virginia and the committee.[29] The owners of the certificates would be the principal beneficiaries of the suit if it was successful, but Virginia's literary and sinking funds together owned nearly $3 million worth of 1871 certificates, so the state also stood to gain and was a genuine principal in the case and not merely acting as a joint trustee with the committee on behalf of the actual owners of the bulk of the certificates. On 24 November 1905 the Virginia Debt Commission authorized the attorney general to file the suit.[30]

Anderson filed a suit in equity against West Virginia in the Supreme Court of the United States on 5 March 1906.[31] Article III, Section 2, Paragraph 2, of the Constitution of the United States granted the Supreme Court original jurisdiction in "Controversies between two or more States." Such cases were an uncommon but regular part of the court's work. They often involved boundary disputes or the interpretation or enforcement of the terms of interstate compacts. In fact, Virginia had sued West Virginia in the Supreme Court late in the 1860s in an unsuccessful attempt to block West Virginia's annexation of Berkeley and Jefferson Counties. But this case was not that simple, and the jurisdictional issues as well as the legal and constitutional issues the counsel for both states, the attorneys for the certificate holders, and the judges had to sort through and settle were complex and subtle. So, too, was the question whether or how the Supreme Court could compel compliance if it issued a judgment declaring West Virginia liable for payment.

Those questions were not new. Back in 1878, when Bradley T. Johnson was a member of the Senate of Virginia and fighting hard for full implementation of the Funding Act of 1871, he had published a learned treatise in the *American Law Review* entitled "Can States Be Compelled to Pay Their Debts?" The doctrine of sovereign immunity protected states from being sued without their consent, which meant that no owners of bonds or certificates residing anywhere could sue Virginia in state or federal court to force it to pay the principal or interest on its bonds. That was how the state got a free pass after 1872, when it first reduced the interest it paid from 6 percent to 4 percent annually, and later when it stopped all payments of interest on 1871 and 1878 bonds. "It has generally been conceded," Johnson wrote in a sentence that is worth repeating, "that State debts rest alone on the faith of the State creating them, and that no remedy exists, under the American system of government, by which the States can be compelled to perform their contracts."[32] The Supreme Court restated the doctrine of sovereign immunity in an 1890 case that also involved state bonds and whether or how federal courts could compel states to pay the principal or interest. In *Hans v. Louisiana* the judges wrote that at the time of the adoption of the Constitution, the "suability of a State without its consent was a thing unknown to the law. This has been so often laid down and acknowledged by courts and jurists that it is hardly necessary to be formally asserted. . . . It is enough for us to declare its existence."[33]

The only exception was the Constitution's grant of original jurisdiction to the Supreme Court to decide controversies between states. But how could the judges, if they determined that a state government had impaired obligations of contract or had established a legal claim for compensation from another state government, compel a legislature to pay an obligation? A state government, unlike a person or a corporation, had little or no non-governmental property that officers of a court could seize and sell for the benefit of a creditor; and there was no judicial precedent for a court coercing a state legislature to obey a judicial order requiring the legislators to appropriate money to pay a creditor or to raise a tax to provide the money. "The legislative department of a State," the Supreme Court declared in *Hans v. Louisiana,* "represents its polity and its will, and is called upon by the highest demands of natural and political law to preserve justice and judgment, and to hold inviolate the public obligations. Any departure from this rule, except for reasons most cogent (of which the legislature, and not the courts, is the judge), never fails in the end to incur the odium of the world and to bring lasting injury upon the State itself. But to deprive the legislature of the power of judging what the honor and safety of the State may require, even at the expense of a temporary failure to discharge the public debts, would be attended with greater evils than such failure can cause."[34] The Supreme Court refused to threaten state legislatures with decrees it might not have the means to enforce. To do so would demean the dignity of a state and the elected representatives of its citizens and also expose the essential impotence of the federal judiciary, which had few or no means of implementing or enforcing such a decree.

Bradley T. Johnson may have had in mind the unfunded portion of the antebellum debt of Virginia—the third of the original principal that the Virginia Deferred Certificates represented—when he wrote in his *American Law Review* article that it was "clear that a State has the right . . . to sue another State in the Supreme Court for debts due to the citizens of the complainant State."[35] Five years later, though, the Supreme Court ruled that Johnson's conclusion was in error. Because the Eleventh Amendment denied jurisdiction to federal courts in suits between a state and a person residing in another state, the legislatures of New Hampshire and New York had enacted laws empowering their governments to sue the government of Louisiana to force it to pay the interest on Louisiana bonds that citizens of their respective states owned. In 1883, in *New Hampshire v. Louisiana,* the Supreme Court decided that the Eleventh Amendment did not allow the indirect action of a state government using the Supreme Court to sue other states to force them to pay debts owed to their citizens, who were the real creditors.[36]

That decision could easily complicate Virginia's case against West Virginia because even though Virginia owned some certificates and was therefore a legitimate creditor, the state was acting primarily in a fiduciary capacity and as a partner with the Brown committee on behalf of the personal interests of the bankers and the owners of Virginia Deferred Certificates, most of whom were not citizens of Virginia. *New Hampshire v. Louisiana* could provide a precedent for the Supreme Court to decline taking the case *Virginia v. West Virginia.*[37]

Other issues, some of them technical, were also involved, such as whether Virginia's failure for nearly thirty-five years to bring a case against West Virginia fell under the equity rule of laches. That rule held that if an interested party failed for so long and unreasonable a time to attempt to vindicate its asserted rights in court that the ability of the other party to defend its rights was impaired, then a court could not or should not hear the suit.[38] Had Virginia waited too long? If not, was West Virginia in fact liable for a portion of the debt? If so, there were many specific questions to be decided, such as which date to select to establish the original principal—1 January 1861, as stated in the West Virginia Constitution of 1863, or the statehood date of 20 June 1863 being the most obvious; whether to credit either state with taxes paid or tax money expended; how to ascertain the value—the whole real value or the value of its taxable property—of the part of Virginia that became West Virginia; and how to calculate the accrued interest if West Virginia was liable to pay interest too.

11 *VIRGINIA V. WEST VIRGINIA*

Attorney General William A. Anderson probably did not suspect or fear when he filed his bill with the Supreme Court of the United States in the case *Virginia v. West Virginia* on 5 March 1906 that he had begun a litigation that would drag on for thirteen years before it was finally settled in 1919—as long as the political tumults dragged on between the passage of the Funding Act of 1871 and the 1884 Democratic General Assembly's acceptance of the Riddleberger Act. Anderson must have anticipated that the complex financial history and the legal issues involved would produce an extended series of briefs and counterbriefs, but he almost certainly did not anticipate how long the time or how voluminous the record of the case would become. Counsel for West Virginia contested every assertion that counsel for Virginia made, and vice versa, and small armies of attorneys and accountants from both states spent months inspecting tax returns, expenditure reports, treasury and auditors' records, and other documents in the archives in Richmond.[1] Anderson remained involved in the litigation until its conclusion, acting with his successors as co-counsel for the state after the close of his second term as attorney general at the end of 1909.

Anderson was pleased with the bill he filed to commence the suit and printed it in full in his annual report for 1906. He did not there publish the eight bulky supplemental documents that he submitted to the Supreme Court containing details about the origins of the public debt, Virginia's first failed attempts to persuade West Virginia to pay a portion of the principal (an old Confederate veteran, Anderson dated them "at the close of the period of 'destruction and reconstruction'"), the succession of funding acts the General Assembly of Virginia subsequently passed that produced the Virginia Deferred Certificates, and the second round of failed attempts Virginia made to open negotiations during the decade before he filed the suit. Anderson and Holmes Conrad, counsel for the Brown committee and the certificate holders but acting as co-counsel with the attorney general, concluded the bill with a request that the Supreme Court "adjudicate and determine the amount due" from West Virginia to Virginia in its multiple capacities as the successor with West Virginia as creator of the debt, as one of the creditors of the West Virginia portion, and as a fiduciary for the certificate holders.[2]

Clarke E. May, the attorney general of West Virginia, and counsel assisting him filed a brief containing that state's objections to all of Anderson's assertions. They also added arguments denying that the Supreme Court had jurisdiction, because Virginia was in reality suing on behalf of the certificate owners and was not a genuine creditor and also because the judges, having no effective means of enforcing such a decree as Virginia sought, could not or should not take the case.[3] In January 1907, no doubt anticipating a decision favorable to Virginia and the certificate owners, the bankers' committee that had secured custody of most of the Virginia Deferred Certificates transferred to the Virginia Debt Commission physical control of the certificates, together with three notarized copies of the names of the owners of each and every certificate and two keys to the lock boxes in which the certificates were deposited in the vaults of the Central Trust Company of New York.[4]

The Supreme Court heard oral arguments on 11 and 12 March 1907.[5] On 27 May, in the first of eight unanimous opinions all styled *Virginia v. West Virginia,* Chief Justice Melville W. Fuller dismissed most of West Virginia's objections without prejudice to its case. The court reserved until later a decision on whether laches should force it to dismiss Virginia's suit and on West Virginia's objection on the ground of "multifarious plaintiffs," that is, questioning whether Virginia was in fact a fully interested party to the suit or merely seeking to use the Supreme Court's original jurisdiction in suits between states as a method of obtaining a ruling favorable to the actual owners of most of the certificates and thereby ridding itself of any residual liability for funding them.

Most importantly, the Supreme Court ruled that the act of Congress that had admitted West Virginia to statehood, the terms under which the General Assembly of the Restored Government of Virginia had agreed to the admission of West Virginia, and the express declaration in the West Virginia Constitution of 1863—"An equitable proportion of the public debt of the Commonwealth of Virginia, prior to the first day of January in the year one thousand eight hundred and sixty-one, shall be assumed by this State, and the Legislature shall ascertain the same as soon as may be practicable, and provide for the liquidation thereof, by a sinking fund to pay the accruing interest, and redeem the principal within thirty-four years"—together constituted "a constitutional and legal compact between the two states." West Virginia was therefore liable for payment of some portion of the original debt of the original state, as Virginia had asserted.[6]

The next step was to calculate the amount. Following another hearing in which counsel for the two states presented their suggestions, on 4 May 1908 the chief justice issued a decree itemizing the specific subjects that a special master should investigate and ascertain prior to the Supreme Court's issuing its final ruling on what West Virginia's "equitable" portion of the antebellum debt was. The special master's charge included seven subjects:

1. The amount of the public debt of the Commonwealth of Virginia on the first day of January, 1861, stating specifically how and in what form the same was evidenced, by what authority of law, and for what purposes the same was created, and the dates and nature of the bonds or other evidence of said indebtedness.
2. The extent and value of the territory of Virginia and of West Virginia June 20, 1863, and the population thereof, with and without slaves, separately.
3. All expenditures made by the Commonwealth of Virginia within the territory now constituting the State of West Virginia since any part of the debt was contracted.
4. Such proportion of the ordinary expenses of the government of Virginia since any of said debt was contracted, as was properly assignable to the counties which were created into the State of West Virginia, on the basis of the average total population of Virginia, with and without slaves, as shown by the census of the United States.
5. And also on the basis of the fair estimated valuation of the property, real and personal, by counties, of the State of Virginia.
6. All moneys paid into the treasury of the commonwealth from the counties included within the State of West Virginia during the period prior to the admission of the latter state into the Union.
7. The amount and value of all money, property, stocks, and credits which West Virginia received from the Commonwealth of Virginia,

not embraced in any of the preceding items, and not including any
property, stocks, or credits which were obtained or acquired by the
commonwealth after the date of the organization of the restored
government of Virginia, together with the nature and description
thereof.[7]

Shortly thereafter and with the agreement of counsel for both states,
the chief justice appointed Charles E. Littlefield as the special master. A
Republican, Littlefield had served in the Maine legislature and as attorney
general of the state before being elected to the United States House of
Representatives in 1899. At the time of his appointment as special master
he was preparing to resign from Congress to resume the practice of law
in New York.[8] The West Virginians recommended him for the appointment. The Virginians had initially favored other men,[9] but Rosewell Page,
then the second auditor of Virginia, in charge of auditing the accounts of
the public debt, later described Littlefield as "a big-hearted, big brained
American lawyer" with whom he had worked easily. "I have had him at my
home," Page wrote, "and been to his New York home, and can speak of him
from long acquaintance and from an examination of his work in this case,
as a notable factor in the settlement."[10]

Littlefield conducted extended hearings in Richmond in 1908 and
1909. He had the immensely difficult task of comparing the data and con-
clusions that counsel for the two states submitted on every aspect of each
of the seven paragraphs of the decree.[11] In the autumn of 1909, while
Littlefield was still sifting through the records and testimony and compil-
ing his report, Anderson predicted ominously in his last annual report as
attorney general, "We can rest assured that the able and resourceful counsel for West Virginia will make every defense, and interpose every obstacle
in the way of a recovery by Virginia, which the ingenuity and learning of
such skillful and experienced counsel can suggest." Anderson was impatient for the case to be resolved, but he also wisely noted in an exception-
ally long run-on sentence, "In view of the magnitude and complexity of
the case, the great mass of accounts and statements, records, statutes, and
documentary and other evidence covering transactions extending over the
forty years prior to January 1, 1861, and embracing a number of important
transactions since that date, which had to be examined, investigated, and
passed upon, and from which the accounts and schedules representing the
contentions of the parties respectively in the different branches of the case

presented by the seven general accounts directed by the seven paragraphs of the decree, had to be derived, the progress of the case cannot be said to have been, under all the circumstances, unduly retarded."[12]

Littlefield issued his report on 17 March 1910.[13] He calculated that the total public debt of Virginia on 1 January 1861 was $33,897,073.82.[14] He ascertained that 37.3686 percent of the land area of the original state and 36.1843 percent of the total surface area, including the bay and rivers, was in what became West Virginia. He calculated that on 20 June 1863, the date of West Virginia's statehood, 21.7812 percent of the whole value of taxable land, 24.5145 percent of the value of all taxable personal property counting slaves, and 33.5231 percent not counting slaves was in West Virginia.[15]

Littlefield also reported in detail on the amount of money the government of Virginia had spent on internal improvements and for the ordinary expenses of operating the government in the counties and cities that became West Virginia between the creation of the first public indebtedness in 1822 and 1 January 1861. The amount was, as many West Virginians had long said, less than the amount of money Virginia had collected in taxes from that portion of the state.[16] Littlefield included detailed accounts of the value of state property in the counties that became West Virginia and of the amount of taxes that had been paid or would have been paid as of 20 June 1863.[17]

Counsel for one or both states submitted variant figures for almost every one of Littlefield's.[18] After the attorneys representing the two states prepared arguments and compiled data to support their claims and to refute those of their opponents, including objections to some of Littlefield's findings, they submitted detailed legal briefs for consideration.[19] The Supreme Court of the United States heard oral arguments on five days in January 1911, and Justice Oliver Wendell Holmes Jr. issued the second unanimous opinion in *Virginia v. West Virginia* on 6 March.

"This case," Holmes wrote in the opening section of his opinion, "is to be considered in the untechnical spirit proper for dealing with a *quasi*-international controversy, remembering that there is no municipal code governing the matter, and that this Court may be called on to adjust differences that cannot be dealt with by Congress or disposed of by the legislature of either state alone."[20] The precise rules of procedure and considerations that would govern an equity proceeding between ordinary litigants therefore need not be binding on the Supreme Court, Holmes explained, because a "state is superior to the forms that it may require of its citizens."[21] For that reason, the judges refused to allow laches or the potential complication arising from multifarious plaintiffs to interfere with the court's responsibility to determine and assess the portion of the principal for which West Virginia was liable. That settled the jurisdictional questions in Virginia's favor.[22]

Holmes repeated the Supreme Court's 1907 conclusion that West Virginia remained bound by the terms of the acts of Congress and the General Assembly of the Restored Government of Virginia and the West Virginia Constitution of 1863 that made West Virginia a state in the Union. Those public acts constituted a constitutionally binding and protected compact, or contract, that rendered irrelevant the specifications about how to calculate the debt that appeared in the August 1861 resolution of the convention that met in Wheeling, which had called the constitutional convention into being.[23] The judges accepted the Virginia argument that the debt had been incurred for the benefit of the whole state and rejected the West Virginia argument that because the western portion of the state had received less than its due or less than it had become liable for to subsidize construction of canals and railroads, it should therefore receive credit for the difference. The judges also rejected the West Virginia argument that the Supreme Court had no authority to declare whether or how much that state should pay because a provision in the West Virginia Constitution of 1863 empowered the legislature of that state alone to ascertain the proportion of the debt of the old state of Virginia for which the new state of West Virginia was responsible.[24]

Holmes and the other members of the Supreme Court declared that the "liability of West Virginia is a deepseated equity, not discharged by changes in the form of the debt, nor split up by the unilateral attempt of Virginia to apportion specific parts to the two states."[25] He continued, "It remains true, then, notwithstanding all the transactions between the old commonwealth and her bondholders, that West Virginia must bear her equitable proportion of the whole debt." Based for the most part on the findings of the special master but taking into account the variant figures that counsel for the two states had submitted, the Supreme Court concluded that "the nearest approach to justice that we can make is to adopt a ratio determined by the master's estimated valuation of the real and personal property of the two states on the date of the separation, June 20, 1863. A ratio determined by population or land area would throw a larger share on West Virginia, but the relative resources of the debtor populations," that is, the taxable value of West Virginia's land and personal property at the time of statehood, "are generally recognized, we think, as affording a proper measure" for calculating the resources available at the time of statehood for paying that state's part of the debt. "It seems to us plain," Holmes continued, "that slaves should be excluded from the valuation. The master's figures without them are, for Virginia, $300,887,367.74, and for West Virginia, $92,416,021.65," or 76.51 percent for Virginia and 23.49 percent for West Virginia, far from the two-thirds, one-third proportion that the General Assembly of Virginia established in the Funding Act of 1871. "Taking .235 as representing the proportion of West Virginia," Holmes concluded, "we have $7,182,507.46 as her share of the principal debt."[26]

The Supreme Court left open for future determination the question whether West Virginia was also liable for accrued interest on the principal, and if so, how to calculate the rate or amount. The court authorized the two states to negotiate the terms of a decree for the court to issue that specified whether or how much interest West Virginia should pay. "As this is no ordinary commercial suit," Holmes reiterated, "but, as we have said, a *quasi*-international difference, referred to this Court in reliance upon the honor and constitutional obligations of the states concerned, rather than upon ordinary remedies, we think it best at this stage to go no farther, but to await the effect of a conference between the parties, which, whatever the outcome, must take place." The members of the Supreme Court deferred generously to the unique dignity and responsibility of each state and issued no idle or toothless threats against West Virginia but nevertheless made their expectations quite clear. Holmes reminded the two states again that the case "calls for forbearance upon both sides. Great states have a temper superior to that of private litigants, and it is to be hoped that enough has been decided for patriotism, the fraternity of the Union, and mutual consideration to bring it to an end."[27]

On 20 April 1911 the chair of the Virginia Debt Commission addressed a letter to Governor William E. Glasscock, who with most other West Virginians was still in shock at the unexpected defeat in the Supreme Court and the size of the debt imposed on the state.[28] The Virginians invited the West Virginians to begin negotiations in conformity with the court's decision. Glasscock relayed the request to the legislature, which was then meeting in special session, but the members took no action. The state's constitution restricted their considerations solely to the other matters for which the governor had convened the special session. The new attorney general of Virginia, Samuel W. Williams, therefore applied to the Supreme Court on 10 October 1911 to request that because of West Virginia's refusal to cooperate the court proceed directly to a final decree.[29]

On 30 October 1911 the Supreme Court turned down the Virginia request. West Virginia's attorney general, William G. Conley, had affirmed that the state's constitution forbade the spring special session of the legislature from considering the Virginia debt; its consideration would have to be postponed until the governor called another special session for that explicit purpose or until the next regularly scheduled biennial session in 1913. He had also argued that the Virginia Debt Commission lacked legal authority to negotiate with West Virginia and that it had authority under the act of March 1900 only to authorize a suit against the state.

In his second opinion for the unanimous Supreme Court, Holmes declared that the negotiations were to take place as a consequence of the court's decision and under its authority, not under any legislative act of either state. "The conference is not for an independent compromise out of court," he continued, "but an attempt to settle a decree" about the interest as a consequence of the 1907 and 1911 decisions. Nevertheless, Holmes wrote, "If the parties in charge of the suit consent" to mutually agreeable terms, "this Court is not likely to inquire very curiously into questions of power if, on its part, it is satisfied that they have consented to a proper decree." As he had in his previous ruling, Holmes made a special point of distinguishing this suit between two states from common suits between ordinary citizens and/or corporations. "A question like the present should be disposed of without undue delay," he explained. "But a state cannot be expected to move with the celerity of a private business man; it is enough if it proceeds, in the language of the English Chancery, with all deliberate speed." Holmes then concluded in a sentence that a preliminary conditional *if* and two negatives made clumsy, "If the authorities of West Virginia see fit to await the regular session of the legislature, that fact is not sufficient to prove that, when the voice of the state is heard, it will proclaim unwillingness to make a rational effort for peace."[30] In practical terms, that meant that nothing would or could happen until the next regularly scheduled session of the West Virginia Legislature early in 1913, so Virginia's attorney general, Samuel W. Williams, promised that at that time he would press Virginia's case "with such diligence as its importance demands and the then existing conditions will warrant."[31]

On 21 February 1913 the next regular session of the West Virginia Legislature created an eleven-member Virginia Debt Commission—significantly, not a West Virginia Debt Commission—and empowered it to negotiate with representatives of Virginia and also "to ascertain and report upon and give the utmost publicity to all the facts in relation to the pending suit." That specifically meant the portion of the principal the Supreme Court had decided West Virginia owed and that the Commonwealth of Virginia itself already owned in the form of Virginia Deferred Certificates in its sinking fund.[32] The creation of the commission represented the legislature's first acknowledgment that West Virginia was bound to pay some portion of the debt. The legislators submitted to the authority of the Supreme Court, but their actions indicated that they preferred to try to negotiate the terms of a better settlement with the Virginia commissioners rather than continue the litigation and risk being compelled to obey what might very well be a more expensive ruling by the Supreme Court.

Most of the West Virginia commissioners had little or no detailed knowledge of the financial and legal histories of Virginia's public debt or its implications for West Virginia.[33] The exception was the commission's chair, John M. Mason, who had paid close attention to the Virginia debt controversy for decades and had published two pamphlets and one short note in the *Virginia Law Register* to demonstrate that West Virginia owed little or no money to Virginia and none to the owners of the Virginia Deferred Certificates.[34] After the West Virginia commissioners hastily organized themselves, they initially received little initial assistance from the state's young new attorney general, who also had no background on the legal history and issues involved,[35] but the West Virginia commissioners nevertheless agreed to meet the Virginia commissioners.

On 25 July 1913 the members of the two debt commissions met in Washington, D.C. In his opening statement, the chair of the Virginia commission, John B. Moon, announced in what he regarded as a generous spirit that in discussing the amount of interest West Virginia should pay on the principal that the Supreme Court had ruled West Virginia owed, "it is not the desire of Virginia nor was it the intention of the Supreme Court that Virginia should ask or demand the full or legal amount of interest upon the principal debt as ascertained in the decision of the court, but that there should be concessions made upon both sides, such as comport with justice and honor and dignity of the two States."

John M. Mason, the chair of the West Virginia commission, objected that "it was not our expectation that this conference was to be confined to the consideration of only the question of interest. Our idea had been that the scope of the conference would be wider, and that we would confer together and take up the whole case, principal and interest. We thought that was what we were to meet here for." During the remainder of the day, through the evening until after midnight, and again on the following day the members of the two commissions exchanged written and oral messages that explained their very different understandings of why they were meeting. Each eventually gave up trying to persuade the other, and they adjourned until 12 August.[36]

The West Virginians soon thereafter postponed the meeting scheduled for 12 August because they had not yet had time to digest all the voluminous data and records of the case.[37] As a consequence of the postponement, Attorney General Samuel W. Williams informed Abraham A. Lilly, the West Virginia attorney general, in September that he had prepared a petition to the Supreme Court "to proceed with a further hearing and determination of said case, and to settle and determine all questions left open by its decision rendered on the 6th day of March, 1911."[38]

In his response to Williams's motion, Lilly laid out in detail how little time the members of the West Virginia commission had had between their appointment and the first conference with the Virginians to master the complexities of the case. He also explained that he and the state's new governor, both of whom had taken office on 4 March of that year, had not had time to become adequately informed about the past history of the case before the July conference. "In view, therefore, of the foregoing considerations," Lilly requested of the Supreme Court, "it is respectfully submitted that the motion of the complainant is premature and ought not to prevail; that no further action should be taken by this court until the West Virginia Commission has had a reasonable opportunity to present its intended proposition of settlement to the Virginia Commission."[39]

Chief Justice Edward D. White issued a brief opinion on 10 November 1913 denying Virginia's second request for proceeding to a final decree and allowing until 13 April 1914 for "the commissioners of West Virginia to complete the work which we are assured they are now engaged in performing for the purpose of effecting a settlement of the controversy."[40]

The West Virginians were indeed at work. Almost immediately after the failed July 1913 meeting between the two state debt commissions, West Virginia's governor, Henry D. Hatfield, hired attorneys to research the financial and legal histories of the debt. They also listened to John M. Mason, who had always believed that if West Virginia should be found liable for any part of the original Virginia debt, Virginia's ownership of railroad and bank stock as well as other resources at the time of the creation of West Virginia would be assets for which West Virginia should be allowed a proportional credit to reduce the amount of West Virginia's liability.[41]

Hatfield's researchers found evidence that Mason had some solid grounds for his beliefs. They ascertained that as of 1 January 1861 the government of Virginia had owned shares of stock in internal improvement companies and banks and held other assets that were available for helping retire the debt. The assets included more than eight hundred thousand dollars in cash in the sinking fund that was specifically dedicated to paying the principal of the debt. The other resources included large numbers of shares of stock in several railroad companies (Richmond, Fredericksburg, and Potomac; Orange and Alexandria; Richmond and Danville; Richmond and Petersburg; Virginia Central; Alexandria, Loudoun, and Hampshire; Manassas Gap) and the James River and Kanawha Company, as well as outstanding loans to other railroads (Virginia and Tennessee; Norfolk and Petersburg), stock in four banks (Farmers' Bank of Virginia; Bank of Virginia; Bank of the Valley; Exchange Bank), securities of the Atlantic, Mississippi, and Ohio Railroad, and also a claim against the government of the United States for unreimbursed expenses incurred during the War of 1812.[42]

The attorneys' calculations revealed that the total value of the assets was about $20.8 million. They, the governor, and the members of the West Virginia commission concluded that according to the Supreme Court's own determination of taxable assets and liabilities, West Virginians had owned 23.5 percent of those assets and that therefore 76.5 percent of their value should be deducted from the principal that the court had ruled West Virginia was liable for paying. The West Virginians also believed that legal precedents made a state government immune from suits to force it to pay interest on its debt and that therefore they had found ways to reduce the amount of money the court had declared the state should pay to a small fraction of what Virginia had insisted on, an amount that would not be onerous.[43]

Six weeks before the Supreme Court's April 1914 deadline, the two debt commissions assembled in Washington, D.C. On 4 March the West Virginia commissioners submitted a proposition to ascertain the true value of all the shares of stock and other assets Virginia had owned at the beginning of 1861 plus interest or dividends earned on that stock in order that the equitable portion of that sum be declared a credit for West Virginia. The West Virginians calculated that their proposal would drastically reduce the debt that state owed from about $7.2 million to a little more than $2.3 million. The astonished Virginia commissioners, who evidently had no idea what the West Virginians were going to suggest, immediately rejected the proposal and reasserted that the only thing remaining to be negotiated after the Supreme Court's previous rulings was the amount of interest West Virginia should pay on the larger principal.[44]

West Virginia's attorney general and associate counsel repeated the commissioners' arguments when the Supreme Court took up the case again in April. They asked for additional time to prepare the necessary legal arguments and compile the necessary financial data.[45] On 8 June 1914 the court unanimously agreed to allow the delay. "We think it must be conceded," Chief Justice Edward D. White wrote, "that, in a case between ordinary litigants, the application of the ordinary rules of legal procedure would render it impossible, under the circumstances which we have stated, to grant the request," which would significantly alter the bases for settlement late in the proceedings. "We are of the opinion, however, that such concession ought not to be here controlling. As we have pointed out, in acting in this case from first to last, the fact that the suit was not an ordinary one concerning a difference between individuals, but was a controversy between states, involving grave questions of public law, determinable by this Court under the exceptional grant of power conferred upon it by the Constitution, has been the guide by which every step and every conclusion hitherto expressed has been controlled. And we are of the opinion that this guiding principle should not now be lost sight of, to the end that, when the case comes ultimately to be finally and irrevocably disposed of, as come ultimately it must, in the absence of agreement between the parties, there may be no room for the slightest inference that the more restricted rules applicable to individuals have been applied to a great public controversy, or that anything but the largest justice, after the amplest opportunity to be heard, has in any degree entered into the disposition of the case. This conclusion, which we think is required by the duty owed to the moving state"—West Virginia, if he meant the suit at hand, Virginia if the whole action—"also in our opinion operates no injustice to the opposing state"—Virginia, if he meant the suit at hand, West Virginia if the whole action—"since it but affords an additional opportunity to guard against the possibility of error, and thus reach the result most consonant with the honor and dignity of both parties to the controversy."[46]

Special Master Charles E. Littlefield conducted another long and intensive inquiry in Richmond. He received more than a thousand pages of testimony in two sessions that lasted in the whole nearly two weeks in August and September 1914 and then in another in New York on 12 December.[47] Littlefield concluded in his report, dated 22 January 1915, that with the credits to which West Virginia was entitled, the principal for which West Virginia could be held liable should be reduced to about $4.3 million and that the combined principal and accrued interest therefore should be reduced by more than $10 million to $11,753,904.41.[48]

On 14 June 1915 Associate Justice Charles Evans Hughes for a unanimous Supreme Court ruled that the principal for which West Virginia had been declared responsible in the 1907 and 1911 decisions should be reduced. Relying in large part on Littlefield's report, he explained that no reliable data existed to ascertain the true market value of the shares of stock on 1 January 1861 or 20 June 1863 or what could be understood as their intrinsic value on either of those dates based on earnings and profits. Nor could the court accurately calculate dividends that the companies could or should have paid to Virginia before West Virginia's statehood. Finding no reliable means of ascertaining any of the alternative values, the court rejected them all and valued each share of stock at its face value. The Supreme Court's adjustment of West Virginia's portion took into account the $150,000 that the Restored Government of Virginia had paid to the new government of West Virginia during the Civil War and also a proportion of an unpaid compensation for expenses incurred during the War of 1812 that Virginia had always maintained the U.S. government still owed the original state. The revised figures persuaded the court to reduce the principal West Virginia owed from almost $7.2 million to a little more than $4.2 million.

The Supreme Court also decided at the same time that the compact West Virginia, the Restored Government of Virginia, and Congress had entered into at the time of West Virginia's statehood clearly required that West Virginia pay interest on its portion of the old debt. The West Virginia Constitution of 1863 explicitly acknowledged that responsibility, and the court therefore did not even bother to reject West Virginia's assertion that no state could be compelled to pay interest. The court fixed the rate of accrued unpaid interest for West Virginia's adjusted principal as closely as it could to the reduced rates of interest Virginia had paid on its portion as a result of the series of funding acts and reductions in interest after the Civil War. To ascertain the amount of interest that had thus legitimately accrued on West Virginia's portion, the justices calculated that Virginia had paid an average annual interest of 4 percent from 1 January 1861 to 1 July 1891 and 3 percent from 1 July 1891 to 1 July 1915. Adding the interest to the adjusted principal made West Virginia's new equitable portion of the debt of old Virginia $12,393,929.50. The Supreme Court directed that West Virginia pay it at the rate of 5 percent annual interest commencing on 1 July 1915.[49]

The decision was a substantial victory for Virginia and for the certificate holders. It shifted Virginia's potential liability for paying the certificates entirely onto West Virginia, and the certificate holders at last appeared assured of receiving payment of at least some of the principal and accrued interest. The then new attorney general of Virginia, John Garland Pollard, concluded that Hughes's decision was definitely "in favor of the Common-wealth of Virginia." He also wrote, "For the successful termination of this long-drawn-out litigation too much credit cannot be given to Honorable William A. Anderson and Honorable Randolph Harrison"—the former, the attorney general who had initiated the suit and who as a former at-torney general continued to act as co-counsel with his successors, and the latter, the most active and longest-serving member of the Virginia Debt Commission.[50]

The Supreme Court's opinion was also a victory for West Virginia in that it significantly reduced the total amount of the old Virginia debt it then had a legal responsibility to pay.[51] On 19 October 1915 the chair of the Vir-ginia Debt Commission wrote to Governor Hatfield, who on 12 November responded in what appeared to be a helpful and conciliatory manner, but the Virginians' pleasure at the outcome of the 1915 case dissipated dur-ing the winter because the legislature of West Virginia did not reconvene and therefore took no steps to appropriate or raise money to pay what the Supreme Court had declared it should pay.[52] Early the following summer, Pollard petitioned the court "to levy upon any property of the State of West Virginia, subject to such levy for the satisfaction of the said judgment and decree, and for such other and further relief in the premises as shall seem just and meet."[53]

To Pollard's request the attorney general of West Virginia objected that only the legislature of the state could act and that it had not met since the Supreme Court's ruling early in 1915. Furthermore, the state had no property that courts could seize and sell to raise the sum that the Supreme Court had stated West Virginia owed. Even though the Constitution of the United States granted jurisdiction to the Supreme Court in suits between states, he pointed out, it did not grant the court authority or provide it with means to enforce a monetary award against a state.[54]

On 12 June 1916 Chief Justice Edward D. White denied Pollard's request and allowed time for the West Virginia Legislature to act in its next regularly scheduled biennial meeting. White acknowledged that "although the Constitution imposes upon this Court the duty, and grants it full power, to consider controversies between states, and therefore authority to render the decree in question, yet with the grant of jurisdiction there was conferred no authority whatever to enforce a money judgment against a state if, in the exercise of jurisdiction, such a judgment was entered."[55]

When the West Virginia Legislature met in January 1917, Governor Hatfield sent a very long special message to the members outlining in detail the history of the Virginia debt controversy, the negotiations and lawsuits it had generated, and the problems West Virginia faced after the most recent Supreme Court decision. Hatfield concluded, "The next step, therefore, in the Debt controversy must be taken by the Legislature of the State of West Virginia, and such step should be taken at its present session." The Supreme Court's decisions left no room for modifying the legal obligation to pay and appeared to leave little room to reduce the amount further. "The narrow limits that have been imposed," Hatfield continued, "leave but few alternatives. To decline to pay the debt means repudiation—and this course I do not believe West Virginians are willing to adopt. I feel justified in saying that our citizenry will be willing to assume any equitable or reasonable amount that their ability to pay will permit for the sake of the Constitution under which we live, for the sake of the Union of which we are a part, and for the high regard in which they hold the highest tribunal of the land, regardless of the unfairness of the embarrassing position which it has always been our State's misfortune to occupy in the public debt controversy."[56]

West Virginia's legislators accepted the authority of the Supreme Court to determine that the state was liable for a portion of the original debt, but they delayed taking any steps toward paying it until they were satisfied that they had reduced the amount as much as possible. And the governor had an idea about how to do that, perhaps one that he had gotten from John M. Mason, who had argued that Congress still owed Virginia a sum of money promised when Virginia donated the land north of the Ohio River to the United States in the 1780s.[57] Hatfield informed the legislators that if West Virginia could by suit or by congressional action obtain payment or credit for a portion of that sum, it would receive a sum sufficient, or a credit sufficient, to reduce significantly the amount of additional money it had to raise to pay off the Virginia Deferred Certificates.[58]

Attorney General John Garland Pollard, impatient because the West Virginia Legislature did not immediately act on Hatfield's first recommendation,[59] boldly moved that the Supreme Court summon all the members of the West Virginia Legislature, or legal counsel on their behalf, and require them to explain "why a writ of mandamus should not issue against them" requiring them as a legislative body to pay the debt.[60] That motion produced the last in the long series of judicial decisions arising from the antebellum Virginia debt.

Pollard's request was unprecedented. The Supreme Court had never issued such an order to a state legislature. West Virginia's attorney general and co-counsel argued at length that the court had no authority to issue a writ of mandamus to the legislators and, moreover, no authority to enforce one. On 22 April 1918 Chief Justice Edward D. White denied Pollard's request. The court refused even to consider the question West Virginia raised about money the U.S. government may have owed Virginia since the 1780s,[61] so West Virginia lost its last chance to reduce further the amount of the debt that the Supreme Court had declared it was supposed to pay. But the West Virginians succeeded in persuading the court to deny Pollard's request for a writ of mandamus, and the chief justice's opinion dealt almost entirely with that potentially momentous subject.

"That judicial power essentially involves the right to enforce the results of its exertion is elementary," White explained, but neither that assertion by itself nor the language of the Constitution provided a method of enforcement. The chief justice suggested that because the Constitution explicitly declared that all laws of Congress were supreme over any law of any state, Congress could by legislation enforce the compact that it, West Virginia, and the Restored Government of Virginia had entered into making West Virginia a state. But the Supreme Court, lacking any obvious effective enforcement methods, declined to act at that time or to issue an order that it could not on its own enforce. Instead, the court directed the two states to return and present arguments on three questions: Did the Supreme Court have authority to issue the writ of mandamus as Pollard requested? If not, did the court have any other authority to direct the West Virginia Legislature to levy a tax? And if so, what means or measures did the Supreme Court have to enforce its rulings? The justices explicitly reserved the right to appoint a special master "for the purpose of examining and reporting concerning the amount and method of taxation essential to be put into effect" in the event that they decided to require West Virginia to pay.[62] Charles E. Littlefield had recently died, and had the appointment of a special master been necessary for a third time, it would have been some other person.

The question whether or how the Supreme Court could constitutionally require or effectively compel the state of West Virginia and/or its legislature to appropriate money, raise taxes, or issue bonds to pay the debt was one of the most interesting and potentially most important of all the constitutional issues that the Virginia debt controversy produced. Legal scholars discussed it seriously at the time. Indeed, the Supreme Court's official reporter appended to the chief justice's 1918 opinion large portions of Pollard's petition and of West Virginia's counterargument on that subject, "believing that they will add to the future, if not to the immediate, value of the report."[63]

Not long before White issued his decision, William C. Coleman wrote an essay for the *Harvard Law Review* that addressed the question, and shortly after the decision the *Review* printed a short, unsigned note on the subject.[64] Later in 1918, Thomas Reed Powell, early in a long and distinguished career of legal scholarship, published in the *Michigan Law Review* an article entitled "Coercing a State to Pay a Judgment: Virginia v. West Virginia." He reviewed the previous rulings of federal courts and predicted that the Supreme Court would issue the requested writ of mandamus or identify some other judicial implement for enforcing its decisions. "The text writers and cases," Powell concluded, "support the principle that mandamus may be used to tell officers what they shall do, even though they must be left free to determine how they shall do it," taking notice of some West Virginians' objections that it was up to the legislature of that state, not the Supreme Court, to decide whether to issue bonds or to raise taxes. "They cannot fail to perform a duty," Powell continued, "merely because they have a choice as to how they shall perform it. The distinction rests on the difference between means and ends. It may be mandatory to achieve a given end, but discretionary to choose between alternative means. Obviously the mandatory duty would fail of enforcement, if those charged with its performance were entitled to say that, since each particular means rested in discretion when considered separately, they all rested in discretion when considered collectively. The distinction is plain and clearly established, even though it easily invites verbal quibbles."

Powell had reviewed the case law that applied to officials of city and county governments or state government officeholders, but there were no precedents relevant to state legislatures. "The only escape from the application of these well-established principles to the case at bar," he wrote, "lies in the fact that they have previously been applied only to what are commonly called 'inferior officers.' The duty in question has usually been imposed by the legislature, and officers have been coerced to do only what the legislature made it their duty to do . . . whereas what Virginia now asks is that the Supreme Court compel West Virginia to make a law."[65] That was the big and unanswered question. Could the Supreme Court compel West Virginia to make a law?

The members of the Supreme Court had repeated in every one of the substantive rulings and in most of the procedural ones that they trusted that West Virginia in its capacity as a state in the Union would abide by the court's determinations, suggesting that they hoped but could not be certain that the state would do its duty as the court had declared it. Because the Supreme Court could not actually force the legislators to act, it very cautiously approached the precipice of issuing an order that it clearly had no legal implements to enforce. The court's direction to counsel for Virginia and West Virginia in 1918 to return later and present arguments for and against the capacity of the Supreme Court to order the West Virginia Legislature to act could have led to at least one more important and perhaps groundbreaking judicial proceeding or to an unusually important constitutional law decision, but it did not. In fact, the two states reached a mutually acceptable agreement that made it unnecessary for them to return to the court at all.

The West Virginia Legislature had abolished the Virginia Debt Commission and in 1915 created the New Virginia Debt Commission.[66] The chair of the old commission, John M. Mason, had died in the meantime and was not a member of the New Virginia Debt Commission. About two months after the chief justice issued his April 1918 opinion in *Virginia v. West Virginia*, West Virginia's new governor, John J. Cornwell, wrote to the Virginia commissioners to suggest that its members enter into negotiations with the New Virginia Debt Commission.[67] Following a preliminary exchange of ideas, the two commissions met informally in Washington on 14 November 1918 and agreed on the outlines of a plan that did not in any substantial way work to Virginia's disadvantage. West Virginia would issue new bonds paying 3.5 percent interest and maturing in twenty years to compensate the owners of the Virginia Deferred Certificates and would make a cash payment of a little more than $1 million to Virginia for the certificates that it owned. The agreement also included a provision that West Virginia retain in escrow or in its treasury about $1.15 million in bonds for later payment to certificate holders who were not parties to the suit.[68]

When the West Virginia Legislature took up the proposal early in 1919, the members objected to holding any bonds in escrow because that would be an admission that West Virginia owed money to the owners of the Virginia Deferred Certificates. In an address to a joint session of the West Virginia Legislature made on behalf of the Virginia commission, Randolph Harrison informed the members that the Virginians did not insist on that as a condition of finally coming to an agreement.[69] Four days later the New Virginia Debt Commission reported that the two states were finally in full agreement and that West Virginia could (as Virginia had done after passage of the Olcott Act of 1892) "go into the market and buy up the bonds if selling below par" and thereby reduce both the amount of interest to be paid in the short term and the total amount of principal before the bonds matured.[70]

West Virginia no longer had any chance to reduce the amount of the debt, and although the legislature could have refused to acknowledge the superior legal authority of the Supreme Court of the United States, its members wisely elected not to contest the issues further. As makers of laws themselves, they had clearly concluded long before 1919 that they were going to have to do what the court directed or negotiate a better settlement with Virginia and abide by its terms. The 3.5 percent interest rate that Virginia and the agents for the certificate holders agreed to was certainly better for West Virginia than the 5 percent the Supreme Court had decreed.

On 1 April 1919 a special session of the West Virginia Legislature adopted a funding act that adhered closely to the terms the two debt commissions had negotiated. The preamble to the law referred to the Supreme Court's decisions and declared that "the state of West Virginia desires to comply with the decree of said court, and to satisfy the same as soon as practicable." The funding act authorized the state to issue $13.5 million in bonds to be dated 1 July 1919, mature in twenty years, and pay an annual interest of 3.5 percent. The legislature also established a sinking fund and directed that the state annually deposit an amount equal to 5 percent of the principal in the fund to pay off the bonds in 1939. The law directed that West Virginia make a cash payment of $1,062,876.16 to Virginia for the Deferred Certificates it owned.[71] By another law passed the same day, the legislature, as the New Virginia Debt Commission recommended, authorized the West Virginia Board of Public Works to purchase the state's own bonds with any surplus money it had and deposit them in the sinking fund.[72]

The bankers' committee and the certificate owners had agreed from the beginning that the committee would distribute the compensation that the Virginia Debt Commission obtained from West Virginia through negotiation or litigation, which freed the government of Virginia from involvement in paying the owners of the Virginia Deferred Certificates who were parties to the suit. Distribution of the proceeds to certificate holders who were not parties to the suit took place under the direction of a special master that the circuit court of the city of Richmond, Virginia, appointed later in 1919.[73] West Virginia later refinanced the debt at an even lower rate of interest, saving the state about $100,000 annually, and by buying back the bonds on the open market it reduced the outstanding principal to about $1.68 million by 1937. When the redemption date of 1 July 1939 arrived, the state treasurer declared the debt paid,[74] sixty-nine years after the last of the original debt of old Virginia had been incurred.

The members of the Virginia Debt Commission met for the last time in Richmond on 28 May 1919 and recorded that West Virginia had deposited the agreed-on sum in the Riggs National Bank, of Washington, D.C., to the credit of Virginia.[75] That concluded Virginia's part of the case on behalf of itself and the owners of the Virginia Deferred Certificates. "All honor to the Virginia Debt Commission," Second Auditor Rosewell Page exulted in Richmond in August 1919, a few months after the West Virginia Legislature passed the funding act, "to the able state officials—the Governors, the Attorney-Generals, and the Legislatures that have accomplished this great work."[76] Page meant, of course, the state officials, governors, attorneys general, and legislators of Virginia who had pursued the case against West Virginia since 1906, not those of West Virginia, although he recognized that they deserved some credit too.

On the other hand, the chief justice and associate justices of the Supreme Court of the United States could have privately said something similar about the governor, the attorney general, and the legislators of West Virginia. They had spared the court from having to decide what, if anything, to do if the West Virginia Legislature refused to accept responsibility for the debt and pay it off. The terms were close to but not quite the same as those specified in Charles Evans Hughes's 1915 decision, but as Oliver Wendell Holmes had indicated in 1911, it was in the best interests of the two states, of the creditors, and ultimately of the Supreme Court itself that the case be settled. If the two states reached a mutually agreeable settlement that did not require the Supreme Court to take additional action, especially the drastic action of issuing what might become an imitation of a futile bull against the comet of the West Virginia Legislature, then all the better for everybody concerned.

And the owners of the Virginia Deferred Certificates too could breathe a long-pent-up sigh of relief, even if they might not have been inclined to heap praise on any of the politicians, attorneys, and jurists. In 1919 the creditors finally received at least something from the certificates first issued in 1871 on a debt created between 1822 and 1861.

12 LEGACIES OF THE
DEBT CONTROVERSY

Virginians paid taxes until the 1944, and West Virginians until 1939, to retire Virginia's pre–Civil War debt, created for the construction of railroads and canals that for the most part had been abandoned, destroyed, or rebuilt even before the General Assembly passed the Funding Act of 1871. Most of the money the state paid to the creditors went to people who lived outside of Virginia, so that people in Virginia could not spend that money on any other projects or public works they desired or needed.

In that and many other ways the debt controversy shaped Virginia's political environment and institutions late in the nineteenth century and early in the twentieth as much as any other one thing. In the 1870s it produced a genuine reconstruction of Virginia's politics by providing the circumstances in which the Readjuster Party won the support of workingmen and farmers of both races and gained control over the state government. Then in the 1880s it set up the reaction against the Readjusters that destroyed that reconstruction and brought to power a political machine more durable, less flexible, and much less democratic than the Readjuster Party.

In the public mind, William Mahone became the personification of the controversy and the party he led. Two years after his six-year term in the United States Senate expired in 1887, Mahone won the nomination of the Republican Party for governor of Virginia and lost to Philip Watkins McKinney. That concluded the political career of the railroad executive and political maverick who had begun as a Conservative Party opponent of Congressional Reconstruction, helped bring the Readjuster Party into being, and then led it to its brief political success. It could be said that he had tried to lead it into a new kind of South so different from the old that it was not then possible for any party to go in that direction or that far.

Mahone died in 1895, by which time he and his old party had become stigmatized as anathema to all the traditions of Virginia's history, and the invented word *Mahoneism* became synonymous in Virginia with bossism. He was indeed an overbearing leader, but his opponents and even many of his supporters objected less to his domineering leadership style and micro-management of the party than to his inclusion of African Americans in his coalition and his acceptance of them as fully enfranchised citizens—that and his affiliation with the Republicans. Because Mahone was so conspicuous, people may have exaggerated his significance and undervalued the importance of the actions and beliefs of other people, especially the men who voted for his party. Nevertheless, Billy Mahone became and remained for several decades after his death one of the most reviled men in the whole of Virginia's history.

All, or virtually all, the African Americans who had supported the Readjusters returned to the Republican Party as soon as possible after the party's disappearance, and a significant number of white Readjusters entered or reentered the Republican Party too. John Paul, for instance, who had declared war on Governor Holliday in 1878, won election to the United States House of Representatives as a Readjuster in 1881, and in 1883 he received a presidential appointment as the federal judge for the Western District of Virginia. His family remained in the Republican Party for decades, and his namesake son also served in Congress in the 1920s and as a federal judge later. The Readjusters' one attorney general, Frank Simpson Blair, flirted with the Greenback Party and then traveled with Mahone from the Conservative Party, through the Readjuster Party, to the Republican Party. His son Robert William Blair was a lifelong Republican and one of the few members of the Constitutional Convention of 1901–2 to oppose disfranchisement of the state's African American voters.[1] By the opening of the twentieth century, though, most white Virginia Republicans no longer defended African American voting or campaigned for African Americans' votes. The number of black voters in the state had been reduced to an insignificant fraction of the electorate, and white Virginia Republicans seldom risked their small chances of winning local or legislative elections by appearing to favor African Americans and thereby offending white voters. But some appreciable portion of the 40 percent or more of white Virginia men who cast ballots for Republican candidates for president and governor at the end of the nineteenth century had probably voted, or their fathers had probably voted, for Readjuster candidates twenty years earlier.

Mahone's Readjuster colleague in the United States Senate and the party's legislative leader in Richmond, Harrison Holt Riddleberger, continued to identify himself as a Readjuster while representing the state in Washington, but in spite of the support for African Americans and the disdain for the Bourbons that he had trumpeted in his 1882 article in the *North American Review,* he did not go as far as Mahone and join the Republican Party. In fact, by the time his Senate term concluded in 1889, he had made peace with the Democrats and publicly denounced Mahone and Mahoneism. Riddleberger's side trip into the Readjuster Party was more typical of the Conservatives and Democrats who had supported some form of debt reduction and then abandoned their Republican and African American allies and subsided into the party of white supremacy.

Sadly, the Readjusters' one governor, William E. Cameron, also gradually abandoned his Readjuster principles and by the end of the century had quietly returned to the Democratic Party. He won election to the Virginia Constitutional Convention of 1901–2 and voted to disfranchise nearly all of Virginia's remaining African American voters and also a large portion of the state's white voters. In that convention, Cameron served with the man he had defeated for governor, John Warwick Daniel, who represented elite white Virginians in the United States Senate from 1887 until his death in 1910. Daniel led the charge within the Democratic Party for the disfranchisement convention and probably watched with pleasure the completion of Cameron's transformation from Readjuster democrat to white supremacy Democrat.

The Constitutional Convention of 1901–2 turned back nearly all of the democratic reforms embodied in the Virginia constitutions of 1851, 1864, and 1869, excepting only the creation of the public school system and the popular election of some local and statewide officials. The convention reintroduced the poll tax as a prerequisite for voting to make it possible for Democratic candidates to win elections without having to cheat. The poll tax, though, created new forms of political corruption and significantly reduced the number of adult male Virginians who could vote. The constitutional provisions and enabling acts that the assembly passed disfranchised about 90 percent of the few African Americans who still voted in Virginia at the beginning of the twentieth century and a large number of white voters. In fact, more white men than black men lost the ability to vote then. The number of voters in the state fell by about 50 percent, from 264,357 in the presidential election of 1900 to a mere 130,842 in 1904. That was fewer than had voted in any presidential election since 1852, when universal white manhood suffrage had just been introduced and the state's population, which still included the western counties that later became West Virginia, was smaller than in 1904 by about 25 percent. The Republican vote in Virginia fell from almost 44 percent in 1900 to about 35 percent in 1904.[2] The Democratic Party thereafter retained control of both houses of the General Assembly, all the statewide offices, most of the state's congressional seats, its two Senate seats, and local offices in most parts of the state until the final decades of the twentieth century.

One man who played an unusually long and large role in that process was William A. Anderson, the attorney general of Virginia who filed the suit against West Virginia in 1906 and acted as co-counsel with his successor attorneys general throughout the litigation. As a young member of the Senate of Virginia, still limping from the leg wound that knocked him out of the Confederate army at Manassas, he voted for the Funding Act of 1871. As a member of the House of Delegates in 1884, he was a co-sponsor of the Anderson-McCormick election law that wrested the conduct of elections out of local hands and gave it to appointees of the Democrats in the General Assembly. In 1900 Anderson devoted his address as president of the prestigious Virginia State Bar Association to an exploration of methods for disfranchising African Americans without appearing to violate the Fifteenth Amendment to the Constitution of the United States.[3] He was president pro tempore of the Constitutional Convention in 1901 when he was elected attorney general for the first time.

The fate of the biracial Readjuster-Republican coalition probably contributed to Virginia's having no genuinely viable Populist movement in the 1890s, when biracial coalitions of farmers upset and then set on new tracks the emergence of Jim Crow regimes in several other Southern states and ushered in what came to be called the Solid South. In Virginia, an appreciable number of Democratic Party leaders supported important parts of the Populist economic reform agenda, but large-scale commercial farmers, not poor farmers as elsewhere, dominated Virginia's agricultural reform organizations.[4] By the 1890s neither the Republicans nor any other white Virginians remained willing to make an alliance with African Americans, and even the Democrats who supported parts of the Populist agenda never contemplated separately mobilizing the state's white farmers either. The former Conservative-Readjuster attorney general James G. Field was by then engaged in large-scale commercial agriculture and was a Democrat, but he was also the 1892 Populist (or People's Party) candidate for vice president. He received very few votes in Virginia, even in his own county. Field was almost the exception that proved the rule. What happened elsewhere in the South in the 1890s, including in neighboring North Carolina, where Republicans, African Americans, and agrarian reformers seized control of the state government, did not happen in Virginia at that time in large part because it had already happened more than a decade earlier, and the state's Democratic Party had made certain in the meantime that it could not happen again.

The issues of race and debt became so inextricably intertwined with partisan politics during the 1870s and 1880s that nobody could have disentangled them had anybody tried. They provided the votes for the Democratic Party that John Strode Barbour reassembled early in the 1880s and that he, John Warwick Daniel, and their successors controlled until 1922. In that year a talented political operative of a new generation, Harry Flood Byrd, took it over as chair of the party's state central committee while he was serving as an influential member of the Senate of Virginia. In 1923 Byrd led the referendum campaign against a proposal for the state to issue bonds for speeding the construction of a modern state highway system. It was the first proposal for a large bond issue since before the Civil War. Byrd helped defeat it, and his pay-as-you-go policy propelled him into the governor's office in the 1925 election.[5] From then until his death in 1966 Byrd directed the Democratic Party organization that Barbour had created in the 1880s with a ruthless efficiency that even Mahone never exercised.

The disfranchisement of a large number of white Virginians at the opening of the twentieth century so far reduced the political influence of lower- and middle-class white people that the remnant of the electorate, unlike in most other Southern states, had little or no chance of electing Progressives or New Dealers to Congress. Nor could they press economic reform programs on the General Assembly, as happened nearly everywhere else in the South at one or more times during the twentieth century. Most supporters as well as adversaries of the dominant leadership of the Virginia Democratic Party from the time of the Readjusters until the middle of the twentieth century or later were committed to white supremacy, as were Progressives and New Dealers elsewhere in the Southern states, but the men who dominated Virginia's politics during that time were not democratic in their white supremacy. They were elitists too, for reasons that stretched back to and beyond the debt controversy and the Readjusters.

In many ways Virginia's twentieth-century Democratic Party very closely resembled its nineteenth-century Conservative Party.

Late in the nineteenth century and throughout much of the twentieth, Democratic candidates did not have to appeal to very many lower- or middle-class voters of either race. The party's leaders therefore included no rabble-rousers such as appeared in most of the other Southern states at one time or another, because there was no voting rabble in Virginia to rouse. Following the establishment of the Democratic Party machine in the 1880s, Virginia produced no colorful demagogic champions of white underdogs or flagrant race-baiters like Tom Watson and Eugene Talmage in Georgia, "Pitchfork" Ben Tillman in South Carolina, James K. Vardaman in Mississippi, or Huey Long in Louisiana, nor any nationally respected Progressives either. Instead, Virginia's political rulers were an almost unbroken run of solemn attorneys and businessmen: the able party organizer and railroad president John Strode Barbour; the railroad lawyer John Warwick Daniel; the enigmatic and secretive railroad lawyer Thomas Staples Martin; the amiable and cautious career politician Claude A. Swanson; and the rigid and intolerant orchard owner and newspaper publisher Harry F. Byrd.[6]

On the other hand, the politics of the debt controversy gave the public school system authorized in the Constitution of 1869 a permanent foundation of firm political support. Determined voters of both races repeatedly defeated the politicians who were willing to starve the school fund (or burn the schools) in order to pay the state's creditors. That required the support of men and women of both races and a willingness of white politicians to cooperate with black politicians for that purpose. The voters' demands ultimately forced Democratic Party politicians to support the public schools.[7] It may be a coincidence, but probably is not, that some of the young men and women who came of age during the intense debates about the schools and the debt entered public life later in the nineteenth century in support of improving the schools, even by raising taxes if necessary. Many of the women who took part in that movement pursued other political objectives even before they gained the vote in 1920 and created the rudiments of a Progressive movement in Virginia and helped found some of the state's first social service agencies. Some of them even formed working partnerships across both class and racial lines for those purposes. To that extent and in that shape, the reforming spirit and some of the democratic impulses of the Readjuster movement survived into the twentieth century among the white women of Virginia.[8]

In the political myths and memories of most of the white people of Virginia, though, the debt controversy and everything associated with it became a mere extension of the destruction of old Virginia in the Civil War and of imagined horrors of Congressional Reconstruction. The reminiscences of a man whose name has not appeared in this narrative of the events of the debt controversy helps explain how and why that was the case. Robert Thomas Barton, of Winchester, [9] was one of the leading attorneys in Virginia during those decades. He published the standard manuals of practice for the state's lawyers in the 1870s and 1880s and was president of the Virginia State Bar Association in 1892. He won election to the House of Delegates when the Democrats defeated the Readjusters in 1883 and as chair of the Committee on Courts of Justice led the unsuccessful attempt to impeach the Readjuster attorney general Frank Simpson Blair. Like nearly all the white participants in the debt saga, Barton had served in the Confederate army. The memories of that service and the deaths of his comrades and family members profoundly influenced him for the remainder of his life, as the services and losses of the other Virginians influenced his contemporaries. After the debt controversy had passed into myth and history, Barton wrote a memoir of his time in the army, but his recollections of the long subsequent political and social upheavals that followed the war also shaped that narrative. He recalled that as a student at the University of Virginia during the secession crisis he had opposed secession as unwise and unconstitutional. He had even maintained that view throughout the war, in which he fought, and for several years afterward. By the end of the century, though, he had changed his mind, perhaps in part as a consequence of the domestic revolutions that the defeat of the Confederacy had allowed to happen, which would not have happened had secession succeeded. Old Virginia would have survived intact, and Northerners, Republicans, and African Americans would never have had a chance to challenge or change it. Having "grown older and read fully on the subject and reflected about it since," Barton wrote, "it has become only an abstract question, I no longer doubt it, and I often wonder that I was ever misled by what seems to me now to have been the sophistry of those who denied the right of secession" in order to preserve old Virginia as a part of the old South.[10]

Race and debt, politics and law, economic change and political control—these were the great public policy issues of the post–Civil War period in Virginia and elsewhere in the South. It was and is impossible to separate any of them from the others. That was perfectly obvious to everybody in Virginia at the time. In that politically charged context, opponents of the Readjusters and their increasingly egalitarian creed began interpreting the debt controversy even before it was resolved and shaped durable narratives to fit the prejudices of their audiences and their own racist and partisan objectives. As early as 1880 the popular humorist George William Bagby entered the lists with a polemical pamphlet that had the frightening title *John Brown and Wm. Mahone: An Historical Parallel, Foreshadowing Civil Trouble.*[11] Nobody had to explain the awful parallel that he perceived, which was war between the races and black domination.

The myths and misunderstandings operated to the disadvantage of the people of Virginia during much of the twentieth century. Inaccurately and unfairly, the Readjusters became the symbol in Virginia of black rule, racial strife, and political corruption. The economic and political problems that the antebellum public debt created in the postbellum period were so intimately associated with Mahone and the Readjusters that through deliberate distortions of them the debt controversy gained a sustained and influential long life in the public memory. It was always tied tightly to the place of African Americans in the state's politics and culture. During the first decades of the twentieth century, Virginia politicians often referred back to the Readjusters and to manufactured memories of race riots and black domination when they needed to add energy to their campaigns. The inaccurate and unfair characterizations of Mahone, the Readjusters, the debt, and how African Americans had participated in politics during the period provided a firm base of support for the undemocratic political machine that dominated Virginia for generations.

Men and women who wrote textbooks, novels, histories, poems, and songs in or about post–Civil War Virginia had created a large and compelling new literature by the end of the nineteenth century that romanticized the long-gone plantation elite, demonized the Republicans and the Readjusters, and portrayed the Democrats who defeated them as a second set of Redeemers every bit as admirable and important as the first Redeemers, who they believed had saved Virginia from Northern radicals and black rule at the end of Congressional Reconstruction. One exaggerated episode became a mythic act of heroism in that cause. During the 1881 election campaign, Mahone and his close allies had circulated pledges for

Readjuster candidates to sign stating that they would vote for all measures the party proposed at the ensuing session of the General Assembly. Four successful candidates for the Senate of Virginia—Conservatives Samuel H. Newberry, of Bland County, and Peyton G. Hale, of Grayson County, and Republicans Alfred M. Lybrook, of Patrick County, and Benjamin F. Williams, of Nottoway County—refused. According to Charles Chilton Pearson, who published the first history of the Readjuster Party in 1919, "It is the popular opinion in Virginia that these men saved the day,"[12] although the party's full legislative agenda passed, and it is not at all evident that the refusal of the so-called Big Four to sign the pledge saved anybody from anything or very much altered the course of events. But they became heroes to enemies of the Readjusters anyway. After the party collapsed a few years later, men who had opposed Mahone for any reason or at any time took the credit.

Even though Pearson almost certainly exaggerated the actual importance of the Big Four, he was correct about the public perception of their role. When in March 1928 the General Assembly commissioned a group portrait of the four together with John E. Massey, the legislators inadvertently or ignorantly transferred the events back in time from the 1880s to the earlier era of Congressional Reconstruction and also accepted the myth that political leaders who were not genuine Virginians had planned to subjugate decent, real Virginians. The legislative authorization for the group portrait praised the men who "in the days of reconstruction fought, with inflexible will, and stood in unbending opposition to the plans and proposals which would had they been carried out, placed the State of Virginia in political bondage."[13]

In that same tradition, and beginning soon after the collapse of the Readjuster Party, the Sons of Confederate Veterans policed and censored textbooks in Virginia, and Virginia members of the United Daughters of the Confederacy and the Daughters of the American Revolution taught the new political catechism to their children and grandchildren. Together with the corps of elite white women who founded the Association for the Preservation of Virginia Antiquities and directed its work for half a century, they all opposed the democratizing trends in nineteenth-century American society generally and the participation of African Americans and non-elite white men in Virginia's public life specifically.

Emma Frances Plecker Cassell, for instance, belonged to and took an active part in almost all of those societies and also led another educational

group, the Children of the Confederacy, to indoctrinate the next generations for the same purpose. She and other women like her made their
understanding of part of the state's past the politically correct historical
orthodoxy.[14] Cassell, as it happened, was the sister of Walter Ashby Plecker,
who during most of the first half of the twentieth century directed the
state's department of vital records and pursued a vicious vendetta against
African Americans, American Indians, and everybody else who was not
demonstrably of pure European derivation or did not behave as he and his
white comrades thought proper.[15]

Just as he had done in forcing the legal issues during the coupon litigation, the aggressive bond attorney William L. Royall also helped shape the
historical literature and the legacy of the debt controversy. He wrote an
anecdotal chapter on the period in his memoirs in 1909; while amusing, it
is of no historical value and contains no useful insights.[16] Royall's *History of
the Virginia Debt Controversy* (1897), however, was more substantive and
subtly influential. He was a belligerent racist, and the political message he
intended to teach was much more about race than about public finance and
the law. That is inescapably clear from the volume's subtitle, *The Negro's
Vicious Influence in Politics.* Through Pearson's later history of the Readjuster Party and the articles and books that relied on it and on Royall's book
for context, Royall's highly charged interpretation became the influential
historical lesson of the nineteenth-century debt controversy. Implementing that lesson, many white Virginians blamed and punished the victims.

For three-quarters of a century or more, the textbooks pupils read in
Virginia's public schools and the popular historical literature the adults read
conformed to that incorrect characterization of that long and important
episode. That was the historical context in which the men of Harry Byrd's
generation operated. They had learned when they were young and had
the message frequently reinforced while they were adults that the federal
government had always been a threat to the right of prosperous elite white
Virginians to govern the state the way they wanted; that federal courts
intruded improperly into state politics and always to the disadvantage of
good government in the elite Virginia tradition; and that African Americans and poor whites were incapable of taking a productive part in politics.
The white political leaders of Byrd's generation and many members of the
following generation deeply distrusted the people and the federal government. And although they probably did not know it at the time because they
were largely ignorant of the details of late-nineteenth-century Virginia pol-

itics, when those politicians began the Massive Resistance campaign to obstruct enforcement of the federal courts' orders to desegregate the state's public schools, they were following in the same long anti-government tradition that the late-nineteenth-century Democrats had pursued with single-minded dedication.[17]

NOTES

ABBREVIATIONS AND SHORT TITLES

Acts	*Acts and Joint Resolutions Passed by the General Assembly of the Commonwealth of Virginia*, with variant titles and session year
Annual Report	*Annual Report of the Attorney General of the Commonwealth of Virginia*, with variant titles and year
Bondholders Report	*Annual Report of the Council of the Corporation of Foreign Bondholders* (London), numbered, with variant titles and year
DVB	John T. Kneebone et al., eds., *Dictionary of Virginia Biography* (Richmond, 1998–)
JHD	*Journal of the House of Delegates of the Commonwealth of Virginia*, with variant titles and session year
JSV	*Journal of the Senate of the State of Virginia*, with variant titles and session year
Maddex, *Virginia Conservatives*	Jack P. Maddex Jr., *The Virginia Conservatives, 1867–1879: A Study in Reconstruction Politics* (Chapel Hill, 1970)
Moore, *Two Paths*	James Tice Moore, *Two Paths to the New South: The Virginia Debt Controversy, 1870–1883* (Lexington, Ky., 1974)
Royall, *History*	William L. Royall, *History of the Virginia Debt Controversy: The Negro's Vicious Influence in Politics* (Richmond, 1897)
Tarter, *Grandees of Government*	Brent Tarter, *The Grandees of Government: The Origins and Persistence of Undemocratic Politics in Virginia* (Charlottesville, 2013)
Virginia vs. West Virginia	Nine bound volumes of printed briefs, exhibits, and other documents, 1906–13, Library of Virginia

VLJ   *Virginia Law Journal*

VMHB   *Virginia Magazine of History and Biography*

Younger and   Edward E. Younger and James Tice Moore, eds., *The*
Moore, *Governors*   *Governors of Virginia, 1860–1978* (Charlottesville, 1982)
of Virginia

INTRODUCTION

1. James G. Randall, "The Virginia Debt Controversy," *Political Science Quarterly* 30 (1915): 553–77; Rosewell Page, "The West Virginia Debt Settlement," *Virginia Law Register,* new ser., 5 (1919): 257–83.

2. William C. Coleman, "The State as Defendant under the Federal Constitution: The Virginia–West Virginia Debt Controversy," *Harvard Law Review* 31 (1917): 210–45; Thomas Reed Powell, "Coercing a State to Pay a Judgment: Virginia v. West Virginia," *Michigan Law Review* 17 (1918): 1–32.

3. Elizabeth J. Goodall, "The Virginia Debt Controversy and Settlement, Part I," *West Virginia History* 24 (1962): 42–74; "Part II," 24 (1963): 296–308; "Part III," 24 (1963): 332–51; "Part IV," 25 (1963): 42–68; "Part V," 25 (1964): 102–29.

4. John V. Orth, "The Virginia State Debt and the Judicial Power of the United States, 1870–1920," in *Ambivalent Legacy: A Legal History of the South,* ed. David J. Bodenhamer and James W. Ely Jr. (Jackson, Miss., 1984), 106–22.

5. Tarter, *Grandees of Government,* 231–54.

6. John O. Peters, *From Marshall to Moussaoui: Federal Justice in the Eastern District of Virginia* (Petersburg, Va., 2013), 79–86.

7. *Report of the Commission Appointed at the Session of 1889–90, to Receive Proposals for Settling the Outstanding Unsettled Obligations of the State,* 14 Jan. 1892, and printed as Senate Doc. 6 with *JSV,* 1891–92 sess., 15–24, and House Doc. 2 with *JHD,* 1891–92 sess., 15–24.

8. William A. Scott, *The Repudiation of State Debts: A Study in the Financial History of Mississippi, Florida, Alabama, North Carolina, South Carolina, Georgia, Louisiana, Arkansas, Tennessee, Minnesota, Michigan, and Virginia* (Boston, 1893), 167–96.

9. Royall, *History.*

10. Charles Chilton Pearson, *The Readjuster Movement in Virginia* (New Haven, Conn., 1917).

11. Reginald Charles McGrane, *Foreign Bondholders and American State Debts* (New York, 1935), 364–81; Benjamin Ulysses Ratchford, *American State Debts* (Durham, N.C., 1941), 197–229.

12. Allen W. Moger, *Virginia: Bourbonism to Byrd, 1870–1925* (Charlottesville, 1968), 21–75; Raymond H. Pulley, *Old Virginia Restored: An Interpretation of the Progressive Impulse, 1870–1930* (Charlottesville, 1968), 29–47.

13. Tarter, *Grandees of Government,* 239–304.

14. See James Tice Moore, "Redeemers Reconsidered: Change and Continuity

in the Democratic South, 1870–1900," *Journal of Southern History* 44 (1978): 357–78, and Moore, "Origins of the Solid South: Redeemer Democrats and the Popular Will, 1870–1900," *Southern Studies* 22 (1983): 285–301, as well as the later comments on those articles and the interpretation of late-nineteenth-century Southern history in John B. Boles and Bethany L. Johnson, eds., *Origins of the New South Fifty Years Later: The Continuing Influence of a Historical Classic* (Baton Rouge, 2003), esp. 131–43, 144–60.

15. Maddex, *Virginia Conservatives*, esp. 44–73, 121–42, 233–34.

16. Moore, *Two Paths*, esp. 83–92.

17. Charles E. Wynes, *Race Relations in Virginia, 1870–1902* (Charlottesville, 1961); Jane Dailey, *Before Jim Crow: The Politics of Race in Postemancipation Virginia* (Chapel Hill, 2000).

18. Carl N. Degler, *The Other South: Southern Dissenters in the Nineteenth Century* (New York, 1974), 264–315; Steven Hahn, *A Nation under Our Feet: Black Political Struggles in the Rural South, From Slavery to the Great Migration* (Cambridge, Mass., 2003), 367–84, 400–411.

19. C. Vann Woodward, *Origins of the New South, 1877–1913* (Baton Rouge, 1951), 92–100; Edward L. Ayers, *The Promise of the New South: Life after Reconstruction* (New York, 1992), 46–47.

20. Tarter, *Grandees of Government*, 189–93, 203.

21. George Harrison Gilliam, "Building a Modern South: Political Economy in Nineteenth-Century Virginia" (Ph.D. diss., University of Virginia, 2013).

22. Boles and Johnson, *Origins of the New South Fifty Years Later.*

1. ORIGINS OF THE DEBT CONTROVERSY

1. House Doc. 1 with *JHD*, 1861 extra sess., tabulation on xliii.

2. Benjamin Ulysses Ratchford, *American State Debts* (Durham, N.C., 1941), 124, 133.

3. Carter Goodrich, "The Virginia System of Mixed Enterprise: A Study of State Planning of Internal Improvements," *Political Science Quarterly* 44 (1940): 355–86. For the larger economic development context, see John D. Majewski, *A House Dividing: Economic Development in Pennsylvania and Virginia before the Civil War* (New York, 2000); Sean Patrick Adams, *Old Dominion, Industrial Commonwealth: Coal, Politics, and Economy in Antebellum America* (Baltimore, 2004); and George Harrison Gilliam, "Building a Modern South: Political Economy in Nineteenth-Century Virginia" (Ph.D. diss., University of Virginia, 2013), 16–96.

4. Ratchford, *American State Debts,* 124, 127.

5. Abraham Lincoln to the Senate and House of Representatives, 4 July 1861, *Congressional Globe,* 37th Cong., 1st sess., appendix, 2.

6. Virgil A. Lewis, ed., *How West Virginia Was Made. Proceedings of the First Convention of the People of Northwestern Virginia at Wheeling May 13, 14, and 15, 1861, and the Journal of the Second Convention of the People of Northwestern Virginia at Wheeling, Which Assembled, June 11th, 1861, and Continued in Session*

until June 25th. Adjourned until August 6th, 1861. Reassembled on that Date; and Continued in Session Until August 21st, When it Adjourned sine die. *With Appendixes and an Introduction, Annotations and Addenda* (Charleston, W.Va., 1909), 287.

7. Charles H. Ambler, Frances Haney Atwood, and William B. Mathews, eds., *Debates and Proceedings of the First Constitutional Convention of West Virginia (1861–1863)*, 3 vols. (Huntington, W.Va., 1939), 3:879. See also John E. Stealey III, *West Virginia's Civil War–Era Constitution: Loyal Revolution, Confederate Counter-Revolution, and the Convention of 1872* (Kent, Ohio, 2013), 84–87, 97.

8. Elizabeth J. Goodall, "The Virginia Debt Controversy and Settlement, Part I," *West Virginia History* 24 (1962): 44–48.

9. *Acts,* 1862 Wheeling extra sess., 3–4.

10. Ibid., 18.

11. *Acts,* 1862–63 Wheeling extra sess., 64–66.

12. Ibid., 68.

13. *Constitution of the State of Virginia, and The Ordinances Adopted by the Convention Which Assembled at Alexandria, on the 13th Day of February, 1864* (Alexandria, 1864), 15.

14. *Acts,* 1863 Richmond extra sess., 88–89.

15. Sara B. Bearss, "Restored and Vindicated: The Virginia Constitutional Convention of 1864," *VMHB* 122 (2014): 156–81.

16. *Acts,* 1865–66 sess., 194–96.

17. Ibid., 1866–67 sess., 482.

18. *Virginia v. West Virginia,* 78 US (1870): 39–65; Vasan Kesavan and Michael Stokes Paulsen, "Is West Virginia Unconstitutional?," *California Law Review* 90 (2002): 291–400.

19. William G. Thomas, *The Iron Way: Railroads, the Civil War, and the Making of Modern America* (New Haven, Conn., 2011), 181–86; Gilliam, "Building a Modern South," 162–63.

20. Robin L. Einhorn, *American Taxation, American Slavery* (Chicago, 2006).

21. Robert Clinton Burton, "The History of Taxation in Virginia, 1870–1901" (Ph.D. diss., University of Virginia, 1962), 4. For one extended examination, see Peter Wallenstein, *From Slave South to New South: Public Policy in Nineteenth-Century Georgia* (Chapel Hill, 1987), 183–95.

22. Wythe Holt, "'To Establish Justice': Politics, the Judiciary Act of 1789, and the Invention of the Federal Courts," *Duke Law Journal* (1989): 1421–1531, esp. 1439–51, 1459–66; Holt, "George Wythe: Early Modern Judge," *Alabama Law Review* 58 (2008): 1009–39, esp. 1017–24.

23. Maddex, *Virginia Conservatives,* 167–69; Amy Feely Morsman, *The Big House after Slavery: Virginia Plantation Families and Their Postbellum Domestic Experiment* (Charlottesville, 2010), 125–57; Jane Turner Censer, *The Reconstruction of White Southern Womanhood, 1865–1895* (Baton Rouge, 2003), 52–152; Jeffrey W. McClurken, *Take Care of the Living: Reconstructing Confederate Veteran Families in Virginia* (Charlottesville, 2009); Cynthia A. Kierner, Jennifer R. Loux, and Megan

Taylor Shockley, *Changing History: Virginia Women through Four Centuries* (Richmond, 2013), 189, 190–91, 195–96, 203.

24. Censer, *Reconstruction of White Southern Womanhood;* Kierner, Loux, and Shockley, *Changing History,* 182–84, 194–96; Catherine A. Jones, *Intimate Reconstructions: Children in Postemancipation Virginia* (Charlottesville, 2015), 180–82. Elizabeth R. Varon's *Appomattox: Victory, Defeat, and Freedom at the End of the Civil War* (New York, 2013) clearly demonstrated that Southern women paid close attention to important political news, even though there is not much good scholarship on that topic, much as Varon's *We Mean to Be Counted: White Women and Politics in Antebellum Virginia* (Chapel Hill, 1998) demonstrated the same before the Civil War even though most historians had overlooked or ignored the abundant evidence.

25. Younger and Moore, *Governors of Virginia,* 33–45.

26. *JHD,* 1865–66 sess., 10–11.

27. *Acts,* 1865–66 sess., 79–80.

28. Ibid., 453–54.

29. House Doc. 1 with *JHD,* 1866–67 sess., 4–5.

30. *Acts,* 1866–67 sess., 499–500.

31. Goodall, "Debt Controversy, Part I," 48–50.

32. *Acts,* 1866–67 sess., 805, 877, 904–5.

33. Dan T. Carter, *When the War Was Over: The Failure of Self-Reconstruction in the South, 1865–1867* (Baton Rouge, 1985); *Statutes at Large,* 39th Cong., 2d sess., 429.

34. Plaques mounted in the Virginia Capitol in 2013 contain complete lists of African American members of the Virginia Convention of 1867–68 and of the Senate and House of Delegates and their years of service in the nineteenth century; the data with numerous biographies is also posted on the web site of the General Assembly's Martin Luther King Jr. Commission. Compiled by editors of the *DVB* at the Library of Virginia, the lists include several men whom Luther Porter Jackson missed and one white man whom he erroneously identified as black when researching his pioneering *Free Negro Office-Holders in Virginia, 1867–1895* (Petersburg, Va., 1946).

35. Richard G. Lowe, "Virginia's Reconstruction Convention: General Schofield Rates the Delegates," *VMHB* 80 (1972): 341–60; Richard L. Hume, "The Membership of the Virginia Constitutional Convention of 1867–1868: A Study of the Beginnings of Congressional Reconstruction in the Upper South," ibid. 86 (1978): 461–84; Richard L. Hume and Jerry B. Gough, *Blacks, Carpetbaggers, and Scalawags: The Constitutional Conventions of Radical Reconstruction* (Baton Rouge, 2008), 35–44, 53–55, 57–69.

36. Tarter, *Grandees of Government,* 255–74.

37. *Constitution of Virginia, Framed by the Convention Which Met in Richmond, Virginia, the Third Day of December, Eighteen Hundred and Sixty-Seven* (Richmond, 1868), 29.

38. Richard G. Lowe, *Republicans and Reconstruction in Virginia, 1856–70* (Charlottesville, 1991), 159–63, 171; Maddex, *Virginia Conservatives,* 67–73.

39. Maddex, *Virginia Conservatives,* 46–66, 121–42, 276–96; Moore, *Two Paths,* 12–26.

40. Brent Tarter, "Daniel, Raleigh Travers," *DVB* 3:689–91.

41. Circular No. 4, Conservative State Committee, 12 Feb. 1868, broadside, Library of Virginia.

42. Lowe, *Republicans and Reconstruction in Virginia,* 164–82; Maddex, *Virginia Conservatives,* 82–85.

43. *JSV,* 1869–70 sess., 27–28; *JHD,* 1869–70 sess., 36.

2. THE FUNDING ACT OF 1871

1. *Acts,* 1863–64 Richmond sess., 3; Emily J. Salmon, "Bennett, Jonathan Mc-Cally," *DVB* 1:444–45.

2. *State Indebtedness,* printed in *Acts,* 1869–70 sess., 648.

3. Benjamin Ulysses Ratchford, *American State Debts* (Durham, N.C., 1941), 179, 254, 583.

4. *Acts,* 1869–70 sess., 8; 1870–71 sess., 67.

5. Records of commissioners printed as Senate Docs. 17 and 20 with *JSV,* 1869–70 sess., and as House Doc. 1 with *JHD,* 1871–72 sess.; records of the West Virginia commissioners printed with *Report of the Committee,* 22 Dec. 1873 (n.p., [ca. 1873]), 9–15, and also as Randolph Harrison, "West Virginia's Contributive Share of the Debt of Virginia," *Virginia Law Register* 10 (1905): 1055–71, on 1060; Rosewell Page, "The West Virginia Debt Settlement," ibid., new ser., 5 (1919): 257–83, on 260–61; Elizabeth J. Goodall, "The Virginia Debt Controversy and Settlement, Part I," *West Virginia History* 24 (1962): 55–65.

6. Younger and Moore, *Governors of Virginia,* 57–67.

7. House Doc. 6 with *JHD,* 1869–70 sess.

8. *JHD,* 1870–71 sess., 8.

9. Ratchford, *American State Debts,* 179.

10. *JSV,* 1870–71 sess., 294–95; *JHD,* 1870–71 sess., 387.

11. Allen W. Moger, "Railroad Practices and Policies in Virginia after the Civil War," *VMHB* 59 (1951): 425–26, 437–38; Robert Clinton Burton, "The History of Taxation in Virginia, 1870–1901" (Ph.D. diss., University of Virginia, 1962), 125, 128–30; George Harrison Gilliam, "Building a Modern South: Political Economy in Nineteenth-Century Virginia" (Ph.D. diss., University of Virginia, 2013), 200–215, 276–85.

12. *Acts,* 1870–71 sess., 378–81, quotation on 379.

13. John S. Wise summarized the allegations in his thinly disguised autobiographical novel, *The Lion's Skin: A Historical Novel and a Novel History* (New York, 1905), 285–87. See also Maddex, *Virginia Conservatives,* 97–99; and Gilliam, "Building a Modern South," 295–96.

14. Moger, "Railroad Practices and Policies," 433, 438–39, 442; Burton, "History of Taxation in Virginia," 125, 128–30; Maddex, *Virginia Conservatives,* 92–94, 143–65; Moore, *Two Paths,* 23–25, 100–102.

15. Maddex, *Virginia Conservatives,* 95–99, 113–20.

16. Ibid., 96–97; Gilliam, "Building a Modern South," 273–74.

17. *State Indebtedness,* in *Acts,* 1872–73 sess., 399–400.

18. Henry A. Wise, quoted in John S. Wise, *Lion's Skin,* 288.

19. Senate Doc. 5 with *JSV,* 1872–73 sess.; Senate Doc. 3 with *JSV,* 1874 sess.

20. *JHD,* 1871–72 sess., 16–25.

21. Enrolled Bills of the General Assembly, 1871–72 sess., 15, Records of the General Assembly, Record Group 78, Library of Virginia.

22. *JHD,* 1871–72 sess., 106–11.

23. Ibid., 111, recording that the delegates had declined to take a vote.

24. *Acts,* 1871–72 sess., 141. The House of Delegates voted 65 to 21 to override the veto (*JHD,* 1871–72 sess., 389), and the Senate, 21 to 10 (*JSV,* 1871–72 sess., 367–68).

25. Senate Doc. 19 with *JSV,* 1871–72 sess.

26. *Acts,* 1871–72 sess., 218.

27. [Bradley T. Johnson], *The Public Debt of Virginia and the Attempt to Repeal the Funding Bill* ([Richmond, 1872]), quotation on 15.

28. John O. Peters, "Bouldin, Wood," *DVB* 2:122–23.

29. *Antoni v. Wright* and *Wright v. Smith,* 62 VA (1872): 833–59, quotation on 837.

30. Ibid., 859–71, quotations on 863, 866–67.

31. William L. Royall, "Constitutionality of the Funding Bill," *VLJ* 2 (1878): 129–46, on 139.

32. Brent Tarter, "Anderson, Francis Thomas," *DVB* 1:133–34.

33. Anderson's concurrence in 62 VA (1872): 871–87.

34. Supreme Court of Appeals Richmond City Orders No. 22 (1872): 650–51. For contrasting learned but partisan expositions of the decision and dissent in the case, see Royall, "Constitutionality of the Funding Bill," *VLJ* 2 (1878): 129–46; and William Green, "The Funding Act," ibid., 193–209.

35. *Wise Bros. &c. v. Rogers,* 63 VA (1873): 169–71, quotations on 171.

36. *Oxford English Dictionary,* s.v. "consol" and "consolidated."

37. John W. Johnston, "Repudiation in Virginia," *North American Review* 134 (1882): 149–60, on 151; Morris Gray, "The Coupon-Legislation of Virginia," *American Law Review* 23 (1889): 924–45, on 927.

38. *Alexandria Gazette,* 27 Mar. 1874.

39. Goodall, "Debt Controversy, Part I," 62–64; John E. Stealey III, *West Virginia's Civil War–Era Constitution: Loyal Revolution, Confederate Counter-Revolution, and the Convention of 1872* (Kent, Ohio, 2013), 483–89, 703; *Constitution and Schedule Adopted in Convention, at Charleston, April 9th, 1872* (Charleston, W.Va., 1874), 34–35.

40. *Report of the Senate Finance Committee,* 22 Dec. 1873, printed as a pamphlet without title ([Charleston, W.Va., ca. 1873]), quotation on 6–7, also in Clarke W. May et al., *Answer of Defendant,* Oct. Term 1907, Exhibit No. 3, 28–32, in *Virginia vs. West Virginia,* vol. 2, 8th imprint, quotation on 31; Goodall, "Debt Controversy, Part I," 5–71.

41. James G. Randall, "The Virginia Debt Controversy," *Political Science Quarterly* 30 (1915): 553–77, on 554–56; Charles Henry Ambler, *Sectionalism in Virginia from 1776 to 1861* (Chicago, 1910), 240–43, 311–19; Stealey, *West Virginia's Civil War–Era Constitution*, 84–87.

42. Goodall, "Debt Controversy, Part I," 66–68.

3. FUNDERS AND READJUSTERS

1. *JHD*, 1872–73 sess., 7–9, quotation on 8.

2. Senate Doc. 8 with *JSV*, 1872–73 sess.

3. Senate Doc. 12 with *JSV*, 1872–73 sess.

4. *Acts*, 1872–73 sess., 160–61.

5. Ibid., 207.

6. Ibid., 13–14.

7. *Second Bondholders Report* (1875), printed with additional information in *Petersburg Index and Appeal*, 8 Mar. 1875.

8. House Doc. 6 with *JHD*, 1872–73 sess.

9. *Acts*, 1872–73 sess., 219–20.

10. Executive Papers of Governor Gilbert Carlton Walker, Record Group 3, Library of Virginia.

11. House Doc. 6 with *JHD*, 1869–70 sess., 31–32.

12. Tarter, *Grandees of Government*, 90.

13. *JHD*, 1901 extra sess., 6.

14. *Acts*, 1873–74 sess., 9.

15. House Docs. 6 and 7 with *JHD*, 1873–74 sess.; House Doc. 9 with *JHD*, 1878–79 sess.

16. Maddex, *Virginia Conservatives*, 114–17; Emily J. Salmon, "Coleman, William D.," *DVB* 3:366–68, and research notes in *DVB* files, Library of Virginia.

17. *Acts*, 1874–75 sess., 420–22.

18. Maddex, *Virginia Conservatives*, 104–13; Younger and Moore, *Governors of Virginia*, 69–79.

19. *Acts*, 1873–74 sess., 264–65.

20. *Third Bondholders Report* (1875), 19–20.

21. *JHD*, 1873–74 sess., 350–52, quotations on 351, 352.

22. Ibid., 343–50, quotation on 347; Maddex, *Virginia Conservatives*, 235.

23. "The Women's Association for the Liquidation of the State Debt. To the Daughters of Virginia—Respectfully Greeting" (undated broadside, probably 1873–75 judging by its characterization of the amount of principal and interest then due), Virginia Historical Society.

24. *JHD*, 1873–74 sess., 482–84.

25. Tipton Ray Snavely, *The Taxation of Negroes in Virginia* (Charlottesville, 1917), 18–20; Richard L. Morton, *The Negro in Virginia Politics, 1865–1902* (Charlottesville, 1919), 90–96; Robert E. Martin, "Negro Disfranchisement in Virginia" (MA thesis, Howard University, 1938), 85–86; Charles E. Wynes, *Race Relations in*

Virginia, 1870–1902 (Charlottesville, 1961), 23–24; Maddex, *Virginia Conservatives,* 197–98.

26. Maddex, *Virginia Conservatives,* 184–203; Pippa Holloway, "'A Chicken-Stealer Shall Lose His Vote': Disfranchisement for Larceny in the South, 1874–1890," *Journal of Southern History* 75 (2009): 931–62.

27. Emily J. Salmon and Edward D. C. Campbell Jr., eds., *The Hornbook of Virginia History,* 4th rev. ed. (Richmond, 1994), 92.

28. W. Dean Burnham, *Presidential Ballots, 1836–1892* (Baltimore, 1955), 817.

29. *Proceedings of a Conference with Virginia Creditors, Including an Exposition of the Debt, Finances, and Taxation of the State by the Governor, on the Tenth Day of November, 1874* (Richmond, 1874), quotation on 4; also printed as House Doc. 1 with *JHD,* 1874–75 sess., and as Senate Doc. 1 with *JSV,* 1874–75 sess.

30. House Doc. 4 with *JHD,* 1874–75 sess., and Senate Doc. 4 with *JSV,* 1874–75 sess.

31. *JHD,* 1874–75 sess., 4–8, quotation on 7.

32. *Acts,* 1874–75 sess., 366–67.

33. The broadside collection of the Library of Virginia preserves samples of the three electoral tickets.

34. John E. Massey, *Debts and Taxes, or Obligations and Resources of Virginia* ([Charlottesville], 1875), quotations on 8, 16; Maddex, *Virginia Conservatives,* 237–39.

35. *Acts,* 1875–76 sess., 203–4.

36. *JHD,* 1876–77 sess., 5–11, quotations on 5, 6.

37. Peter S. Carmichael, *The Last Generation: Young Virginians in Peace, War, and Reunion* (Chapel Hill, 2005).

38. Nelson Morehouse Blake, *William Mahone of Virginia: Soldier and Political Insurgent* (Richmond, 1935); Maddex, *Virginia Conservatives,* 248–54.

39. Younger and Moore, *Governors of Virginia,* 81–93.

40. Brent Tarter, "Daniel, Raleigh Travers," *DVB* 3:689–91.

41. Maddex, *Virginia Conservatives,* 248–56; Moore, *Two Paths,* 53–59.

42. *JHD,* 1877–78 sess., 137–38.

43. Senate Doc. 24 with *JSV,* 1877–78 sess., quotation on 25.

44. Bradley T. Johnson, "Can States Be Compelled to Pay Their Debts?," *American Law Review* 12 (1878): 625–59, quotations on 625, 626.

45. Donald W. Gunter, "Barbour, James," *DVB* 1:331–33.

46. A Bill Imposing Taxes on Real and Personal Property to Meet the Necessary Expenses of the Government and to Pay the Interest on the Public Debt, Enrolled Bills of the General Assembly, 1877–78 sess., 192–95, Records of the General Assembly, Record Group 78, Library of Virginia.

47. Maddex, *Virginia Conservatives,* 261–64.

48. William Bland Whitley, "Daniel, John Warwick," *DVB* 3:681–85.

49. *Richmond Daily Whig,* 30 Jan. 1878.

50. John W. Daniel to W. T. Taliaferro, 19 Sept. 1879, in Richmond *Daily Dispatch,* 24 Sept. 1879.

51. *JHD*, 1877–78 sess., 425–30, quotations on 425–26, 427, 428.

52. Ibid., 434.

53. Maddex, *Virginia Conservatives*, 204–17.

54. "Conference of Re-Adjusters," *Richmond Daily Whig*, 28 Feb. 1878.

55. *JSV*, 1877–78 sess., 407–15.

56. *Acts*, 1877–78 sess., 230–33.

4. THE READJUSTER PARTY

1. Jane Turner Censer, *The Reconstruction of White Southern Womanhood, 1865–1895* (Baton Rouge, 2003), 153–206; Cynthia A. Kierner, Jennifer R. Loux, and Megan Taylor Shockley, *Changing History: Virginia Women through Four Centuries* (Richmond 2013), 189–90, 203–4.

2. *JHD*, 1878–79 sess., 26.

3. *Fourth Bondholders Report* (1877), 54–56.

4. *JHD*, 1878–79 sess., 5–25, quotation on 5.

5. *Acts*, 1878–79 sess., 29–30.

6. *Virginia State Debt. Report of Mr. John Collinson and Mr. E. R. Leland, to the Council of Foreign Bondholders, and the Funding Association of the U.S.A., (Limited), on the Funding Act, 1879* (London, 1879), 4.

7. *Acts*, 1878–79 sess., 75–76.

8. Robert W. Hughes, letter to the editor, 6 Jan. 1879, printed in Staunton *Valley Virginian*, 16 Jan. 1879, and also in *Richmond Daily Whig*, 18 Jan. 1879; [James C. Lamb], "The 'Coupon Killers,'" *VLJ* 7 (1883): 513–26, on 522.

9. Senate Doc. 23 with *JSV*, 1878–79 sess.

10. Maddex, *Virginia Conservatives*, 268–71; Moore, *Two Paths*, 62–64.

11. *Acts*, 1878–79 sess., 264–68.

12. *Williamson v. Massey*, 74 VA (1880): 237–50.

13. Brent Tarter, "Blair, Francis Simpson," *DVB* 1:537–39.

14. John T. Kneebone, "Brisby, William Henry," *DVB* 2:234–35.

15. *Richmond Daily Whig*, 26, 27 Feb. 1879 (quotations); Richmond *Daily Dispatch*, 26, 27 Feb. 1879.

16. Charles E. Wynes, *Race Relations in Virginia, 1870–1902* (Charlottesville, 1961), 26–38; Jane Dailey, *Before Jim Crow: The Politics of Race in Postemancipation Virginia* (Chapel Hill, 2000); Tarter, *Grandees of Government*, 245–50.

17. *Seventh Bondholders Report* (1880), 8–9.

18. Maddex, *Virginia Conservatives*, 256–75.

19. *Seventh Bondholders Report* (1880), 66–67.

20. *JHD*, 1879–80 sess., 37–51.

21. Compare lists of city and county superintendents in 1880 with 1882 and 1883 lists in the official annual reports of the superintendent of public instruction.

22. *JHD*, 1879–80 sess., 63.

23. Ibid., 9–19.

24. Senate Doc. 3 with *JSV*, 1879–80 sess.

25. Senate Doc. 12 with *JSV*, 1879–80 sess.; Robert Clinton Burton, "The History of Taxation in Virginia, 1870–1901" (Ph.D. diss., University of Virginia, 1962), 149–52.

26. *JHD*, 1885–86 sess., 422.

27. A Bill to Reestablish the Public Credit, Enrolled Bills of the General Assembly, 1879–80 sess., 363–88, Records of the General Assembly, Record Group 78, Library of Virginia.

28. *JSV*, 1879–80 sess., 440–43, quotation on 440.

29. Ibid., 443, recording that the Senate tabled the motion to take up the bill.

30. Ibid., 401–2, 411; *JHD*, 1879–80 sess., 471.

31. William Bland Whitley, "Christian, Joseph," *DVB* 3:231–32.

32. *Clarke v. Tyler*, 71 VA (1878): 134–45, quotation on 144; also reported in part in *VLJ* 2 (1878): 222–32.

33. 71 VA (1878): 145–50, quotation on 146.

34. Peter Wallenstein, "Burks, Edward Calohill," *DVB* 2:409–11.

35. 71 VA (1878): 150–65.

36. *Hartman v. Greenhow*, Supreme Court of Appeals Richmond City Orders No. 25 (1878): 93.

37. *Hartman v. Greenhow*, 102 US (1881): 672–86, quotation on 684.

38. *Eighth Bondholders Report* (1881), 71–75, quotation on 73.

39. Younger and Moore, *Governors of Virginia*, 95–109; James Tice Moore, "Cameron, William Evelyn," *DVB* 3:533–36.

40. *Richmond Daily Whig*, 15, 16 Mar. 1881, quotations from 16 Mar.

41. Moore, *Two Paths*, 68–71.

42. *Richmond Daily Whig*, 3, 4 June 1881.

43. Moore, *Two Paths*, 67, 73.

44. Richmond *Daily Dispatch*, 5, 6 Aug. 1881. The following account of the campaign is derived from Tarter, *Grandees of Government*, 246–47.

45. John S. Wise, *The Lion's Skin: A Historical Novel and a Novel History* (New York, 1905), 303.

46. Joseph Patrick Harahan, "Politics, Political Parties, and Voter Participation in Tidewater Virginia during Reconstruction, 1865–1900" (Ph.D. diss., Michigan State University, 1973).

47. W. Dean Burnham, *Presidential Ballots, 1836–1892* (Baltimore, 1955), 817.

48. Corruption of the electoral process is well documented in Ronald E. Shibley, "Election Laws and Electoral Practices in Virginia, 1867–1902: An Administrative and Political History" (Ph.D. diss., University of Virginia, 1972), esp. 60–214; Wythe Holt, *Virginia's Constitutional Convention of 1901–1902* (New York, 1990), 59–74; and Tarter, *Grandees of Government*, 262–64. The published vote totals are therefore not entirely reliable.

49. Official returns printed in *JHD*, 1881–82 sess., 33; 1885–86 sess., 21; 1889–90 sess., 49.

50. "Free Schools, Free Ballot, and a Fair Count," broadside, Library of Virginia.

51. Moore, *Two Paths*, 83–92, 128–29, 140–52.

5. READJUSTMENT, REFORM, AND REACTION

1. *JHD*, 1881–82 sess., 9–14.

2. Fred W. M. Holliday, *Letters of Travel*, 8 vols. (Baltimore, 1897); John d'Entremont, "Virginians Encounter the World: The Travels in India of Moncure Conway and Frederick Holliday," paper presented at the Virginia Forum, James Madison University, 31 Mar. 2012.

3. *JHD*, 1881–82 sess., 99–103, quotations on 101.

4. *Acts*, 1881–82 sess., 88–98.

5. Robert Clinton Burton, "The History of Taxation in Virginia, 1870–1901" (Ph.D. diss., University of Virginia, 1962), 211.

6. Charles Chilton Pearson, *The Readjuster Movement in Virginia* (New Haven, Conn., 1917), 142–51; Allen W. Moger, *Virginia: Bourbonism to Byrd, 1870–1925* (Charlottesville, 1968), 21–75; Raymond H. Pulley, *Old Virginia Restored: An Interpretation of the Progressive Impulse, 1870–1930* (Charlottesville, 1968), 29–47; Jane Dailey, *Before Jim Crow: The Politics of Race in Postemancipation Virginia* (Chapel Hill, 2000), 48–102; Carl N. Degler, *The Other South: Southern Dissenters in the Nineteenth Century* (New York, 1974), 264–315; Steven Hahn, *A Nation under Our Feet: Black Political Struggles in the Rural South, From Slavery to the Great Migration* (Cambridge, Mass., 2003), 367–84, 400–411; Moore, *Two Paths*, esp. 83–92; Tarter, *Grandees of Government*, 245–50.

7. James Tice Moore, "The University and the Readjusters," *VMHB* 78 (1970): 87–101; Moore, "Battle for the Medical College: Physicians, Politicians, and the Courts, 1882–1883," *Virginia Cavalcade* 31 (1982): 158–67.

8. Burton, "History of Taxation in Virginia," 85–119, with railroad data on 67–68, 96–100, 106.

9. *JHD*, 1881–82 sess., 74.

10. Ibid., 1883–84 sess., 17–23, quotation on 20.

11. *Address of the Readjuster Members of the Legislature to the People!* (Richmond, 1882).

12. John W. Johnston, "Repudiation in Virginia," *North American Review* 134 (1882): 149–60, quotation on 159–60.

13. H. H. Riddleberger, "Bourbonism in Virginia," ibid., 416–30, quotations on 425, 427.

14. William Mahone to John D. Long, 11 Feb. 1882, reprinted in *Richmond Daily Whig*, 15 Mar. 1882.

15. Alan B. Bromberg, "Barbour, John Strode," *DVB* 1:334–36.

16. Allen W. Moger, "Railroad Practices and Policies in Virginia after the Civil War," *VMHB* 59 (1951): 423–57; Moger, "The Origin of the Democratic Machine in Virginia," *Journal of Southern History* 8 (1942): 183–209.

17. Charles E. Wynes, *Race Relations in Virginia, 1870–1902* (Charlottesville, 1961), 68–110.

18. Mahone's Brigade, William Mahone Papers, Duke University.

19. Tarter, *Grandees of Government*, 241–42, 248–50.

20. "Public Free Schools!," broadside ([ca. 1883]), Library of Virginia.

21. Richmond *Daily Dispatch*, 26 July 1883.

22. Dailey, *Before Jim Crow*, 103–54.

23. Moger, *Virginia: Bourbonism to Byrd;* Pulley, *Old Virginia Restored;* William A. Link, *A Hard Country and a Lonely Place: Schooling, Society, and Reform in Rural Virginia, 1870–1920* (Chapel Hill, 1986).

24. *Acts,* 1883–84 sess., 7–8.

25. Senate Doc. 3 with *JSV,* 1884 extra sess.; Tarter, "Blair, Francis Simpson," *DVB* 1:537–39; *Blair v. Marye,* 80 VA (1885): 485–502.

26. *Acts,* 1884 extra sess., 146–51.

27. Ronald E. Shibley, "Election Laws and Electoral Practices in Virginia, 1867–1902: An Administrative and Political History" (Ph.D. diss., University of Virginia, 1972), esp. 60–214; Wythe Holt, *Virginia's Constitutional Convention of 1901–1902* (New York, 1990), 59–74; Tarter, *Grandees of Government,* 262–64.

28. Quoted passage from John Warwick Daniel, address at Fincastle, Virginia, 23 Oct. 1883, printed in Richmond *Daily Dispatch,* 26 Oct. 1883.

29. Moore, *Two Paths,* 73, 79, 93, 99, 110, 112, 113.

30. Wynes, *Race Relations in Virginia,* 131.

31. *JHD,* 1885–86 sess., 21.

6. THE COUPON KILLERS

1. [James C. Lamb], "The 'Coupon Killers,'" *VLJ* 7 (1883): 513–26; *Eleventh Bondholders Report* (1884), 111.

2. An early analysis of the legislation and resulting court cases that is decidedly unsympathetic to the anti-coupon laws is Morris Gray, "The Coupon-Legislation of Virginia," *American Law Review* 23 (1889): 924–45.

3. *Acts,* 1881–82 sess., 10–12, quotation on 10.

4. House Docs. 6 and 8 with *JHD,* 1881–82 sess.

5. Frank Simpson Blair, *Annual Report* (1883), 9.

6. [Lamb], "Coupon Killers," 516.

7. *Commonwealth v. Weller & Sons,* 82 VA (1887): 725.

8. *Willis and Wife v. Miller,* 29 Fed. Rep. (1886): 238–44, quotation on 239–40.

9. [Lamb], "Coupon Killers," 517–18.

10. *Acts,* 1881–82 sess., 37–39.

11. Ibid., 342.

12. Ibid., 537.

13. This fact does not appear in the court's official order book but was stated in Chief Justice Morrison R. Waite's 1883 opinion for the Supreme Court of the United States in *Antoni v. Greenhow,* 107 US (1883): 769–812, on 774.

14. *Antoni v. Greenhow,* Supreme Court of Appeals Richmond City Orders No. 26 (1882): 373–74.

15. *Antoni v. Greenhow,* 107 US (1883): 769–82, quotation on 775.

16. Ibid., 784–801, quotation on 797.

17. Ibid., 801–12, quotations on 806, 808.

18. William L. Royall, "Constitutionality of the Funding Bill," *VLJ* 2 (1878): 129–46, on 145.

19. *Antoni v. Greenhow,* 107 US (1883): 779–80.

20. [Lamb], "Coupon Killers," 515–16.

21. *Commonwealth v. H. M. Smith Jr.,* 76 VA (1882): 477–86.

22. *Commonwealth v. Taylor,* Supreme Court of Appeals Richmond City Orders No. 26 (1882): 397, and described in [Lamb], "Coupon Killers," 516–17.

23. Royall, *History,* 83; *In Re Ayers,* 123 US (1887): 443–516, on 447.

24. *Baltimore & Ohio Railroad Co. v. Allen,* 17 Fed. Rep. (1883): 171–76, quotation on 175; also reported in part in *VLJ* 7 (1883): 409–12.

25. *Baltimore & Ohio Railroad Co. v. Allen,* 17 Fed. Rep. (1883): 176–97.

26. [Lamb], "Coupon Killers," 513–26, esp. 518.

27. *The Coupon and Tax Question. May a State be Enjoined from Collecting her Taxes by a Federal Court? If She Can be at all, Then Under What Circumstances? Opinion of Hon. Robert W. Hughes, U.S. District Judge for the Eastern District of Virginia, Sitting Alone, in Circuit Court, 15th May, 1883, in a Case from the Western District of Virginia* (n.p., [1883]).

28. [Lamb], "Coupon Killers," 518.

29. *Commonwealth v. Guggenheimer,* 78 VA (1883): 71–75; reported also in *VLJ* 8 (1884): 96–98.

30. *Commonwealth v. Guggenheimer,* 78 VA (1883): 74–75.

31. *Acts,* 1884 extra sess., 121–22.

32. Senate Doc. 9 with *JSV,* 1883–84 sess.

33. *Eleventh Bondholders Report* (1884), 110, 112.

34. Moore, *Two Paths,* 100.

35. *JHD,* 1883–84 sess., 17–19, quotations on 17, 18.

36. *Acts,* 1883–84 sess., 721–22.

37. Ibid., 561, 603.

38. Ibid., 590.

39. *Smith v. Greenhow,* 109 US (1884): 669–71; Stanley I. Kutler, *Judicial Power and Reconstruction Politics* (Chicago, 1968), 143–60; William M. Wiecek, "The Reconstruction of Federal Judicial Power, 1863–1875," *American Journal of Legal History* 13 (1969): 333–59.

40. *Acts,* 1883–84 sess., 251.

41. *Taylor v. Williams,* 78 VA (1884): 422–30; also reported in *VLJ* 8 (1884): 216–21.

42. *Acts,* 1883–84 sess., 527.

43. Blair, *Annual Report* (1883), 9.

44. *Dunnington v. Ford,* 80 VA (1885): 177–79, quotation on 179.

45. *Harvey and Another v. Commonwealth of Virginia,* 20 Fed. Rep. (1884): 411–22; also reported in part in *VLJ* 8 (1884): 400–409.

46. *Harvey and Another v. Commonwealth of Virginia,* 20 Fed. Rep. (1884): 413.

47. Blair, *Annual Report* (1883), 9–10.

48. *Commonwealth v. Maury* (1884), reported in *VLJ* 8 (1884): 494–502.

49. Senate Doc. 5 with *JSV*, 1884 extra sess.

50. *Faure v. Sinking Fund Commissioners*, 25 Fed. Rep. (1884): 641–47, quotations on 642, 647; date of ruling in Hughes's revised opinion printed in the *Richmond State*, 2 Sept. 1884.

51. *Acts*, 1884 extra sess., 30–31.

52. Ibid., 163–64. For an account of the enactment of the Wickham Amendment and its effects, see *Richmond Dispatch*, 27 Jan. 1888.

53. *Richmond State*, 2 Sept. 1884.

54. John O. Peters, *From Marshall to Moussaoui: Federal Justice in the Eastern District of Virginia* (Petersburg, Va., 2013), 83–85.

55. *Colonel Frank G. Ruffin's Letter: A Terrible Arraignment: Mahoneism Unveiled! The Great Plot to Sell out Virginians to the Republican Party Exposed* ([Richmond, 1882]); *An Appeal to the 31,527 Re-Adjuster Democrats of Virginia* ([Richmond], 1883).

56. *An Examination of Judge Robert W. Hughes' Decision in the Case of John P. Faure, vs. The Commissioners of the Sinking Fund of Virginia, By Frank G. Ruffin. Respectfully Submitted to The General Assembly of Virginia* (Richmond, 1884).

57. *A Reply, to a Pamphlet Assailing his Political and Official Conduct, by Robert W. Hughes, A Citizen of Virginia* (n.p., [1884]).

58. Frank G. Ruffin, *Judge Robert W. Hughes in the Case of Jno. P. Faure vs. the Commissioners of the Sinking Fund of Va.* (Richmond, 1884).

59. James Tice Moore, "Cameron, William Evelyn," *DVB* 2:534.

7. THE COUPON CASES

1. *Eleventh Bondholders Report* (1884), 111; *Thirteenth Bondholders Report* (1886), quotation on 153.

2. *Poindexter v. Greenhow*, 114 US (1885): 270–306.

3. *White v. Greenhow*, ibid., 307–8.

4. *Chaffin v. Taylor*, Supreme Court of Appeals Richmond City Orders No. 27 (1884): 226.

5. *Chaffin v. Taylor*, 114 US (1885): 309–10.

6. *Chaffin v. Taylor*, Supreme Court of Appeals at Staunton Orders No. 2 (1885): 308; *Chaffin v. Taylor*, 116 US (1886): 567–72.

7. *Allen v. Baltimore and Ohio Railroad Company*, 114 US (1885): 311–17.

8. *Carter v. Greenhow*, ibid., 317–23; *Pleasants v. Greenhow*, ibid., 323–24.

9. *Marye v. Parsons*, ibid., 325–38, with opinion of court on 325–30.

10. *Marye v. Parsons*, ibid., 330–38, quotation on 338.

11. *Moore v. Greenhow*, ibid., 338–40.

12. *Acts*, 1885–86 sess., 453.

13. *Jones v. Commonwealth of Virginia*, 25 Fed. Rep. (1885): 666–69.

14. *Stewart v. Virginia*, 117 US (1886): 612–15.

15. William L. Royall, "Constitutionality of the Funding Bill," *VLJ* 2 (1878): 129–46, on 145; Harlan in *Antoni v. Greenhow*, 107 US (1883): 808.

16. *Thirteenth Bondholders Report* (1886), 157–58; *Fourteenth Bondholders Report* (1887), 140–41, quotation on 141.

17. *Fourteenth Bondholders Report* (1887), 145; *Fifteenth Bondholders Report* (1888), 195–96; *Sixteenth Bondholders Report* (1889), 178–81; *Seventeenth Bondholders Report* (1890), 160–62.

18. *Gorman v. Sinking Fund Commissioners*, 25 Fed. Rep. (1885): 647–54.

19. *Norfolk Trust Co. v. Marye* (1885), ibid., 654–66.

20. *Greenhow v. Vashon*, 81 VA (1886): 336–54, quotation on 351.

21. *Royall v. Virginia*, 116 US (1886): 572–84; *Sands v. Edmunds*, ibid., 585–87.

22. *Barry v. Edmunds*, ibid., 550–66, quotation on 566.

23. *Ex Parte Royall*, 117 US (1886): 241–54.

24. *Ex Parte Royall*, ibid., 254–55.

25. John V. Orth, "The Virginia State Debt and the Judicial Power of the United States, 1870–1920," in *Ambivalent Legacy: A Legal History of the South*, ed. David J. Bodenhamer and James W. Ely Jr. (Jackson, Miss., 1984), 106–22, on 121 n. 44, citing a personal communication from Wythe Holt.

26. *Acts*, 1885–86 sess., 36–37, quotation on 37.

27. *Fifteenth Bondholders Report* (1888), 193.

28. *Acts*, 1885–86 sess., 40.

29. Ibid., 86.

30. Ibid., 312.

31. Ibid., 467–69, quotation on 467.

32. Ibid., 228.

33. Ayers, quoted in *Strickler and Wife v. Yager*, 29 Fed. Rep. (1886): 244–45, on 245.

34. Instructions described in statement of evidence in *Willis and Wife v. Miller*, ibid., 240–44, on 241.

35. *Acts*, 1885–86 sess., 384, with index cross-reference on 596; Bradley in *McGahey v. Virginia*, 135 US (1890): 662–721, on 680; *Fifteenth Bondholders Report* (1888), 190.

36. *Cornwall v. Commonwealth*, 82 VA (1886): 644–46; *Newton v. Commonwealth* and *Burruss v. Commonwealth*, ibid., 647–49; all three also reported in part in *VLJ* 11 (1887): 90–94.

37. *Commonwealth v. Weller & Sons*, 82 VA (1887): 721–26, quotation on 723; also reported in part in *VLJ* 11 (1887): 166–69.

38. *Commonwealth v. Booker & Co.* and *Same v. Fifty-Seven Others*, 82 VA (1887): 964–65.

39. *Commonwealth v. Jones*, ibid., 789–800, quotations on 793, 793–94; reported also in *VLJ* 11 (1887): 152–61.

40. *Commonwealth v. Maury*, 82 VA (1887): 883–89, quotation on 888; reported also in *VLJ* 11 (1887): 161–66.

41. *Willis and Wife v. Miller*, 29 Fed. Rep. (1886): 238–44; also reported in part in *VLJ* 10 (1886): 712–13.

42. *Strickler and Wife v. Yager*, 29 Fed. Rep. (1886): 244–45.

43. Ibid., 245.

44. *Royall v. Virginia*, Supreme Court of Appeals Richmond City Orders No. 28 (1887): 186.

45. *Royall v. Virginia*, 121 US (1887): 102–5, quotations on 104, 105.

46. *In Re Royall*, 125 US (1888), 696–97; *W. L. Royall v. Commonwealth of Virginia*, and *Ex Parte William L. Royall*, Supreme Court of Appeals Richmond City Orders No. 28 (1888): 502–4, 628–29.

8. THE COUPON CRUSHER

1. Younger and Moore, *Governors of Virginia*, 111–20.

2. Rufus Adolphus Ayers, *Annual Report* (1887), 13.

3. *JHD*, 1885–86 sess., 420–23, quotation on 421.

4. Senate Doc. 17 with *JSV*, 1887 extra sess.

5. *JHD*, 1887 extra sess., 4–11, quotation on 8.

6. *Fifteenth Bondholders Report* (1888), 190–91; Royall, *History*, 102–6.

7. The 1889 edition, published in Ashland, was printed with the revised title *Report on the Public Debt of Virginia to the Senate, by Bradley T. Johnson*.

8. *Fourteenth Bondholders Report* (1887), 143–46.

9. Senate Doc. 7 with *JSV*, 1887 extra sess., quotation on 2.

10. Senate Docs. 10, 11, 17, and 18 (including more than 100 pages of stenographic transcriptions of negotiation sessions) with *JSV*, 1887 extra sess.; *Fifteenth Bondholders Report* (1888), 191–92; Sir Edward Thornton and S. N. Braithwaite, *Virginia State Debt: Report to the Council of Foreign Bondholders of Negotiations Conducted at Richmond* (London, 1887).

11. Royall, *History*, 83–84.

12. *JHD*, 1887 extra sess., 9–10, quotation on 9.

13. Royall, *History*, 86, and so described in *New York Times*, 8 June 1887, and *Fifteenth Bondholders Report* (1888), 192.

14. *Acts*, 1887 extra sess., 257–60; *Fifteenth Bondholders Report* (1888), 192–93.

15. Royall, *History*, 88–89.

16. *James P. Cooper, et al. v. Morton Marye, et al.*, printed in full in *In Re Ayers*, 123 US (1887): 443–516, on 454–55.

17. Edward L. Ayers, "Ayers, Rufus Adolphus," *DVB* 1: 260–62.

18. *In Re Ayers*, 123 US (1887): 455–57; *New York Times*, 8 June 1887.

19. *In Re Rufus A. Ayers*, 8 Oct. 1887, in the Circuit Court for the Eastern District of Virginia, printed in full in *In Re Ayers*, 123 US (1887): 445–84, quotation on 457.

20. Ibid., quotation on 456.

21. Rufus Adolphus Ayers, *Annual Reports* (1887), 11–13; (1888), 9.

22. Full record in *Transcription of Record in the Supreme Court of the United States, of the Virginia Coupon Controversy* (Washington, D.C., 1887).

23. *In Re Ayers*, 123 US (1887): 443–516, on 485–508.

24. Ibid., 508–10, quotation on 508–9.

25. Ibid., 510–16, quotation on 516.

26. *Acts,* 1887 extra sess., 437.

27. Ibid., 516–17.

28. Ibid., 522.

29. Ibid., 530.

30. Ibid., 304.

31. Ibid., 534–35.

32. *JHD,* 1887–88 sess., 16–22, quotations on 20, 20, 22.

33. Senate Docs. 4 and 5 with *JSV,* 1887–88 sess.

34. *Sixteenth Bondholders Report* (1889), 178–81, quotation on 181.

35. *Seventeenth Bondholders Report* (1890), 167–85.

36. Rufus Adolphus Ayers, *Annual Report* (1889), 10–12.

37. *McGahey v. Commonwealth,* 85 VA (1888): 519–25; reported in part in *VLJ* 13 (1889): 28–30.

38. *Commonwealth v. Hurt,* 85 VA (1888): 918–20; and reported in *VLJ* 13 (1889): 270–71.

39. *Smith v. Clark,* Virginia Supreme Court of Appeals Staunton Orders No. 2 (1889): 550; and reported unofficially in *VLJ* 13 (1889): 695–96.

40. *Mallan Bros. v. Bransford,* 86 VA (1890): 675–78; and reported in part in *VLJ* 14 (1890): 153–55.

41. *JHD,* 1889–90 sess., 19–25, quotations on 22, 23.

42. House Doc. 4 with *JHD,* 1889–90 sess.

43. Younger and Moore, *Governors of Virginia,* 121–34.

44. House Doc. 6 with *JHD,* 1889–90 sess., quotation on 3.

45. Ibid., quotations on 2.

46. Text omitted from *Acts,* 1889–90 sess., but included in commission's 1892 report as Senate Doc. 6 with *JSV,* 1891–92 sess., and as House Doc. 1 with *JHD,* 1891–92 sess.

47. *McGahey v. Virginia, Bryan v. Virginia,* and *Cooper v. Virginia,* 135 US (1890): 662–95, quotation on 693.

48. *Ellett v. Virginia,* ibid., 696–98.

49. *Cuthbert v. Virginia,* ibid., 698–701.

50. *Ex Parte Brown,* ibid., 701–9.

51. *Hucles v. Childrey,* ibid., 709–12.

52. *Vashon v. Greenhow,* ibid., 713–20.

53. Ibid., quotation on 721.

9. THE OLCOTT ACT OF 1892

1. Royall, *History,* 97–98.

2. R. Taylor Scott, *Annual Report* (1891), 7.

3. R. Taylor Scott, *Annual Reports* (1890), 6–8; (1891), 4–6, 7–10; (1892), 6–7, 24 (quotation).

4. *Edwin Parsons v. C. A. Slaughter, C. H. Phillips, and W. W. Hunter,* 63

Fed. Rep. (1894): 876–81; also reported in R. Taylor Scott, *Annual Report* (1894), 19–23.

5. *Nineteenth Bondholders Report* (1892), 8–10, 260.

6. Senate Doc. 6 with *JSV*, 1891–92 sess., and House Doc. 2 with *JHD*, 1891–92 sess.

7. Ibid.

8. Ibid., 11.

9. Ibid., quotation on 12.

10. *JSV*, 1891–92 sess., 224–25; *JHD*, 1891–92 sess., 251.

11. *Acts*, 1891–92 sess., 533–42.

12. *Twentieth Bondholders Report* (1892), 12–14, 277–89; *Twenty-First Bondholders Report* (1894), 340–47.

13. *JHD*, 1893–94 sess., 17–19, quotations on 17, 18, 19.

14. *Acts*, 1893–94 sess., 100–102.

15. Ibid., 260–62.

16. Ibid., 381.

17. *Commonwealth v. McCullough*, 90 VA (1894): 597–620, quotations on 605, 606, 607.

18. Ibid., 618–19.

19. *Tax-Receivable Coupons Received on Judgments Since the Repeal of the Tax-Receivable Coupon Act*, in *Statement of the Debt of Virginia*, in *Acts*, 1920 sess., 873.

20. *McCullough v. Virginia*, 172 US (1898): 102–33, quotations on 106, 108–9.

21. Ibid., quotations on 112–13.

22. Ibid., quotations on 116–17, 123.

23. Ibid., 124–25.

24. Ibid., 125–33, quotation on 129.

25. Andrew Jackson Montague, *Annual Report* (1899), 3.

26. *JHD*, 1899–1900 sess., 23.

27. *Acts*, 1893–94 sess., 100–102; 1895–96 sess., 160–62; 1897–98 sess., 316–17; 1899–1900 sess., 270–71.

28. *Tax-Receivable Coupons Received on Judgments Since the Repeal of the Tax-Receivable Coupon Act*, in *Statement of the Debt of Virginia*, in *Acts*, 1920 sess., 873.

29. *JHD*, 1901–2 sess., 19, 24–25.

30. *Acts*, 1906 sess., 6–7.

31. Ibid., 1936 sess., 342–47.

32. Ibid., 1942 sess., 788–89; Senate Doc. 1 with *JSV*, 1944 sess., 1.

10. UNFINISHED BUSINESS

1. John O. Peters, *Tale of the Century: A History of the Bar Association of the City of Richmond, 1885–1985* (Richmond, 1985), 28–29; text of address printed in *Richmond Dispatch*, 8 Feb. 1895, and with some variations as John Randolph Tucker, "Reminiscences of Virginia's Judges and Jurists," *Virginia Law Register*, supplement to vol. 1, no. 3 (1895): 1–47.

2. *Acts,* 1893–94 sess., 862–67, quotation on 865.

3. Tarter, *Grandees of Government,* 262–65.

4. Description of legislative maneuvering in J. M. Mason, *The West Virginia Debt and the Resolutions of the Virginia Legislature Appointing Commissioners to Adjust It* (Charles Town, W.Va., 1894).

5. Younger and Moore, *Governors of Virginia,* 135–46.

6. *JHD,* 1893–94 sess., 658–60, quotations on 658, 659.

7. *Acts,* 1893–94 sess., 867–69, quotations on 868.

8. Senate Doc. 10, with *JSV,* 1895–96 sess., 4–13, quotation on 5.

9. Ibid., 4–5, quotation on 5.

10. Record Book of the Virginia Debt Commission, Record Group 84, acc. 21739, Library of Virginia, 14–15.

11. Elizabeth J. Goodall, "The Virginia Debt Controversy and Settlement, Part I," *West Virginia History* 24 (1962): 65–72.

12. *Sixth Bondholders Report* (1879), 57–58; *Sixteenth Bondholders Report* (1889), 186; *Nineteenth Bondholders Report* (1892), 280.

13. Printed in *Reply Brief for Virginia upon Motion to Refer the Cause to a Master,* William A. Anderson, Oct. Term 1907, *Virginia vs. West Virginia,* vol. 2, 7th imprint, 53.

14. Senate Doc. 10, with *JSV,* 1895–96 sess., 1–3.

15. Printed in *Reply Brief for Virginia upon Motion to Refer the Cause to a Master,* William A. Anderson, Oct. Term 1907, *Virginia vs. West Virginia,* vol. 2, 7th imprint, 53.

16. No meetings are recorded in the official Record Book of the Virginia Debt Commission.

17. Senate Doc. 6 with *JSV,* 1899–1900 sess., 5, 6–8.

18. Ibid., 4.

19. *Acts,* 1899–1900 sess., 902–3.

20. Printed in *Reply Brief for Virginia upon Motion to Refer the Cause to a Master,* William A. Anderson, Oct. Term 1907, *Virginia vs. West Virginia,* vol. 2, 7th imprint, 55.

21. Brent Tarter, "Anderson, William Alexander," *DVB* 1:161–63.

22. Record Book of the Virginia Debt Commission, 36.

23. Senate Doc. 1 with *JSV,* 1906 sess., 14–21, 41–46.

24. Printed in *Reply Brief for Virginia upon Motion to Refer the Cause to a Master,* William A. Anderson, Oct. Term 1907, *Virginia vs. West Virginia,* vol. 2, 7th imprint, 55–56.

25. Senate Doc. 1 with *JSV,* 1906 sess., 22–25; Goodall, "Debt Controversy, Part I," 74.

26. Senate Doc. 1 with *JSV,* 1906 sess., 25–45, also printed as Randolph Harrison, "West Virginia's Contributive Share of the Debt of Virginia," *Virginia Law Register* 10 (1905): 1055–71.

27. Goodall, "Debt Controversy, Part I," 296.

28. *South Dakota v. North Carolina,* 192 US (1904): 286–354.

29. William A. Anderson, *Annual Report* (1905), 65–67, quotation on 65.

30. Senate Doc. 1 with *JSV*, 1906 sess., 42–45; Record Book of the Virginia Debt Commission, 92.

31. William A. Anderson, *Annual Report* (1906), 9.

32. Bradley T. Johnson, "Can States Be Compelled to Pay Their Debts?," *American Law Review* 12 (1878): 625–59, quotation on 625.

33. *Hans v. Louisiana*, 134 US (1890): 1–21, quotations on 16, 21.

34. Ibid., quotation on 21.

35. Johnson, "Can States Be Compelled to Pay Their Debts?," 653.

36. *New Hampshire v. Louisiana*, 108 US (1883): 76–91.

37. John V. Orth, "The Virginia State Debt and the Judicial Power of the United States, 1870–1920," in *Ambivalent Legacy: A Legal History of the South*, ed. David J. Bodenhamer and James W. Ely Jr. (Jackson, Miss., 1984), 106–22.

38. *Black's Law Dictionary*, s.v. "laches."

11. *VIRGINIA V. WEST VIRGINIA*

1. William A. Anderson, *Annual Report* (1908), 6; Elizabeth J. Goodall, "The Virginia Debt Controversy and Settlement, Part III," *West Virginia History* 24 (1963): 332–33. The full record of the case is in the Records of the Supreme Court of the United States, Record Group 267, Original Jurisdiction, 267.3.3, National Archives and Records Administration. Other pertinent archival materials include Records of the Virginia Debt Commission, 1894–26, Record Group 84, Library of Virginia; attorney general's records in Department of Law, Record Group 5, Library of Virginia; William Alexander Anderson Papers, University of Virginia Library; as well as nine bound volumes in the Library of Virginia entitled *Virginia vs. West Virginia*, which contain many of the briefs, exhibits, and arguments of the case through 1913, and several large volumes containing briefs and exhibits published by the attorneys general of West Virginia.

2. William A. Anderson, *Annual Report* (1906), 96–107, quotations on 102, 107; bill and exhibits bound in *Virginia vs. West Virginia*, vol. 2, 2nd and 3rd imprints, and in vol. 4, 1st imprint.

3. J. G. Carlisle, Brief on Demurrer for West Virginia, Oct. Term 1906, bound in *Virginia vs. West Virginia*, vol. 1, 1st imprint.

4. Records of the Virginia Debt Commission, including the two keys.

5. Briefs, exhibits, and arguments of counsel printed in Clarke E. May, *Proceedings in the Equity Suit of the Commonwealth of Virginia vs. The State of West Virginia, with an Appendix* (Charleston, W.Va., 1907), 1:1–413; briefs and arguments summarized in Elizabeth J. Goodall, "The Virginia Debt Controversy and Settlement, Part II," *West Virginia History* 24 (1963): 303–4.

6. *Virginia v. West Virginia*, 206 US (1907): 290–322, quotation on 320.

7. *Virginia v. West Virginia*, 209 US (1908): 534–37, quotation on 535–36.

8. Anderson, *Annual Report* (1908), 6.

9. Goodall, "Debt Controversy, Part II," 307–8.

10. Rosewell Page, "The West Virginia Debt Settlement," *Virginia Law Register,* new ser., 5 (1919): 257–83, quotation on 275.

11. The legal briefs are in A. A. Lilly, *Debt Suit: Virginia v. West Virginia . . .* (Charleston, W. Va., 1913), 1–563; transcriptions of hearings published in *Record Part Two: Being the Evidence Taken and Proceedings Had Before the Special Master Hon. Charles E. Littlefield at Richmond Virginia November 16th, 1908, to July 2nd, 1909* (n.p., [ca. 1910]), bound in *Virginia vs. West Virginia,* 3:211–899. One of the legal advisers for Virginia published his testimony as a separate pamphlet, *Argument of John B. Lightfoot Jr., on Behalf of the Plaintiff, Before Special Master Charles E. Littlefield, November 6, 1909* (n.p., [ca. 1909]).

12. William A. Anderson, *Annual Report* (1909), 7.

13. [Charles E. Littlefield], *Report of Special Master,* reprinted in Lilly, *Debt Suit,* separately paginated.

14. Ibid., 29–30.

15. Ibid., 37–38.

16. Ibid., 39–141.

17. Ibid., 142–80.

18. Ibid., 181–93; Goodall, "Debt Controversy, Part III," 338–42.

19. Samuel W. Williams, *Annual Report* (1910), 5; legal briefs and related documents printed in Lilly, *Debt Suit.*

20. *Virginia v. West Virginia,* 220 US (1911) 1–36, quotation on 27.

21. Ibid., 28.

22. Ibid., 27, 33, 36.

23. Ibid., 28–29.

24. Ibid., 29–31.

25. Ibid., 33.

26. Ibid., 34–35.

27. Ibid., 35–36, quotation on 36.

28. Goodall, "Debt Controversy, Part III," 343–46.

29. Samuel W. Williams, *Annual Report* (1911), 5–6, with texts of correspondence and related documents printed on 7–18; Attorney General Samuel W. Williams, *Motion of the Complainant,* Oct. Term, 1911, containing texts of all the correspondence and related documents, in *Virginia vs. West Virginia,* vol. 2, 11th imprint; texts also in Record Book of the Virginia Debt Commission, Record Group 84, acc. 21739, Library of Virginia, 116–17, 121–23, 124; Goodall, "Debt Controversy, Part III," 347–50.

30. *Virginia v. West Virginia,* 222 US (1911): 17–20, quotations on 19–20.

31. Samuel W. Williams, *Annual Report* (1912), 5.

32. *Acts of the Legislature of West Virginia, Thirty-First Regular Session, 1913* (Charleston, W.Va., 1913), 621–22, quotation on 622.

33. Elizabeth J. Goodall, "The Virginia Debt Controversy and Settlement, Part IV," *West Virginia History* 25 (1963): 42–47.

34. J. M. Mason, *The Facts about West Virginia's Equitable Proportion of the Debt Incurred by Virginia before She was Divided* ([Charles Town, W.Va., ca. 1881]);

Mason, *The West Virginia Debt and the Resolutions of the Virginia Legislature Appointing Commissioners to Adjust It* (Charles Town, W.Va., 1894); Mason, "West Virginia's Debt and the Supreme Court," *Virginia Law Register* 5 (1899): 202–4.

35. Response of A. A. Lilly, 13 Sept. 1913, printed in Samuel W. Williams, *Annual Report* (1914), 26–33, and in *Virginia vs. West Virginia*, vol. 1, 18th imprint.

36. Transcription of negotiations printed in Samuel W. Williams, *Annual Report* (1913), 7–23, quotations on 7, and also incorporated into Record Book of the Virginia Debt Commission, 126–58.

37. A. A. Lilly, *Proceedings in the Virginia Debt Case . . . 1913* (Charleston, W.Va., 1913), vi–vii, 26; Goodall, "Debt Controversy, Part IV," 49–51.

38. Williams, *Annual Report* (1913), 23.

39. Response of A. A. Lilly printed in ibid., 26–33, and in *Virginia vs. West Virginia*, vol. 1, 18th imprint.

40. *Virginia v. West Virginia*, 231 US (1913): 89–91, quotation on 91.

41. Mason, *Facts about West Virginia's Equitable Proportion of the Debt;* Mason, *West Virginia Debt and the Resolutions of the Virginia Legislature Appointing Commissioners to Adjust It.*

42. Documented statement of war claim in R. Taylor Scott, *Annual Report* (1894), 37–138.

43. *Special Message of His Excellency, Henry D. Hatfield, Governor, to the Legislature of West Virginia, February 5, 1915, together with the Report of the Virginia Debt Commission Made Pursuant to the Requirements of a Joint Resolution of the Legislature Adopted February 21, 1913* ([Charleston, W.Va., 1915]), esp. 4–6; Goodall, "Debt Controversy, Part IV," 54–57.

44. John Garland Pollard, *Annual Report* (1914), 139–47, and also in *Virginia Debt Suit: Statement of Negotiations between the Debt Commissioners of the Two States, Washington, D.C., March 4, 1914* ([Charleston, W.Va., 1914]), 2–19; proposal also incorporated into Record Book of the Virginia Debt Commission, 170–83; Goodall, "Debt Controversy, Part IV," 57–61.

45. Goodall, "Debt Controversy, Part IV," 61–66.

46. *Virginia v. West Virginia*, 234 US (1914): 117–22, quotation on 121.

47. Pollard, *Annual Report* (1914), 5; *Special Message of His Excellency, Henry D. Hatfield, Governor, to the Legislature of West Virginia, February 5, 1915*, 7; [Charles E. Littlefield], *Volume I, Record of Hearings*, and *Volume II, Defendant's and Plaintiff's Exhibits* (Charleston, W.Va., 1914).

48. *Special Message of His Excellency, Henry D. Hatfield, Governor, to the Legislature of West Virginia, February 5, 1915*, 9–12; Elizabeth J. Goodall, "The Virginia Debt Controversy and Settlement, Part V," *West Virginia History* 25 (1964): 102–12.

49. *Virginia v. West Virginia*, 238 US (1915): 202–42.

50. Pollard, *Annual Report* (1915), 7.

51. Goodall, "Debt Controversy, Part V," 113–14.

52. Texts in Record Book of the Virginia Debt Commission, 208–10, and Pollard, *Annual Report* (1916), 276–78; Goodall, "Debt Controversy, Part V," 115.

53. Pollard, *Annual Report* (1916), 276.

54. Henry D. Hatfield, *Special Message of Governor Hatfield to Legislature of 1917, on Subject of the Virginia Debt* ([Charleston, W.Va., 1917]), 16–17.

55. *Virginia v. West Virginia*, 241 US (1916): 531–32, quotation on 532.

56. *Special Message of Governor Hatfield to Legislature of 1917*, quotations on 17, 18.

57. Mason, "West Virginia's Debt and the Supreme Court."

58. *Special Message of Governor Hatfield to Legislature of 1917*, 20–58.

59. Goodall, "Debt Controversy, Part V," 117–20.

60. John Garland Pollard, *Annual Report* (1917), 311–18, quotation on 318.

61. *Virginia v. West Virginia*, 246 US (1918): 565–606, at 590–91.

62. Ibid., quotations on 591, 605–6.

63. Ibid., 567–79, quotation on 567.

64. William C. Coleman, "The State as Defendant under the Federal Constitution: The Virginia–West Virginia Debt Controversy," *Harvard Law Review* 31 (1917): 210–45; "The Virginia–West Virginia Debt Controversy," ibid. 31 (1918): 1158–61.

65. Thomas Reed Powell, "Coercing a State to Pay a Judgment: Virginia v. West Virginia," *Michigan Law Review* 17 (1918): 1–32, quotations on 21–22.

66. *Acts of the Legislature of West Virginia Regular and Extraordinary Sessions 1915* (Charleston, W.Va., 1915), 324–27; *Special Message of Governor Hatfield to Legislature of 1917*, 16.

67. Record Book of the Virginia Debt Commission, 218–20.

68. *Address on Behalf of the Virginia Debt Commission before the Legislature of West Virginia in Joint Session in Relation to the Settlement of the Decree of the Supreme Court of the United States in Favor of Virginia, in the Suit of the Commonwealth of Virginia v. State of West Virginia by Randolph Harrison, Lynchburg, Va., Charleston, West Virginia, February 4, 1919* ([Lynchburg, 1919]), 8; *Report of the New Virginia Debt Commission, February 8, 1919* ([Charleston, W.Va., 1919]), 5.

69. *Acts of the Legislature of West Virginia Regular Session 1919* (Charleston, W.Va., 1919), 499–500, 507–9; *Address on Behalf of the Virginia Debt Commission before the Legislature of West Virginia*, 9.

70. *Report of the New Virginia Debt Commission*, 8–9, quotation on 8; Goodall, "Debt Controversy, Part V," 127–29.

71. *Acts of the Legislature of West Virginia, Extraordinary Session 1919* (Charleston, W.Va., 1919), 19–29, quotation on 20.

72. Ibid., 18–19.

73. John R. Saunders, *Annual Report* (1919), 6; Saunders, *Annual Report* (1920), 7–8; Page, "West Virginia Debt Settlement," 280.

74. Goodall, "Debt Controversy, Part V," 129.

75. Record Book of the Virginia Debt Commission, 245–46; Saunders, *Annual Report* (1920), 7.

76. Page, "West Virginia Debt Settlement," 283.

12. LEGACIES OF THE DEBT CONTROVERSY

1. Brent Tarter, "Blair, Robert William," *DVB* 1:551–52.

2. Charles E. Wynes, *Race Relations in Virginia, 1870–1902* (Charlottesville, 1961); Allen W. Moger, *Virginia: Bourbonism to Byrd, 1870–1925* (Charlottesville, 1968); Raymond H. Pulley, *Old Virginia Restored: An Interpretation of the Progressive Impulse, 1870–1930* (Charlottesville, 1968); Wythe Holt, *Virginia's Constitutional Convention of 1901–1902* (New York, 1990); Tarter, *Grandees of Government,* 232–304; voter tabulations from Herman L. Horn, "The Growth and Development of the Democratic Party in Virginia since 1890" (Ph.D. diss., Duke University, 1949), 102–13.

3. William A. Anderson, "Virginia Constitutions," in *Report of the Twelfth Annual Meeting of the Virginia State Bar Association* (Richmond, 1900), 145–78.

4. William DuBose Sheldon, *Populism in the Old Dominion: Virginia Farm Politics, 1885–1900* (Princeton, 1935). See also Brent Tarter, "Beverley, James Bradshaw," Tarter, "Beverley, Robert," and James Tice Moore, "Cocke, Edmund Randolph," *DVB* 1:468–69, 474–76, 3:326–29.

5. Henry C. Ferrell, "The Role of Virginia Democratic Party Factionalism in the Rise of Harry Flood Byrd, 1917–1923," *East Carolina College Publications in History* 2 (1965): 146–66; Joseph A. Fry and Brent Tarter, "The Redemption of the Fighting Ninth: The 1922 Congressional Election in the Ninth District of Virginia and the Origins of the Byrd Organization," *South Atlantic Quarterly* 77 (1978): 352–70; Stanley Willis, "'To Lead Virginia out of the Mud': Financing the Old Dominion's Public Roads, 1922–1924," *VMHB* 94 (1986): 425–52; Ronald L. Heinemann, *Harry Byrd of Virginia* (Charlottesville, 1996), 19–42.

6. Tarter, *Grandees of Government,* 262–75, 281–304.

7. Robert Clinton Burton, "The History of Taxation in Virginia, 1870–1901" (Ph.D. diss., University of Virginia, 1962), 174–76, 187, 213–14, 231–32; Catherine A. Jones, *Intimate Reconstructions: Children in Postemancipation Virginia* (Charlottesville, 2015), 184–87.

8. Raymond H. Pulley, "The May Movement of 1899: Irresolute Progressivism in the Old Dominion," *VMHB* 75 (1967): 186–201; William A. Link, *A Hard Country and a Lonely Place: Schooling, Society, and Reform in Rural Virginia, 1870–1920* (Chapel Hill, 1986), 76–81, 89–94; Sandra Gioia Treadway, "New Directions in Virginia Women's History," *VMHB* 100 (1992): 21–23; Cynthia A. Kierner, Jennifer R. Loux, and Megan Taylor Shockley, *Changing History: Virginia Women through Four Centuries* (Richmond, 2013), 202–3.

9. Waverly K. Winfree, "Barton, Robert Thomas," *DVB* 1:376–77.

10. Margaretta Barton Colt, *Defend the Valley: A Shenandoah Family in the Civil War* (New York, 1994), 49–50.

11. George William Bagby, *John Brown and Wm. Mahone: An Historical Parallel, Foreshadowing Civil Trouble* (Richmond, 1880).

12. Charles Chilton Pearson, *The Readjuster Movement in Virginia* (New Haven, Conn., 1917), 152–53, quotation on 153 n. 44.

13. *Acts,* 1928 sess., 1082. See also *The "Big Four" and John E. Massey,* Senate Doc. 7 with *JSV,* 1932 sess.

14. Fred Arthur Bailey, "Free Speech and the Lost Cause in the Old Dominion," *VMHB* 103 (1995): 236–66; James Michael Lindgren, *Preserving the Old Dominion: Historic Preservation and Virginia Traditionalism* (Charlottesville, 1993); Tarter, *Grandees of Government,* 258–60; Kierner, Loux, and Shockley, *Changing History,* 207–9; Jennifer Davis McDaid, "Cassell, Emma Frances Plecker," *DVB* 3:121–22. See also Caroline E. Janney, *Burying the Dead but Not the Past: Ladies' Memorial Associations and the Lost Cause* (Chapel Hill, 2008); and Janney, *Remembering the Civil War: Reunion and the Limits of Reconciliation* (Chapel Hill, 2013).

15. J. Douglas Smith, "The Campaign for Racial Purity and the Erosion of Paternalism in Virginia, 1922–1930," *Journal of Southern History* 68 (2002): 65–106; Paul A. Lombardo, *Three Generations, No Imbeciles: Eugenics, the Supreme Court, and Buck v. Bell* (Baltimore, 2008); Gregory Michael Dorr, *Segregation's Science: Eugenics and Society in Virginia* (Charlottesville, 2008); Tarter, *Grandees of Government,* 275–76, 310–11.

16. William L. Royall, *Some Reminiscences* (New York, 1909), 102–53.

17. Tarter, *Grandees of Government,* 340–54.

INDEX

African Americans: driven out of public life, 80, 143–44, 175, 181–82; enter politics, 2–3, 9, 18–19, 20, 40–41; and Readjuster Party, 56–58, 63–64, 66–67, 76–77

Allen v. Baltimore and Ohio Railroad Company (1885), 103

American Bond-Funding and Banking Association, Ltd., 41–42

Anderson, Francis Thomas, 31–32, 62, 88

Anderson, William Alexander, 147, 153, 156–57, 166, 177

Anderson-McCormick Act, 80, 144, 177

Antoni, Andrew, 29–30, 85

Antoni v. Greenhow: 1882, 85; *1883*, 85–87, 105

Antoni v. Wright and *Wright v. Smith* (1872), 30–32, 56, 61, 62, 108, 114; overruled, 136–37

Arthur, Chester A., 43, 73

Association for the Preservation of Virginia Antiquities, 182

Atkins, Thomas Stanley, 97

Ayers, Edward L., 8

Ayers, Rufus Adolphus, 112, 120–21. See also *In Re Ayers* (1887); *In Re Rufus A. Ayers* (1878)

Bagby, George William, 181

Baltimore & Ohio Railroad Co. v. Allen (1883), 89–90, 107

Barbour, James, 49, 55, 56, 65, 76

Barbour, John Strode, 76, 80, 178, 179

Barbour Bill (1878), 49–51, 93

barratry, 112

Barry, Robert P., 109

Barry v. Edmunds (1886), 109

Barton, Robert Thomas, 180

Bennett, Jonathan McCally, 33–34

"Big Four," 181–82

Blair, Frank Simpson, 56, 68, 80, 175; attorney general, 65–66, 90, 95, 97, 180

Blair, Robert William, 175

Blair v. Marye (1885), 80

Bond, Hugh Lenox, 89, 114–15, 120–21

bonds: century, 134; consols, 32; coupon, 25; McCulloch or ten-forty, 55, 85–86; 'peelers ('pealers), 32; registered, 25; taxed, 35–36, 45, 62–63. See also coupons; funding acts

Bouldin, Wood, 30

Bourbons, 73, 74–75

Bowen, Henry, 68

Bradley, Joseph P., 104–5, 112, 128–29

Brewer, David A., 138–40

Brisby, William H., 57

Brown, John Crosby, 147

Brown Committee, 147, 154, 172

Bryan v. Virginia (1890), 128–29

Burks, Edward Calohill, 62

Burruss v. Commonwealth (1886), 113

Byrd, Harry Flood, 178, 179, 183

Cameron, William E., 64–65, 69, 72, 92, 101, 176

Carrington, Isaac H., 55
Carter v. Greenhow (1885), 104
Cassell, Emma Frances Plecker, 182–83
Chaffin v. Taylor: 1885, 103; *1886,* 103
chapmerty, 112
Children of the Confederacy, 183
Christian, Joseph, 61–62
Circuit Court for the Eastern District of
   Virginia, U.S., 104, 105, 106, 107–8,
   114–15, 125; *Edwin Parsons v. C. A.
   Slaughter, C. H. Phillips, and W. W.
   Hunter* (1894), 131; *Faure v. Sinking
   Fund Commissioners* (1884), 98–100;
   *Gorman v. Sinking Fund Commis-
   sioners* (1885), 107; *Harvey and An-
   other v. Commonwealth of Virginia*
   (1884), 95–97; *In Re Rufus A. Ayers*
   (1878), 120–21; *James P. Cooper, et
   al. v. Morton Marye, et al.* (1887),
   120; *Jones v. Commonwealth of
   Virginia* (1885), 105–6; *Norfolk Trust
   Co. v. Marye* (1885), 107; *Strickler
   and Wife v. Yager* (1886), 115; *Willis
   and Wife v. Miller* (1886), 114–15.
   See also Hughes, Robert W.
Circuit Court for the Western District
   of Virginia, U.S., 125; *Baltimore &
   Ohio Railroad Co. v. Allen* (1883),
   89–90, 107
Clarke, James, 61
Clarke v. Tyler (1878), 61–62
Cleveland, Grover, 66, 132
Coleman, William C., 3, 169
Coleman, William D., 38
Commissioners of the Sinking Fund,
   Virginia, 37–38, 99–100
Commonwealth v. Booker & Co. and
   Commonwealth v. Fifty-Seven Others
   (1887), 113
Commonwealth v. Guggenheimer
   (1883), 90–91
Commonwealth v. H. M. Smith Jr.
   (1882), 88, 90–91
Commonwealth v. Hurt (1888), 126
Commonwealth v. Jones (1887), 113–14

Commonwealth v. Maury: 1884, 97;
   1887, 114
Commonwealth v. McCullough (1894),
   136–38
Commonwealth v. Taylor (1882), 88
Commonwealth v. Weller & Sons
   (1887), 113
Conley, William G., 160
Conrad, Holmes, 154
Conservative Party, 7–8, 9, 19–20, 21,
   65–66, 76, 179; divided, 43, 46–47
Constitution, U.S., contracts clause,
   30–31, 48–49
constitutions, Virginia. *See* Virginia
   constitutions
Cooper, James P., 120
Cooper v. Virginia (1890), 128–29
Cornwell, John J., 170–71
Cornwall v. Commonwealth (1886), 113
Corporation of Foreign Bondholders,
   38–39, 63, 102, 111, 112, 117, 120,
   124; denounces Readjuster Party, 58;
   negotiates with government, 54, 55,
   119, 127–28; opposes Riddleberger
   Act, 91–92, 106–7, 125
corruption, 2, 26–27, 47–48
coupon brokers, 37, 45, 97, 123–24, 131
Coupon Crusher, 119–20, 125–26, 130
Coupon Killers, 70; No. 1, 83–84, 89–
   91, 92, 130, 131; amended, 85, 110,
   111, 127; constitutionality challenged,
   105–6; declared constitutional, 85–87;
   No. 2, 84–85, 89–90, 91, 95, 102–3
coupons, 25, 37, 97–100; contracts, 30,
   63, 102–4, 105, 128–29, 138–40; contract status denied, 30–31, 136–38;
   forged or spurious, 83, 86, 110–14;
   license taxes, 94, 95–97, 108–10,
   113–14, 115–16; payment of fines
   with, 61; payment of taxes with, 28,
   38, 42, 82, 99–100; revenue effects,
   28, 38, 82, 117–18, 126–27, 130–31,
   138, 141; tax receivable, 4, 25, 27, 29,
   30–31, 32, 56, 61, 88, 89, 134–35; tax
   receivable status denied, 30–31, 61.

See also Coupon Crusher; Coupon
    Killers
creditors, 17, 22, 23, 38–39, 63, 91–92,
    106–7, 124, 130–33; accept reduc-
    tion in interest, 53–54; negotiate with
    government, 36, 41–42, 54–55; paid
    for Virginia Deferred Certificates,
    172–73. *See also* Brown Committee;
    Corporation of Foreign Bondhold-
    ers; Olcott Committee; Virginia Debt
    Commission (1890–92); Virginia
    Debt Commission (1894–1926)
Cuthbert v. Virginia (1890), 129

Dailey, Jane, 8
Daniel, John Warwick, 49–50, 51, 65,
    80, 176, 178, 179
Daniel, Raleigh Travers, 19–20, 47
Danville Riot, 79
Daughters of the American Revolution,
    182
debt, personal, 16–17, 19–20
debt, Virginia, 11–12, 22; controversy,
    3–10; interest rate, 11, 26, 27; interest
    rate reduced, 29, 35, 38, 41–42, 54,
    55, 70. *See also* finding acts
debt commission. *See* Virginia Debt
    Commission (1890–92); Virginia
    Debt Commission (1894–1926)
Degler, Carl N., 8
Democratic Party, 5, 9, 43, 74, 75–76,
    81, 177–79; accepts Riddleberger
    Act, 79–80
Dunning, William A., 6
Dunnington v. Ford (1885), 95

*Edwin Parsons v. C. A. Slaughter,
    C. H. Phillips, and W. W. Hunter*
    (1894), 131
elections: *1852*, 176–77; *1869*, 20; *1873*,
    38; *1877*, 46–47; *1879*, 58; *1880*,
    66; *1881*, 64–66, 67–68, 74; *1883*,
    75–76, 80; *1884*, 66; *1885*, 67, 81,
    117; *1888*, 66; *1889*, 67, 174; *1900*,
    176; *1904*, 176

Eleventh Amendment, 89–90, 104,
    151–52
Ellett v. Virginia (1890), 129
English, William, 43
English Committee of Virginian Bond-
    holders, 127
Ex Parte Brown (1890), 129
Ex Parte Royall (1886), 109
Ex Parte William L. Royall (1888), 116

Farr, Richard Ratcliffe, 59
Faure, John P., 98
Faure v. Sinking Fund Commissioners
    (1884), 98–100
Field, James G., 47, 61, 62, 65, 105,
    177–78
Field, Stephen J., 63, 86, 87, 105, 122
First National Bank of New York,
    145–46
Fulkerson, Abram, 56, 68
Fuller, Melville W., 154
Funders 43, 54, 65–66
funding acts: *1871*, 24–27, 32–33,
    44–45, 83–84; *1878*, 52, 53; *1879*
    (McCulloch Act, Broker's Act),
    55–56, 59, 61; *1882* (Riddleberger
    Act), 70–71, 83–84, 88–90, 92, 98–99,
    128, 132; *1892* (Olcott Act), 9–10,
    133–135, 141; *1919* (West Virginia),
    171–72, *1936*; 142
Funding Association of the United
    States of America, 54, 55

Garfield, James A., 43, 66
Glasscock, William E., 159
Goodall, Elizabeth J., 4
*Gorman v. Sinking Fund Commission-
    ers* (1885), 107
Grant, Ulysses S., 19
Greenhow, Samuel C., 85, 93, 102,
    103, 115
Greenhow v. Vashon (1886), 108, 136

Habeas Corpus Act (1867), 110
Hahn, Steven, 8

Hale, Peyton G., 182
Hamilton, Alexander, 2, 23–24
Hancock, Winfield Scott, 43
Hans v. Louisiana (1890), 151
Harlan, John Marshall, 86–87, 105, 122–23
Harrison, Benjamin, 66. *See also* Virginia Debt Commission (1894–1926)
Harrison, Randolph, 148, 166, 171
Hartman v. Greenhow: 1878, 62–63; *1881,* 63
Harvey and Another v. Commonwealth of Virginia (1884), 95–97
Hatfield, Henry D., 162–63, 166, 167
Henry, Patrick, 16
Holliday, Frederick William Mackey, 47, 51–52, 53–54, 59, 69; vetoes Barbour Bill, 50–51; vetoes Riddleberger Bill, 60–61
Holmes, Oliver Wendell, Jr., 157–59, 160, 173
Hooper, Benjamin S., 68
Hucles v. Childrey (1890), 129, 136, 139
Hughes, Charles Evans, 165–66, 173
Hughes, Robert W., 54, 89–90, 96–97, 98–101, 105–6, 107–8, 114, 124
Hunter, James Mercer Taliaferro, 41

In Re Ayers (1887), 121–23, 130
In Re Rufus A. Ayers (1878), 120–21

James P. Cooper, et al. v. Morton Marye, et al. (1887), 120
Jefferson, Thomas, 16, 24
Jefferson, William T., 57
Johnson, Bradley T., 29, 30, 47, 48–49, 150, 151
Johnston, John W., 73–74
Jones v. Commonwealth of Virginia (1885), 105–6
Judiciary Act (1875), 94, 96

Kemper, James Lawson, 38, 40, 41–42, 45–46

laches, 152, 154, 158
Lacy, Benjamin Watkins, 90–91, 95, 113
Lee, Fitzhugh, 117, 118, 124, 125, 126–27; elected governor, 67, 81, 117; proposes Coupon Crusher, 119
Libbey, Harry, 68
Lilly, Abraham A., 162
Littlefield, Charles E., 156–57, 165, 169
Lybrook, Alfred M., 182

Mallan Bros. v. Bransford (1890), 126
Marye v. Parsons (1885), 104
McCorkle, William A., 146
McCulloch, Hugh, 41, 55
McCullough v. Virginia (1898), 138–41
McGahey v. Commonwealth (1888), 125–26
McGahey v. Virginia (1890), 128–29, 130, 136
McGrane, Reginald Charles, 7
McKinney, Philip Watkins, 65, 127, 128, 131, 132, 133–34, 135, 174
MacKinnon, John J., 41–42
Maddex, Jack P., Jr., 7, 8–9
Madison, James, 24
Mahone, William, 46–47, 56, 59, 64, 68, 75–77, 79, 124; reputation, 100, 174–75, 181–82
Marye, Morton, 97, 108
Mason, John M., 161–62, 163, 167–68, 170
Massey, John E. ("Parson"), 44–45, 56, 59, 81, 182
massive resistance, 184
Matthews, Stanley, 102–3, 105, 109, 121–22
May, Clarke E., 154
Mayo, Joseph, 38
Mayo, Robert M., 68
Medical College of Virginia, 71
Meredith, Wyndham R., 97–98
Moger, Allen W., 7
Montague, Andrew Jackson, 140–41
Moore, James Tice, 7–8
Moore v. Greenhow (1885), 105

New South, 8–9, 10
Newberry, Samuel H., 182
New Hampshire v. Louisiana (1883), 152
Newton v. Commonwealth (1886), 113
Norfolk Trust Co. v. Marye (1885), 107

O'Ferrall, Charles T., 145, 146
Olcott, Frederick P., 132
Olcott Committee, 132, 134, 145
Orth, John V., 4

Page, Rosewell, 3, 156, 172
Panic of 1873, 38, 42
Parsons, Edwin, 104, 131
Paul, John, 51, 68, 175
Pearson, Charles Chilton, 6, 182
Peckham, Rufus W., 140
Peters, John O., 5
Pierpont, Francis H., 17
Pleasants v. Greenhow (1885), 104
Plecker, Walter Ashby, 183
Poindexter, Thomas, 102
Poindexter v. Greenhow (1885), 102–3, 105–6, 112, 123
poll tax, 40, 59, 70, 73, 74, 176
Pollard, John Garland, 166, 168–69
populists, 177–78
Powell, Thomas Reed, 3–4, 169–70
Pulley, Raymond H., 7

Randall, James G., 3
Ratchford, Benjamin Ulysses, 7
Readjuster Party, 174, 181; coalition with Republican Party, 63–64, 74; creation, 3, 9, 56–57; demise, 77–78, 82; reforms, 57–59, 69–70, 71–72, 73, 74–75
Readjusters, 43, 44–45, 56
Republican Party, 43, 74, 66–67, 81, 144, 175, 177; coalition with Readjuster Party, 63–64, 74
repudiation, 15–16, 17–18, 50, 54, 60, 61–62, 71, 133–34; in West Virginia, 167

Richardson, Robert Alexander, 108, 113–14, 136–38
Riddleberger, Harrison Holt, 56, 72, 74–75, 80, 176
Riddleberger Bill (1880), 60–61. See *also* funding acts
Royall, William L., 30, 31, 87, 102, 119–20, 121, 130; consults in London, 106–107; *History of the Virginia Debt Controversy*, 6, 183; litigant, 108–9, 109–10, 112, 115–16
Royall v. Virginia: 1886, 109, 113; *1887* (Va. Supreme Court of Appeals), 115; *1887* (U.S. Supreme Court), 115–16
Ruffin, Frank G., 100–101, 124, 127
Ruffner, William Henry, 59

Sands, William H., 108–9
Sands v. Edmunds (1886), 109
schools, 4, 5, 60–61, 79, 136–37, 139; politics, 53, 65–66, 79, 179–80; Readjuster policies, 59, 69, 71, 72–73, 74–75. See *also* taxes
Scott, R. Taylor, 130–31
Scott, William A., 6
Simonton, Charles Henry, 131
slavery and taxation, 15
Smith v. Clark (1889), 126
Smith v. Greenhow (1884), 93–94
Sons of Confederate Veterans, 182
South Dakota v. North Carolina (1904), 148–49
sovereign immunity, 48, 104, 121, 140–41, 150–51
Staples, Waller Redd, 30–31, 62, 105, 114
State Female Normal School (Longwood University), 71
Stewart v. Virginia (1886), 106
Strickler and Wife v. Yager (1886), 115
Supreme Court, U.S., 140, 150, 168–70, 172–73; special master, 156–57, 165, 169
Supreme Court, U.S., cases: *Allen v. Baltimore and Ohio Railroad*

Supreme Court, U.S., cases (continued)
Company (1885), 103; Antoni v.
Greenhow (1883), 85–87, 105; Barry
v. Edmunds (1886), 109; Bryan v.
Virginia (1890), 128–29; Carter
v. Greenhow (1885), 104; Chaffin
v. Taylor (1885), 103; Cuthbert v.
Virginia (1890), 129; Ellett v. Virginia
(1890), 129; Ex Parte Brown (1890),
129; Ex Parte Royall (1886), 109;
Hans v. Louisiana (1890), 151 ; Hartman v. Greenhow (1881), 63; Hucles
v. Childrey (1890), 129, 136, 139; In
Re Ayers (1887), 121–23, 130; Marye
v. Parsons (1885), 104; McCullough
v. Virginia (1898), 138–41; McGahey
v. Virginia (1890), 128–29, 130, 136;
Moore v. Greenhow (1885), 105;
New Hampshire v. Louisiana (1883),
152; Pleasants v. Greenhow (1885),
104; Poindexter v. Greenhow (1885),
102–3, 105–6, 112, 123; Royall v.
Virginia (1886), 109, 113; Royall v.
Virginia (1887), 115–16; Sands v.
Edmunds (1886), 109; South Dakota
v. North Carolina (1904), 148–49;
Stewart v. Virginia (1886), 106;
Vashon v. Greenhow (1890), 129,
136, 139; Virginia v. West Virginia
(1870), 14, 150; Virginia v. West Vir-
ginia (1907), 154–55; Virginia v. West
Virginia (1908), 155–56; Virginia v.
West Virginia (Mar. 1911), 157–59;
Virginia v. West Virginia (Oct. 1911),
160; Virginia v. West Virginia (1913),
162; Virginia v. West Virginia (1914),
164–65; Virginia v. West Virginia
(1915), 165–66; Virginia v. West
Virginia (1916), 167; Virginia v. West
Virginia (1918), 168–69; White v.
Greenhow (1885), 103
Supreme Court of Appeals, Virginia,
30–32, 72, 84, 85, 140, 143; Antoni
v. Greenhow (1882), 85; Antoni v.
Wright and Wright v. Smith (1872),
30–32, 56, 61, 62, 108, 114, 136–37;
Blair v. Marye (1885), 80; Burruss v.
Commonwealth (1886), 113; Chaffin v. Taylor (1886), 103; Clarke v.
Tyler (1878), 61–62; Commonwealth
v. Booker & Co. and Commonwealth
v. Fifty-Seven Others (1887), 113;
Commonwealth v. Guggenheimer
(1883), 90–91; Commonwealth v.
H. M. Smith Jr. (1882), 88, 90–91;
Commonwealth v. Hurt (1888), 126;
Commonwealth v. Jones (1887),
113–14; Commonwealth v. Maury
(1887), 114; Commonwealth v. Mc-
Cullough (1894), 136–38; Commonwealth v. Taylor (1882), 88; Commonwealth v. Weller & Sons (1887), 113;
Cooper v. Virginia (1890), 128–29;
Cornwall v. Commonwealth (1886),
113; Dunnington v. Ford (1885), 95;
Ex Parte William L. Royall (1888),
116; Greenhow v. Vashon (1886),
108, 136; Mallan Bros. v. Bransford
(1890), 126; McGahey v. Commonwealth (1888), 125–26; Newton v.
Commonwealth (1886), 113; Royall
v. Virginia (1887), 115; Smith v.
Clark (1889), 126; Taylor v. Williams
(1884), 94–95; Williamson v. Massey
(1880), 56; Wise Bros. &c. v. Rogers
(1873), 32

taxes, 35, 37, 39–40, 54, 71–72, 96–97;
school taxes, 49–51, 59, 93, 108, 129.
See also coupons
Taylor, James Craig, 30
Taylor v. Williams (1884), 94–95
Tucker, John Randolph, 143
Tyler, J. Hoge, 141

Underwood, John C., 18
United Daughters of the Confederacy,
182
University of Virginia, 71
U.S. Circuit Court for the Eastern District of Virginia. See Circuit Court for
the Eastern District of Virginia, U.S.

U.S. Circuit Court for the Western District of Virginia. *See* Circuit Court for the Western District of Virginia, U.S.

U.S. Supreme Court. *See* Supreme Court, U.S.

Vashon v. Greenhow (1890), 129, 136, 139

Virginia Agricultural and Mechanical College (Virginia Tech), 71

Virginia auditor of public accounts, 36, 38, 42, 54, 55, 59, 80, 94, 95, 112–13; reports, 35, 91, 97–98. *See also* Massey, John E.

Virginia Commissioners of the Sinking Fund, 37–38, 99–100

Virginia constitutions: *1851*, 11; *1864*, 13–14; *1869*, 18–19, 19–20, 30, 31, 108, 139, 179; *1902*, 175, 176–77; amendments to 1869 constitution, 40, 69

Virginia debt. *See* debt, Virginia

Virginia Debt Commission (1890–92), 6, 128, 130

Virginia Debt Commission (1894–1926), 145–47, 150; negotiates with West Virginia, 146, 154, 161–62, 163–64, 170–71, 172

Virginia Deferred Certificates, 34, 35, 145–47, 148, 153–54; *1871*, 24–25; *1878*, 52; *1879*, 55; *1882*, 70; West Virginia funds, 171–73

Virginia Literary Fund, 31, 59–60

Virginia Normal and Industrial School (Virginia State University), 71

Virginia Restored Government, 12–15, 22

Virginia second auditor, 28, 37, 38, 42, 59, 80, 93; reports, 83, 124, 127. *See also* Page, Rosewell; Ruffin, Frank G.

Virginia Supreme Court of Appeals. *See* Supreme Court of Appeals, Virginia

Virginia treasurer, 37–38, 45, 55, 56, 62, 95, 99, 107, 112, 120; pays interest, 35–36, 42; replaced, 59, 80; reports, 83; signs bonds, 110–11. *See also* Hunter, Robert Mercer Taliaferro

Virginia v. West Virginia: 1870, 14, 150; *1907*, 154–55; *1908*, 155–56; Mar. *1911*, 157–59; Oct. *1911*, 160; *1913*, 162; *1914*, 164–65; *1915*, 165–66; *1916*, 167; *1918*, 168–69

Waite, Morrison R., 85–86, 106, 116

Walker, Gilbert Carlton, 20, 22–24, 27, 28, 35, 36; vetoes bill, 29; vetoes resolution, 28–29

Walker, James A., 47

Walton Act, 144

West Virginia, 3; constitution (1863), 12–13, 148, 152, 154–55, 158, 165; constitution (1872), 33; declines to pay Virginia debt, 17, 33–34, 146, 147, 148; funding act (1919), 171–73; liable for interest, 159, 161–62, 163, 165–66, 171; liable for part of principal, 155–56, 157, 159, 165–66; New Virginia Debt Commission (1915–19), 170–71; Virginia Debt Commission (1913–15), 161–62, 163–64, 170. See also *Virginia v. West Virginia*

White, Edward D., 162, 164, 167, 168

White v. Greenhow (1885), 103

Wickham, Williams Carter, 99

Williams, Benjamin F., 182

Williams, John C., 94–95

Williams, Samuel W., 160, 162

Williamson v. Massey (1880), 56

Willis and Wife v. Miller (1886), 114–15

Wise, Henry A., 27–28, 36, 44, 66, 81

Wise, John Sergeant, 66, 67, 68, 81

Wise Bros. &c. v. Rogers (1873), 32

women, 16–17, 39–40, 53, 179–80, 182–83

Women's Association for the Liquidation of the State Debt, 39–40

Woodward, C. Vann, 8

Wynes, Charles E., 8